Lawless Lawfare

Advance Praise for *Lawless Lawfare*

"*Lawless Lawfare* details the establishment's tactics in usurping the court system in an attempt to score political points. It threatens to upend the separation of powers and thwart the will of the voters—something I know the dangers of firsthand, as the lawfare was waged against me."

—Texas Attorney General Ken Paxton

"Political prosecutions are something I know all about given what happened to me. My prosecution was the playbook that the Washington establishment later deployed against President Trump in an attempt to defeat a political opponent. My hope is he is the one who can put an end to the weaponization of America's judicial system."

—Governor Rod Blagojevich

"I've worked in the journalistic trenches with Alex Swoyer, breaking international news and breaking down the complexities of legal battles. She is a brilliant attorney and writer whose *Lawless Lawfare* breaks new ground in the crucial effort to document one of the most egregious abuses of power in American history."

—Joel Pollak, Breitbart News Senior Editor at Large

Lawless Lawfare

Tipping the Scales of Justice to Get Trump and Destroy MAGA

ALEX SWOYER

Published by Bombardier Books
An Imprint of Post Hill Press
ISBN: 979-8-89565-079-0
ISBN (eBook): 979-8-89565-080-6

Lawless Lawfare:
Tipping the Scales of Justice to Get Trump and Destroy MAGA

Cover Design by Jim Villaflores

This is a work of nonfiction. All people, locations, events, and situations are portrayed to the best of the author's memory.

Post Hill Press
New York • Nashville
posthillpress.com

Published in the United States of America
1 2 3 4 5 6 7 8 9 10

TABLE OF CONTENTS

To my daughter, Fiona Joon.
May you always seek—*and speak*—the truth.

FOREWORD
BY MIKE DAVIS

The weaponization of our judicial system is the single greatest threat to our republic today. Over the past several years, we have seen a anti-democratic pattern unfold: the use of lawfare—abusing legal and judicial processes for political gain—to target political opponents, particularly President Donald J. Trump and his supporters. The consequences of this trend extend beyond one man or one political movement. This republic-ending lawfare strikes at the very heart of our democracy, eroding the foundational principles of fairness, due process, and equal application of the law.

That is why Alex Swoyer's book is not only timely but essential. Alex meticulously documents the rise of lawfare, exposing the tactics used by leftist actors to manipulate the courts, discredit opponents, and consolidate their power. Her work is the result of years of dedicated investigative reporting, deep legal knowledge, and firsthand experience in Washington, D.C.'s political and judicial arenas.

I first met Alex during one of the most pivotal battles of my career—the confirmation fight for Justice Brett Kavanaugh. As a former law clerk to Justice Neil Gorsuch and a veteran of judicial nominations, I knew what was at stake. The left's attempt to derail Kavanaugh's confirmation was not just about one Supreme Court seat. It was a preview of the broader strategy they would soon unleash with full force: weaponizing the legal system to achieve victories they could not win at the ballot box. Amid the media frenzy, Alex stood out as a reporter who sought truth over narrative. She was sharp, thorough, and unwavering in her commitment to journalistic integrity. It was clear then—as it is now—that she was more than just a reporter. She was a guardian of the truth.

With over a decade of experience covering the intersection of law and politics, Alex possesses an in-depth understanding of the judicial system and its vulnerabilities. Unlike many of her media peers, Alex's legal background allows her to spot irregularities that others overlook—like the unconstitutional decisions handed down by Judges Tanya Chutkan and Juan Merchan against President Trump. She recognizes how small manipulations of courtroom procedures and judicial rulings can have republic-ending consequences in shaping political outcomes. And, most importantly, she understands that lawfare is not just a theoretical concern. It is an immediate and ongoing threat to our nation's legal and political institutions.

The left's use of lawfare is relentless. We saw it in the Russia collusion hoax, where baseless accusations led to years of politically motivated investigations. We saw it in the sham Trump impeachments, where the legal process was twisted into a partisan weapon. We see it now in the barrage of criminal and civil cases aimed at President Trump, including the politically driven prosecutions over classified documents, January 6, and even the dubious claims by E. Jean Carroll. These cases are not about justice. They want to ensure that President Trump and his supporters are buried under an avalanche of legal attacks so they won't effectively fight back.

Through my work at the Article III Project (A3P), I am on the front lines of this battle. We fought back against these radical judges who wanted to legislate from the bench. I personally filed complaints against judges who abuse their positions to serve their leftist ends. And I made it my mission to ensure that the judiciary remains independent, fair, and accountable. But make no mistake—this is a fight that requires vigilance from all who care about our constitutional republic.

That is why Alex's book is so crucial. She lays out, step-by-step, how lawfare is deployed as a political weapon. She exposes the individuals and institutions driving this effort, from deep-state bureaucrats to activist judges to media operatives who amplify false narratives. She connects the dots between seemingly disparate legal attacks, showing how they are part of a coordinated strategy to undermine not just President Trump but any political movement that dares to challenge the left's dominance. And she warns of the dire consequences should this weaponization of our legal system go unchecked.

This book is not just about the past. It exists as a warning for the future. After all, if we fail to learn from our past, we're doomed to repeat it in the future. Today, it is Trump and his allies who are in the crosshairs. Tomorrow, it's anyone who dares to challenge the prevailing political order. The erosion of legal fairness does not happen overnight. It happens incrementally, through small abuses that gradually become acceptable. That is why we must act now to expose and dismantle this dangerous trend before it becomes irreversible.

As you read this book, pay close attention to the patterns Alex uncovers. Observe how the same tactics are refined and redeployed across different cases. Consider the broader implications of a legal system that is easily weaponized against political enemies. And most importantly, recognize that the fight against lawfare is not just about one man or one election. It is about preserving the very foundations of our constitutional republic.

I am grateful to Alex Swoyer for her dedication to this critical issue. Her work is a testament to the importance of fearless journalism in the face of overwhelming pressure. She takes on the tough questions, challenges the prevailing narratives, and provides a much-needed roadmap for understanding the legal battles that will define the future of our nation.

For anyone who cares about the rule of law, the integrity of our judicial system, and the survival of American democracy, this book is a must-read. It is a wake-up call, a warning, and a call to action. Read it, absorb it, and join the fight to restore justice in America.

Mike Davis, founder and president, Article III Project
Former Law Clerk to Justice Neil Gorsuch

INTRODUCTION

As a legal affairs reporter and a lawyer for roughly a decade, it has been somewhat effortless for me to present balanced reporting for *The Washington Times*. All I have had to do when I write about a newsworthy lawsuit is access the legal filings from both the plaintiff and defendant, quote from each party, and ensure the various sides have a chance to shed light on the legal claims. So long as both parties were represented in my article, I felt I had done a balanced job.

Sounds easy, right?

You would think so. But I noticed that when it came to the lawsuits plaguing President Donald Trump, my colleagues in the media were not giving him that same balanced coverage that I had strived to implement in all of my legal reporting and analysis.

I found myself griping daily—to myself and to close confidants—about witnessing the abuse of the courts and America's justice system in what I viewed as purely political gamesmanship. It felt as though Trump Derangement Syndrome took over America's courtrooms. For starters, four criminal indictments against a former president—and a top presidential candidate—came in the span of four short months during a presidential campaign season.

The irony of the timing was not lost on me—or the voters, as the 2024 election results revealed.

As I read and reviewed each complaint or indictment against Trump, I would moan about the warped nature of the legal charges to a group of friends I had kept in touch with since my law school days. I did not consider all of them diehard Trump supporters. Many of my fellow attorney friends, I am sure, would have liked to see a different Republican nominee than Trump in 2024. But we all agreed, nonetheless, that the legal charges Trump was facing were unprecedented, novel, and often suspect at best.

That's when it hit me that the topic of lawfare deserved its own book, specifically the lawfare targeted at Trump, his inner circle, and the Make America Great Again movement as a whole.

With my Capitol Hill credentials and access to federal courtrooms in the District of Columbia and at the US Supreme Court, I felt I could help Americans—from both sides of the aisle—better understand the political nature of the legal battles dominating the mainstream news coverage over the past few years.

I did not necessarily set out to write a pro-Trump book, but Democratic lawmakers, progressive lawyers, and biased judges made it all too easy to compile *Lawless Lawfare*. It was because of their actions that Trump and his allies became viewed as victims of a one-sided system of justice. To most Americans, Lady Justice did not appear to be blind. Many of the individuals tainted by the injustice were willing to share with me their experiences, which I have included in *Lawless Lawfare*.

The online *Cambridge Dictionary* defines lawfare as "the use of legal action to cause problems for an opponent." Lawfare, as I see it in the Trump era, involved usurping America's courtrooms to fight political—rather than legal—battles.

That's exactly what I aim to highlight throughout *Lawless Lawfare*, as I bring the reader through what happened during, and leading up to, the 2024 election. In fact, I make the argument that the lawfare against Trump actually began during his 2016—not his 2024—campaign, with the Russian collusion narrative. It then continued on in the form of impeachments and later indictments.

I wanted *Lawless Lawfare* to expose the strange and often superficial legal battles that Democrats and the Washington establishment unfairly lobbed against Trump, his allies, and his supporters. My findings, which are detailed in this book, include the slanted media coverage and the damage lawfare caused not just to the presidency and the MAGA movement, but also to the legacy media and America's judiciary.

While the financial expense of it all is explored in *Lawless Lawfare*, the emotional and physical toll that the endless political persecutions took upon various individuals that found themselves caught up in Trump's legal web are also detailed by some of the people who were willing to bring me inside their personal and legal trials and tribulations.

Surprisingly, though, many of the people you will hear from throughout *Lawless Lawfare* view themselves as serving a purpose. They see themselves as standing up for democracy and the separation of powers—which they fear lawfare threatens to destroy.

Those insiders, who have been impacted in one way or another by the MAGA-targeted lawfare, told me how Trump and his new administration can best combat the weaponization of law enforcement and our nation's justice system to ensure politically biased lawfare never happens again.

Everyone I spoke to afflicted by Democrats' political prosecutions said the mission of it was clear: to silence, to intimidate, and to defeat. It was as if the Washington establishment and Democrats had read out of the playbook of former Venezuelan President Hugo Chavez, who was known for jailing hundreds of his political enemies.

The MAGA-targeted litigation was meant to drain any and all political opposition financially, mentally, and emotionally until they either complied, died, or were locked up. Thankfully, it did not work, and Americans saw through the dangerous scheme.

The Washington establishment and the Democratic Party underestimated MAGA's will to "fight, fight, fight."

THE COST OF LAWFARE

For the Trump family, the lawfare deployed by Democrats and the Washington establishment during the past several years was deeply personal, so much so that the family is not yet ready to talk about all its negative impacts, according to Lara Trump.

But she, the wife of Eric Trump and daughter-in-law of President Trump, said it was so damaging that even financial institutions did not want to work with them, despite the Trumps being one of the wealthiest and most successful families in America.

"We all, as a family, have experienced things," Trump, who also helped lead the Republican National Committee during the 2024 campaign, told me. "I won't even go into the personal side of this for us, which has affected our ability to get a loan for a house or a mortgage or whatever it is. We all in the Trump family have been negatively impacted by what these people have tried to do in the name of politics.

"I mean, most people will never know the half of it because we don't publicly talk about it," she added. "But it is absolutely outrageous, and it really does feel like we live in another country sometimes—not America—the stuff that we have gone through."

From the moment Trump launched his 2016 campaign, he was under scrutiny by the Federal Bureau of Investigation, which ended up probing him for more than two years for allegedly working with Russia to win the 2016 campaign.

When the Russia investigation failed to land any luck for Democrats, they turned to impeaching him not once, but twice.

Eventually, civil lawsuits ensued.

But the worse of it may have been the four criminal prosecutions he faced, making history as the first time a former president ever stood trial and was convicted of a crime.

Don Jr., the eldest son of the president, said he does not think his father is bothered by being labeled a "felon" or a "convict." He told me that, like the mug shot taken in Fulton County, Georgia, over Trump's state prosecution there, it has all become "sort of a symbol for standing against the corrupt swamp establishment and standing with the tens of millions of everyday, commonsense Americans who supported him."

"In a weird way, the courtroom sketches, the phony witch hunts, the failed Democrat ads, and the mug shot—it all became sort of a badge of honor, because it represents a courageous and bold stand against abuse of power. It's a political comeback story like we've never seen. And no, I'm not tired of winning," Don Jr. said.

He also credited the love and loyalty of the American people for motivating the Trump family to continue to campaign despite the mountain of lawfare.

> In fact, the lawfare only made us that much more driven and eager to deliver on the promises to restore equal justice and equal application of our laws. We're a family of builders—and when

> you're building something, you don't stop until the job is finished. The more the corrupt left-wing lawfare cabal tried to bring him down, the stronger my father became. Because once the corruption got to a certain point, we had no choice but to work harder than ever to deliver a massive victory in November.

Lara Trump, for her part, said that one day the family will feel comfortable coming out and talking more specifically about the way the political targeting that started nearly ten years ago has impacted each of them, adding that "it has upended all of our lives."

> It has been very, very damaging to all of our lives in ways probably people couldn't fathom. When that day comes, I think people will be utterly shocked by the things that have happened to our family and we made it through. I am grateful to the American people that they saw through all the lies and the lawfare and all the nonsense. But it is a really scary process that, had things gone the opposite way in this election, I don't know what that would have meant for our family, for my father-in-law, and for this country as a whole, because I think once you go past a certain point, I don't know that you get this country back. So, I feel like we are very fortunate right now.

Had the election not turned out in his favor, she said the family expected Trump to be put in jail. The same sentiment was echoed by Don Jr.

> I fully believe that had my father-in-law not won the election on November fifth, he would have spent some time in jail. That was their goal—was to put him in jail, to have the optics of that to send it out as a warning to people out there: Don't try to go against the grain so much, because this is ultimately what could happen to you. Don't be outspoken, because this is what could ultimately happen to you.

Don Jr. said the only way Democrats—including corrupt judges and prosecutors—could beat his father would have been to lock him up.

"They knew the only way they could beat him wasn't at the ballot box, but to jail him," he said.

> They used the justice system as an arm of the Democratic Party, with the ultimate goal of putting their political opponent behind bars based on lies, smears, due process denial, and all the rest. It was a disgrace. But the American people also woke up to exactly what they were doing to destroy the fabric of the nation. And it's why the Democrat Party is now a total dumpster fire, and that's putting it mildly.

Through the years, it was not just the Trump family who were personally impacted by the lawfare. Those around them also saw the law being manipulated in order to target political opposition.

General Michael Flynn was one of those supporters at the forefront of the lawfare. He said the bending of the law cost him his career and damaged his son's marriage.

Above all, it silenced him.

He had been an ally of President Trump's since before the 2016 election, when he would introduce him at campaign rallies. Flynn's military experience and the fact that he had worked a top position during the Obama administration helped bolster Trump's bid, at the time.

Flynn spent more than three decades in the military and became the director of the Defense Intelligence Agency in 2012 under Obama. Trump, after he defeated Hillary Clinton in 2016, made Flynn his national security advisor, a role in which he only served for three weeks before coming under scrutiny by the Federal Bureau of Investigation probing alleged Russia collusion in the Trump campaign. They nabbed Flynn for a phone call to his Russian counterpart during the transition period in December of 2016, after the November election but before Inauguration Day in January.

"I couldn't tell my story at all because publishers, they would be attacked. Businesses would be attacked. Jobs—like me getting jobs—I've had to really scratch out a living," Flynn said of the past eight years since Democrat lawfare took his position as US National Security Adviser away from him.

While military personnel with credentials like Flynn retire and sit on boards where they earn millions, Flynn was left struggling.

"I go through the four years of the Trump administration in excruciating pain, and the next four years, I'm out fighting for Trump and fighting for the country, and I am trying to scratch out a living. I wrote books. I made a movie. I'm out speaking. I am doing everything I can to basically recover what was taken from me illegally," Flynn said.

All because his name was tarnished during the Russia investigation.

> The costs are unimaginable. There is really only a very small handful that really can kind of understand what you go through. But for me, it was very public. I mean, all these other things that have happened—even Peter Navarro and Steve Bannon going off to prison—all those things happen after all this—I was like the piñata for the entirety of the Russiagate thing, because I had pled guilty, and now I am cooperating, and the whole thing was based on a lie. It was based on a Hillary Clinton hit piece.

"I haven't given up," Flynn added. "Bannon hasn't given up. Peter Navarro hasn't given up. Rudy Giuliani hasn't given up. There are others that have given up, though, trust me."

Some of the Trump allies he named were confidants in the first administration that were also indicted in the course of Democrats' litigation crusade. But Flynn said if anything good came out of it all, it is that his immediate family has been made stronger. (The strength of family is something Lara Trump also said helped the Trump family make it through.)

"It strengthened them, because they all knew who I was, and they didn't believe anything," Flynn said of his relatives.

> But my immediate family, particularly my son, it basically ruined his marriage... For my own, we are fine in our marriage and all that, but boy, I will tell you, it was tough times going through all that, emotionally, financially. It was destructive. That is a constant battle because now, as you fight back—now I am in the process of trying to fight back; but the emotional side of this thing is that there are so many people who believe and still believe what happened.

Stephen K. Bannon, whom Flynn referenced, had worked on Trump's 2016 campaign after having led the conservative news site Breitbart. Following the 2016 victory, he went to work at the White House as Trump's chief strategist.

But he was not there long before he quickly came under scrutiny by law enforcement, which became a pattern for those in the president's inner circle, as I will continue to explore more in later chapters.

During the first investigation into the president, known to some as "Russia collusion" and to others as the "Russian hoax," Bannon told me he spent $2 million on legal fees just battling that narrative alone.

And that, of course, is not all.

Bannon is still paying lawyers, as he's been fighting a pending prosecution in New York. Bannon did plead guilty in February to one count in the New York prosecution, in exchange not to do jail time.[1] More on that case later. But for Bannon, he plans to go all the way to the Supreme Court in another dispute involving the legitimacy of the January 6 House of Representatives committee that subpoenaed him over January 6 contacts. He refused to comply and spent four months in prison.

He said the lawfare during his time at the White House did not interfere with the administration's work, but it stymied their goal of draining the swamp and dismantling the administrative state.

"It's insanity," he said. "It didn't affect my work at the time, but I tell people, anyone who goes into government now has to get their head examined, because it is so brutal what they do to you."

Trump had pardoned Bannon in a dispute in 2021 over allegedly misusing funds that had been donated by Trump supporters to build a wall along the southern border.

He was—and still is—in Democrats' crosshairs.

Most recently, Manhattan District Attorney Alvin Bragg—the same prosecutor who convicted Trump in his Manhattan hush-money trial—has charged Bannon with money laundering, among other charges related to the build-the-wall donations. Bannon pleaded guilty in February to one charge—to defraud—which makes it so he cannot lead a charity or fundraise for a nonprofit.[2] But he was able to avoid going to trial and doing any more time in jail in this episode of lawfare. Since the Biden Justice Department could not continue to prosecute Bannon due to the pardon, Bragg

---

1 Aaron Katersky, "Steve Bannon pleads guilty in border wall fraud case, avoids jail time," ABC News, February 11, 2025, https://abcnews.go.com/Politics/steve-bannon-pleads-guilty-border-wall-fraud-case/story?id=118664692

2 Ibid.

had decided to do their bidding in state court, where the pardon does not apply.

In terms of his January 6 subpoena fight, meanwhile, Bannon says he does not want a pardon for the time he did behind bars last year.

> I don't want a pardon because mine was a misdemeanor, and I served my time. What I want to do is go to the Supreme Court and have the January 6th Committee ruled as illegitimate. That's what is key to me. My thing is the separation of powers. Was it a legitimate committee or not? Did the president have the power to do executive privilege? I think I win on both of those.

Bannon has always been defiant.

When I worked under him at Breitbart, he would tell us to be honey badgers, because they do not give a damn. He would urge his reporters to be fearless in our pursuit of the truth and expose any corruption inside Washington. In fact, his Capitol Hill home was often referred to as the "Breitbart embassy," since he and Breitbart clearly were not part of the Washington establishment. Outliers in the DC swamp.

He has the ability to read the pulse of Trump's populist base, which has made Democrats fear him. Bannon pushed back, though, when I suggested that he has been singled out, saying he wears the lawfare badge proudly.

"I feel empowered because I know I am doing my job. If they [he said, referencing the Deep State] are not trying to come after me, and fuck me and crush me and put me in prison, then I know I am not doing something right."

Peter Navarro, similarly, has noted the extent of his legal fees in his fight against the congressional subpoena litigation, which also led to his lock-up. He said that cost him $1.7 million.[3] Navarro served as a trade and economic advisor to Trump during his first administration and, like Bannon, refused to comply with a subpoena from the House's January 6th Committee, landing him behind bars for a few months in 2024, too.

Others in Trump's inner circle, though—like former New York City Mayor Rudy Giuliani, who served as Trump's personal lawyer—have been financially decimated by the lawfare.

Giuliani was partly the face of Trump's 2020 election fraud legal challenges, traveling to various swing states to make arguments that the election should be investigated, not certified.

His advocacy led to civil and criminal lawsuits against himself and others.

In 2023, he had more than $1 million in unpaid legal fees,[4] and subsequently faced a whopping $146 million judgment in a defamation lawsuit involving Giuliani's questioning of Georgia election workers' conduct.[5] Giuliani has had to turn over his personal jewelry, accounts, Manhattan home, vehicle, and luxury

---

3 Giulia Carbonaro, "Former Trump Official Peter Navarro Says He Faces $1.7M in Legal Costs," *Newsweek*, September 2, 2023, https://www.newsweek.com/former-trump-official-peter-navarro-faces-1-7m-legal-costs-1824161

4 Katelyn Polantz, "Rudy Giuliani's former attorneys sue him for more than $1.3 million in unpaid legal fees," CNN, September 19, 2023, https://www.cnn.com/2023/09/18/politics/rudy-giuliani-legal-fees-lawsuit/index.html

5 Alex Wolf, "Giuliani Loses NYC Apartment, Trump Fees to Poll Workers," *Bloomberg Law*, October 22, 2024, https://news.bloomberglaw.com/bankruptcy-law/giuliani-loses-nyc-apartment-trump-legal-fees-to-poll-workers

watch collection to help satisfy some of that judgment.[6] He also faced losing his Florida condo.[7]

Giuliani was found to have defamed a female election worker in Georgia and her daughter for accusing them of tampering with ballots, and counting some from suitcases, in Atlanta during the 2020 election.[8] They said that they had faced threats as a result of his claims and that he has continued to repeat the allegations of election fraud.[9]

Giuliani, who is reportedly worth between $1 million and $10 million, had sought to enter bankruptcy court over the verdict.[10]

His financial—and legal—troubles do not stop there.

Giuliani is also a defendant, like Trump, in Fulton County, Georgia, where a now-defunct prosecutor had tried to charge them and others with conspiracy to undermine the 2020 election.

John Eastman, like Giuliani, knows the Georgia charges all too well, as he is also a co-defendant alongside the president.

Eastman was the lawyer who counseled Trump on how exactly he could contest the 2020 election certification in

---

6 Ibid.

7 Katelyn Polantz, "Federal judge slams Rudy Giuliani as 'outrageous and shameful' as she holds him in contempt in 2020 election defamation case," CNN, January 10, 2025, https://www.cnn.com/2025/01/10/politics/rudy-giuliani-contempt-hearing-defamation-case/index.html

8 Jeff Amy, "Georgia election workers settle defamation lawsuit against conservative website," Associated Press, October 11, 2024, https://apnews.com/article/ruby-freeman-shaye-moss-gateway-pundit-settlement-3c55e2c7cf75cf0f8dc6496da14b094e

9 Polantz, "Federal judge slams Rudy Giuliani…," https://www.cnn.com/2025/01/10/politics/rudy-giuliani-contempt-hearing-defamation-case/index.html

10 Mark Osborne, "Rudy Giuliani loses bid to dismiss $148 million defamation judgment in Georgia election workers case," ABC News, April 15, 2024, https://abcnews.go.com/Politics/rudy-giuliani-loses-bid-dismiss-148-million-defamation/story?id=109264527

Washington, DC, amid allegations of fraud. He advised, through a memo, that former Vice President Mike Pence could reject Congress's certification of the results on January 6, 2021.

For his legal advocacy, Eastman has faced a barrage of lawsuits alongside the Georgia indictment. And he also lost his ability to practice law in the state of California after being punished by the state's disciplinary board.

Eastman told me he does not regret being put at the forefront of the sweeping lawsuits where he has had to fend off these legal battles, all because he's been painted as the legal architect of January 6, 2021.

> Our country is on the precipice of losing the consent of the govern, of losing important freedoms that our founders bequeathed to us and for whatever reason, I've been cast into the front lines of that battle and I can't think of a place more important to be to make sure we hand off to my kids and grandkids the same freedom I inherited.

"So, I do not regret my representation of President Trump, or anything I did trying to expose illegality in the 2020 election," he added.

Eastman does, though, regret the direction the legal industry has gone in tolerating lawfare.

> I do regret that my profession and my colleagues' profession have so signed on to this lawfare because of their antipathy to President Trump that I have had to deal with, what I have

> had to deal with, over the last three years. It's preposterous, but I am not backing down from it. I happen to be in a position to fight against it. I am well-armored for that fight.

The lawfare that the Democrats have deployed against Trump and his inner circle is a strategy, Eastman insisted. I heard this same argument from others, too, who were prosecuted, jailed, and drowned in legal debt.

The American people, most of all, appeared to have believed it was all a political strategy as well, seeing through it on November 5, 2024, and electing Trump back to the White House.

Eastman said the goal of Democrats through their lawfare is not only to disbar lawyers like him who support conservatives or their causes, but also to silence any challenge to the status quo and shred free speech rights.

"It is clear what they are doing," Eastman explained. "They are trying to silence the American people who have a different view—that the false narrative being forced down our throats by the government. This is Orwellian. We fed the lie, you must not only repeat the lie, but you must come to believe the lie."

Eastman has a legal team working in six different states after facing eighteen legal battles over his decision to represent Trump and counsel him on the 2020 contest. One lawsuit went after both Eastman and Mark Zuckerberg, the founder of Facebook and someone who was known to support Democrat causes. The two, Eastman and Zuckerberg, were not on the same sides in 2020, ironically.

> One of my favorite ones was some guy in North Carolina filed suit against a whole lot of people

> and named me as the lead defendant. Why? I have no idea, but it was me and Rudy Giuliani and Sean Hannity and Fox News and Donald Trump Jr., and a whole lot of people, and Mark Zuckerberg—which was kind of weird because he was funding the other side—and one of the allegations was this was all billionaire oligarchs trying to undermine our democracy.

"I somehow missed that I am a billionaire," Eastman added, "but anyway, that got dismissed. It was frivolous, but the judge wouldn't award sanctions against this guy, and it cost $40,000 to get it dismissed. It was ridiculous."

In the Georgia prosecution, part of Eastman's bond condition is not to speak to witnesses or co-defendants. He told me that not communicating with co-defendants is doable since there are just seventeen others, but the number of witnesses is more than one hundred people. Calling that bar "insane," he wants to see the Georgia prosecution go away, now that the prosecutor who lobbed the charges against him, Trump, Giuliani, and the other co-defendants was removed from the case for unethical actions surrounding her funding of the prosecution. Fulton County District Attorney Fani Willis had hired her boyfriend, Nathan Wade, to act as a special prosecutor, while paying him generously from county funds. Willis's testimony defending her unethical actions was must-see TV as it was televised live. I will expand more on the tainted Fulton County actions later—I promise.

Meanwhile, aside from Georgia's criminal case, Eastman also takes issue with the California bar, for which he has been a member for more than twenty years. It has tried to take away his license to practice law over his counseling of the president.

"The bar organizations themselves are so politically biased," he told me.

As Trump's lawyer, Eastman had a duty to counsel Trump on how to constitutionally launch a challenge, he insists. As a result, however, he has been targeted over such legal advice. This is something that is supposed to be sacred and confidential in the legal profession: the attorney-client relationship.

"Not only do you have the right to provide legal counsel on contested issues, but when you are retained as a lawyer, you have an ethical duty to zealously advocate for that client, raising every plausible argument based on fact and law that you can," he said, adding that if a constitutional interpretation is not settled by a court, then you are obligated to push the view that best supports your client.

His client just happened to be the commander in chief, challenging what he saw as suspect election results in key swing states.

"I happen to think the positions I staked out were right; but even if ultimately they were wrong or the weaker argument, you still have an ethical duty to press them if there is any plausible argument for them," Eastman said.

The danger of the precedent that has been set with Eastman—the criminalizing of lawyers for counseling an unpopular client—is dangerous to the legal profession. It will have a chilling effect, and attorneys may not want to take on controversial clients.

"It is a huge problem," Eastman said, "and they are doing it because of Trump Derangement Syndrome, which I am convinced is a real thing, and one of the symptoms is blindness to the consequences to the action. In their zealous efforts to get Trump, no matter what, they are throwing out the baby with the bath water. They are throwing out the rule of law to get Trump."

Eastman says his bar challenge has been the longest and most expensive disciplinary proceeding "in history," and he chastised the California bar as being selective in their pursuit of disciplining lawyers. His license has been suspended and a recommendation of permanent disbarment was made.

> The people that were responsible for the Russia hoax and the blatant lies that tied this country up for years, including Eric Swalwell and Adam Schiff, both members of the California Bar—and I know somebody filed bar complaints against them, and those never have gone anywhere—and what they did is a lot more egregious than what I did, even if you assume what they say I did was true, and it is not; so the bar system itself has become corrupted.

Eastman was pointing to now-Senator Adam Schiff of California, who constantly told the public during the first Trump administration, when he was in the House of Representatives, that he had seen evidence of collusion between the Trump campaign and Russia. Eric Swalwell, also a California lawmaker, served as a prosecutor against Trump during his second impeachment. Both Democrats have been mouthpieces, helping spread the lawfare against Trump and his allies through the media.

Eastman, though, also called out the Texas bar for being politically motivated—like California—in its attempt to pursue discipline against pro-Trump lawyer Sidney Powell and Texas Attorney General Ken Paxton.

"The fact that they had to go through that process at all is a scandal," Eastman said.

Powell faced a bar complaint for representing Trump in several swing-state lawsuits looking to challenge the 2020 results. And Paxton, too, filed a petition with the Supreme Court against four swing states, saying the alleged fraud disenfranchised Texas voters. Both Texas bar complaints ultimately failed, and Powell and Paxton are still actively able to practice in their home states.

Paxton told me that there are actually rules in his state that say a lawyer cannot be disciplined for an out-of-state case. But that didn't stop the Texas Bar Association from trying.

"The Supreme Court didn't discipline us. They said we didn't have standing. Otherwise, you are chilling lawyers from making legal arguments that may be creative; but now you are going to oversee an elected official and say, 'We are going to control you because we control your license, we will just take it away,'" he said of the weaponized judicial process he experienced.

"I know so many conservative lawyers, so many attorneys general, who had their license—they go after their licenses. I have friends in California, who lost their license because they're conservative," he added.

Paxton, who was first elected more than a decade ago in 2014, said lawfare has increased significantly in the past four years under the Biden Justice Department.[11] He has been a Trump ally and defender as Texas's top cop. Paxton has faced a lawsuit from the US Securities and Exchange Commission, which accused him of an alleged nondisclosure.[12] The case was dismissed in his favor. And additionally, on top of defending his law license

---

[11] Alex Swoyer, "Watch: Firebrand Texas AG Ken Paxton anticipates new ally in Trump Justice Department," *The Washington Times*, January 16, 2025, https://www.washingtontimes.com/news/2025/jan/16/ken-paxton-firebrand-texas-attorney-general-anticipates-ally-donald/

[12] Ibid.

against the state bar association for his 2020 election challenge, he also had to battle lawmakers, as well as state prosecutors, in an impeachment trial.[13]

Paxton told me the cost of lawfare for him was "immense."

"It is every day. It never stops. I've gone through, like, six major things—from the SEC to three criminal indictments in the state, to the FBI investigating me for four years, to impeachment. I mean, I have incurred over $16 million in legal defense. What they do is try to drain you financially, and then you have to say, 'Okay, I am guilty'—not because you are: because you can't pay," Paxton said.

> I am thinking about what they did to me, so here is the order—just some of it. They ran an election against me, spent $20–30 million running George P. Bush against me, but as soon as I win, I get impeached. I think, "I just got in office. These people just elected me, and now you're taking it away, you elected officials." So, I go through four months of that. As soon as that is over, I am going to trial on three felonies that have been sitting around for ten years, not in my county, but they moved me to a Democratic county with all Democratic judges. I worked that out, got that resolved, then the FBI began investigating me again. The day I win that case in Houston, the FBI is knocking on my door, and they are knocking on other peoples' doors. They just keep coming after you.

---

13 Ibid.

Although the lawfare against Trump and his inner circle began with the Russia collusion investigation, which was launched during his 2016 campaign, the legal assault spread like wildfire after January 6, 2021. That fateful day was responsible for two out of four of the president's criminal prosecutions, and indictments against some of his staff, supporters, and allies like Giuliani and Eastman.

Some of Trump voters, too, who were charged and convicted in the January 6, 2021 Capitol riot, believe they were likewise at the epicenter of the lawfare targeting the MAGA movement. The weaponization of the justice system dinged everyday Americans, as I will continue to explore in later chapters.

But as for the January 6 defendants, now that they were pardoned—and videos were released showing some of them being led through the Capitol by police officers—there is a sense of vindication among them. They feel America saw the truth of January 6 and that not all of them were violent, as had been painted by Democrats, President Biden's Justice Department, and the mainstream media.

One of them feeling vindicated and liberated is Brandon Straka.

Straka garnered nearly a million social media followers between his Instagram and X accounts, as he founded the Walk Away Campaign, which is a grassroots movement launched in 2018 where former liberal voters walk away from the Democratic Party. He was an online celebrity in the conservative world. That is, up until January 6. After that, he says he felt blacklisted.

On that historic day, he was outside the US Capitol during the protests where he shared a roughly eight-minute video of the scene. Although he never went inside the Capitol building—nor committed any violence—he was charged by the feds with entering and remaining on restricted grounds, impeding a law enforcement officer, and disorderly conduct.[14] The complaint alleged he urged people to stop the vote certification inside the Capitol.

For sharing that eight-minute video, where he stood outside an entrance to the Capitol, he was looking at roughly thirty years in prison.[15]

Straka pleaded guilty to one count and was released on thirty-six months of probation, which included three months of home detention, as well as a $5,000 fine and $500 in restitution.[16] He was sentenced to federal supervision, which expired just after Trump entered office when he, along with roughly 1,500 other January 6 defendants, were pardoned.

Still, the years-long experience cost him not just financially, but also mentally and emotionally.

Straka told me the hardest part is seeing the MAGA movement turn its back on him and fellow January 6 defendants without pushing to shed light on the injustices surrounding the feds' treatment of them. Some legal experts have said the way the federal prosecutors categorized violence that day was different than had been applied in other criminal proceedings, as they appeared to want to make an example out of the Trump supporters. But using criminal prosecutions to make an example out of a political opponent is not the right answer—it is lawfare. The facts of each case must support the elements of a crime, and if an accused is found guilty, he or she should be sentenced consistent with others who are similarly situated. But we did not see that with the

---

14 Straka, Brandon. Case No. 1:21-cr-579, US Justice Department, February 4, 2022, https://www.justice.gov/usao-dc/case-multi-defendant/file/1441146/dl

15 *Real Walk Away*, Instagram, January 21, 2025, https://www.instagram.com/p/DFG58P7t2Ir/?img_index=1&igsh=YzNzbzN3bGJibWNh

16 Ibid.

MAGA lawfare. We saw January 6 defendants treated much more harshly than other federal rioters.

"My January sixth arrest, I experienced what I called the 'trifecta,' which means, I was criminally charged, I was civilly sued, and I had to go against the January 6th Committee," Straka told me when discussing the cost of lawfare. "Between those three things, I spent about $350,000 on lawyers and legal fees getting through all that, and interestingly, the worst of it was the civil case, actually. I spent more on the civil case than I did the criminal case."

Straka said in terms of his criminal prosecution, he knew he was going to take a plea deal, but the case was continued five times, and it took a year and a half between arrest and sentencing, costing him between $100,000 and $125,000.

"I spent another $200,000 on the civil case. That was a real nightmare," he told me.

The civil suit involved a liberal-funded group that represented roughly half a dozen black and brown Capitol police officers that sued Straka and more than a dozen others under the Ku Klux Klan Act, which is aimed at preventing the deprivation of civil rights of minorities. The Ku Klux Klan Act, as I will detail in later chapters, has been used against Trump supporters outside of Washington, DC, as well. It was an attempt by Democrats and Big Law to try to silence MAGA advocacy.

Straka, meanwhile, said it was alleged in his KKK Act lawsuit that he and his fellow defendants—whom he did not know—were white supremacists that wanted to attack black and brown officers at the Capitol.

He was eventually released from the lawsuit on procedural and jurisdictional grounds, but that took two years. He said the costliest part of the lawsuit was the discovery; however, through the discovery process it was uncovered that none of the officers suing him were on the side of the Capitol where he was on January 6—or at the time he was there.

"One of them was literally in Maryland," Straka told me. "But he is suing me for aiding and abetting his battery—but he wasn't even on Capitol grounds when I was there."

In terms of the January 6 Committee deposition Straka had to give, he said that "was the easiest of all the shit," although he had to turn over hundreds of documents to the lawmakers.

"The emotional piece is I am not even through it," he said. "I am emotionally drained. I feel really betrayed. I feel abandoned."

The whole ordeal damaged relationships he had with conservative influencers and media personalities.

"A lot of my relationships with people in media or, like, conservative influencers or pundits, went quiet—didn't have my back. To me, in some ways, that has been the worst part," he said, as his work largely relies on the grassroots support. "How do you then pick back up and go back to work, knowing you feel differently now about the people you are working with and what you're doing?"

Some of the conservative influencers Straka knew had online shows with millions of followers, but declined to have any January 6 defendants on to tell their side of the story. He said that conservatives—and media—not asking tough questions led to the snowball effect of the MAGA-targeted lawfare.

"I wasn't even accused of violence. I wasn't even accused of going in the building. It was like, what was so scary about my case that you can't have me on your show to talk about what they are doing?" Straka said.

> But like, nobody would do it. So, it was like in the darkness and in the silence, the DOJ and the FBI were allowed to do anything and everything they want. And it just got bigger and bigger and bigger and bigger, and by the time anybody started giving a shit, it was just a nightmare.

Straka acknowledged that conservative media sensation Tucker Carlson and House GOP leadership releasing the security video of the so-called "insurrection" helped change public opinion related to January 6 defendants. That, coupled with the fact that they were being treated judicially different than other federal rioters had been, in terms of their sentencing.

Many rioters at a federal courthouse in Portland, Oregon, in 2020, during the criminal justice wave following the death of George Floyd—a black man killed by a white police officer—received diversion agreements, where they could simply do community service to erase their charges.

No January 6 defendants—not even the ones that remained outside the Capitol and free of violence—were offered diversion agreements.

"Public opinion has changed quite a bit," Straka told me, as more sunshine has been shed on how January 6 defendants have been treated. "I think public advocacy was a big part of it. I have been for three years now speaking out on a regular basis about the injustices of January 6—what has happened to the defendants, what the government is doing, what Big Tech is doing," he said.

"Nothing will change if the January 6 defendants continue to be ignored and nobody sits down with us and asks us about what we went through and why we pled guilty, about why we pled guilty to things we weren't guilty of," Straka added, noting that some of them are contemplating suing for restitution. "Our names and reputations are permanently destroyed."

Straka, unlike many January 6 defendants, escaped jail time. Some were left behind bars and put in solitary confinement.[17] At least five were driven to suicide, according to a post on Instagram from Straka's Walk Away Campaign.[18]

January 6, 2021 was a terrible day for thousands—and for the country. The violence committed was reprehensible, but so was the abuse of the justice system to make examples of political opponents.

And that day was used against President Trump, too, in an attempt to criminalize his belief and advocacy that the 2020 election was tainted with fraud.

Trump—like his MAGA base—also knows the financial cost of the lawfare.

The president himself is facing more than $673 million in legal penalties—just between his civil fraud verdict and the defamation judgment in favor of E. Jean Carroll, who claimed Trump raped her in the 1990s at a department store in New York City. That $673 million does not include what he is spending on his legal representation—or other legal penalties—as he battles his New York, Georgia, and federal prosecutions.

Trump has the finances and the support—through his political action committee—to help foot legal bills, though, unlike others caught up in Democrats' lawfare.

An Associated Press report from February of 2024 showed that Trump's Save America PAC had spent 84 percent of its

---

17 Ibid.

18 Ibid.

funding at the time towards legal fees.[19] In October of 2024—roughly a month before the November election—the PAC had spent about $60 million toward paying Trump's legal fees.[20]

There's nothing illegal about using a PAC or a party—like the Republican National Committee, hypothetically—to help foot legal bills.[21] The only elections-law bar is that a candidate cannot use campaign money for personal expenses.[22]

President Joe Biden used help from the Democratic National Committee to pay his lawyers for their work on Special Counsel Robert Hur's probe, which looked into his alleged mishandling of classified documents.[23] His probe resulted in zero charges, but Trump's classified-documents investigation landed him again in federal court. It was one of many double standards that are highlighted in later chapters, during the sequence of lawfare episodes that plagued the president.

The RNC, however, did not endorse paying Trump's legal bills during the 2024 election.[24] But maybe it should have, since

---

19 Richard Lardner and Aaron Kessler, "Trump spent $76 million over last two years on attorneys as legal troubles mount ahead of election," Associated Press, February 2, 2024, https://apnews.com/article/trump-spent-millions-legal-fees-2024-presidential-campaign-3384cbfc2df69d3e97ba9e47c2384312

20 Alison Durkee, "Trump Fundraising Group Routed $7 Million To Cover His Legal Bills Last Quarter," *Forbes*, October 16, 2024, https://www.forbes.com/sites/alisondurkee/2024/10/16/trump-fundraising-group-routed-7-million-to-cover-his-legal-bills-last-quarter/

21 Alex Swoyer, "Nothing illegal about spending donor money on legal bills and Trump voters approve," *The Washington Times*, May 6, 2024, https://www.washingtontimes.com/news/2024/may/6/nothing-illegal-about-spending-donor-money-on-lega/

22 Ibid.

23 Ibid.

24 Ibid.

supporters of the president appear to have been up for the lawfare fight.

Robert Cahaly, chief pollster at the Trafalgar Group, told me back in May of 2024 that most Trump voters do not object to their donations going towards fighting the "political prosecution" of Trump.[25]

"The Trump voters see this as one and the same. Campaign or legal fees are part of the larger fight against the left. They don't see a line between them," he said, adding that less than 10 percent of Trump supporters objected to it.[26]

The Democrats' lawfare against Trump also cost American taxpayers more than $86 million.

American taxpayers paid roughly $32 million for Special Counsel Robert Mueller's probe into the debunked Russia collusion allegations that resulted in no charges;[27] more than $7.6 million went to Special Counsel John Durham's probe,[28] where he was basically reviewing the foundation of Mueller's work; and more than $47 million was spent toward Special Counsel Jack

---

25 Ibid.

26 Ibid.

27 Kevin Breuninger, "Robert Mueller's Russia probe cost nearly $32 million in total, Justice Department says," CNBC, August 2, 2019, https://www.cnbc.com/2019/08/02/robert-muellers-russia-probe-cost-nearly-32-million-in-total-doj.html

28 Landon Mion, "Legal pursuits of Trump come at high cost for taxpayers, former president's PAC 'Save America': report," Fox Business, August 15, 2023, https://www.foxbusiness.com/politics/legal-pursuits-trump-high-cost-taxpayers-former-presidents-pac-save-america-report

Smith,[29] who saw both his criminal prosecutions against Trump fizzle with the 2024 landslide reelection of the president to the White House. Smith was the one who charged President Trump with federal election fraud in Washington, DC, and mishandling classified documents in the Southern District of Florida, where Mar-a-Lago is located.

More than money, the lawfare has done damage across the political spectrum in Americans' trust of the court and judicial system.

A Gallup poll in December of 2024 found that Americans had lost trust in the judicial system during the past four years, though it did not cite a specific reason for the sharp decline.[30] The public's trust in the courts dropped to 35 percent, a 24-point low since 2000.[31] It only takes a bit of common sense to understand that Americans were tired—and concerned—about what they saw happening to Trump, being criminally targeted by political opponents with the threat of jail time.

Without public trust in the system of justice, one of our nation's three branches of government—the judiciary—falls.

House Judiciary Committee Chairman Jim Jordan has overseen probes into the lawfare as the top Republican lawmaker on the panel. He told me the loss of trust in the judiciary, potentially

---

29 Alec Schemmel, "Special Counsel Jack Smith's federal Trump cases cost taxpayers more than $50 million, financials show," Fox News, November 26, 2024, https://www.foxnews.com/politics/special-counsel-jack-smiths-federal-trump-cases-cost-taxpayers-more-than-50-million-financials-show

30 Alex Swoyer, "Americans lost trust in judicial system over the past four years, Gallup survey finds," *The Washington Times*, December 17, 2024, https://www.washingtontimes.com/news/2024/dec/17/americans-lost-trust-judicial-system-past-four-yea/

31 Ibid.

over lawfare, is coupled with Americans viewing their First Amendment liberties as being under attack, citing the online censorship taking root during the Biden administration.

> All that plays into the concern about faith and trust in the institutions and their government. And the best thing you can do about it is you win elections. And the American people spoke up pretty loud and pretty clearly on Election Day, and I think it was this issue—the weaponization of federal agencies against "we the people"—I think was one of the key issues on peoples' minds. Certainly the border, certainly inflation were top of mind; but I think also the weaponization of government. So when you put the right people in office and you put the right people running these agencies…that will be just huge for protecting American's rights and liberties and equal application of the law. That is how you combat it. That is how you change it. That is how you prevent it from happening in the future—you win elections, and you have the right people on these respective agencies.

Unfortunately, Democrats are not concerned with the cost of their lawfare. They kept pursuing it until it became overkill.

RUSSIAN "COLLUSION" ILLUSION, WHERE IT ALL BEGAN

"The investigation did not establish that members of the Trump Campaign conspired or coordinated with the Russian government in its election interference activities."[32]
—Special Counsel Robert Swan Mueller III

That just might be the most important sentence gleaned from Special Counsel Robert Mueller's 448-page report detailing his investigation into alleged "collusion"—or lack thereof—between the Russian government and Donald Trump's 2016 campaign.

Really, that should have been the end of it. But it wasn't.

And it still isn't nearly a decade later.

---

32 Special Counsel Robert S. Mueller III, *Report On The Investigation Into Russian Interference In The 2016 Presidential Election*, Volume I of II, US Justice Department, March 2019, https://www.justice.gov/archives/sco/file/1373816/dl

Russia was the start of Democrats' lawfare against Trump, and it began during his 2016 campaign, even before he entered the White House after his first election victory.

"It started when Jim Comey lied," House Judiciary Committee Chairman Jim Jordan, an Ohio Republican, told me during our interview about the Trump lawfare.

Jordan has spent years probing the Russia hoax and the abuses within the Federal Bureau of Investigation and the Justice Department, which have largely come to light from whistleblowers in the executive branch. He oversees the US House of Representatives' Judiciary Committee as its top Republican lawmaker. Comey served as head of the FBI from 2013 to 2017, until Trump eventually fired him.

"He went to the FISA court and spied on the president's campaign back in 2016," Jordan said of Comey.

Jordan was referencing the Foreign Intelligence Surveillance Act that has come under scrutiny in the years since. A judge on the secretive court had said the FBI had provided "unsupported" information to obtain a warrant to spy on a former Trump campaign advisor.[33]

Part of that partisan spying is what laid the groundwork for the controversial probe into Trump's 2016 campaign, where Mueller took over the investigation following Comey's termination in May of 2017.

The manipulating of FISA warrants to obtain the ability to spy was one of many errors made by the Washington establishment in their mission to nab Trump at the start of their lawfare,

---

33 Eric Tucker, "Secretive FISA court rebukes FBI over errors in Russia probe," Associated Press, December 17, 2019, https://apnews.com/secretive-fisa-court-rebukes-fbi-over-errors-in-russia-probe-bf5b3cfee4930501ca86242f446f353e

which began nearly a decade ago under the guise of Russia collusion.

As a bar-licensed attorney and member of the Capitol Hill press, I had access to the halls of the Capitol where the Russian rumors echoed for years—and on occasion, they still do.

Russia, for one reason or another, has become the favorite punching bag of the Washington establishment and Democrats. That is, aside from Trump. Most foreign experts, though, point to China as where the real focus and scrutiny should be. But for whatever reason, the press and Washington, DC, insiders cannot take their eyes off the Russian ball. As my *Washington Times* colleague Susan Ferrechio reported less than two months before Election Day 2024, "Russian collusion is back."[34]

It's quite something that it always seems to return during campaign season.

Ferrechio, who has covered politics for three decades, highlighted that Christopher Steele—the ex-British spy who nearly a decade ago helped launch the Federal Bureau of Investigation's spiraling Russian probe into Trump's 2016 team, known as Crossfire Hurricane—had authored a book that would publish just before the 2024 election.

Timing can be everything.

Steele is the one responsible for the infamous dossier that suggested Russia had dirt on Trump, such as recorded tapes of Trump in 2013 having prostitutes urinate on a bed once used by the Obamas in a Moscow hotel room.

---

[34] Susan Ferrechio, "Democrats say Trump colluding with Russia; Steele book claims democracy threat," *The Washington Times*, September 12, 2024, https://www.washingtontimes.com/news/2024/sep/12/democrats-revive-russian-collusion-charges-to-fram/

It was his dossier that is believed to have, in part, helped launch the federal investigation into the president's 2016 campaign, leading to the FISA warrants, which was not standard practice. Lawyers and law enforcement officials have a duty to exercise candor when presenting a court with a warrant request. Clearly, a warrant that rests on a salacious dossier that was funded by a political opponent, as Steele's was, should have been given the most skeptical of evaluations. Yet our federal investigators used it to help obtain the ability to spy on Trump's allies.

To detail the lawfare—meaning the use of the judicial system against an opponent—it is important to start from the very beginning. When it comes to Trump, from my experience reporting on the president's many prosecutions—and persecutions—the MAGA-targeted lawfare began with the faux Russia allegations. It was Democrats' launching pad for what later became their legal warfare.

Mueller's report dropped in March of 2019 following a roughly two-year investigation. But his quintessential finding that there was no collusion was not, unfortunately, the end of it for the media. The press continued its hyper-focus on potential criminal conduct surrounding Trump and Russian dealings.

Instead of seeing the president cleared of wrongdoing, Americans at the time read headlines from National Public Radio saying, "Mueller Report Doesn't Find Russian Collusion, But Can't 'Exonerate' On Obstruction."[35] The Public Broadcasting

---

[35] Carrie Johnson, "Mueller Report Doesn't Find Russian Collusion, But Can't 'Exonerate' On Obstruction," NPR, March 24, 2019, https://www.npr.org/2019/03/24/706318191/trump-white-house-hasnt-seen-or-been-briefed-on-mueller-investigation-report

Service article read, "Mueller report finds no Trump-Russia collusion, but does not exonerate president, attorney general says."[36]

Mueller did not bring charges against the Trump campaign; however, his report detailed a few interactions between Trump allies and Russian personnel. The mention of these brief exchanges suggested sinister actions, but in reality, no one was charged with acting as a foreign agent as part of Trump's campaign, or even doing anything illegal with the Russians. Instead, they were dinged by the law for having allegedly lied about their foreign conversations.

One of them was George Papadopoulos. He served as the Trump campaign's 2016 foreign policy advisor. In spring of 2016, he spoke with a London professor who suggested the Russians had dirt on Hillary Clinton. But no meeting came about the tip on damaging information.[37]

Later in the summer, Trump campaign officials, including Trump's son Don Jr. and his son-in-law Jared Kushner, met with a Russian lawyer on the similar belief that there would be incriminating information shared about Trump's political opponent. But nothing was apparently shared at that meeting, either.[38]

Some Trump critics believed that where there is smoke, there must be fire. But that theory failed to ignite for Mueller, his team, and Washington Democrats hot on the faux Russia trail.

About a month after the meeting between the Russian lawyer and Trump's family members, another campaign foreign policy

---

[36] Associated Press, "Mueller report finds no Trump-Russia collusion, but does not exonerate president, attorney general says," PBS, March 24, 2019, https://www.pbs.org/newshour/politics/barr-sends-principal-conclusions-of-mueller-report-to-congress

[37] Mueller, "Report On The Investigation Into Russian Interference," https://www.justice.gov/archives/sco/file/1373816/dl

[38] Ibid.

advisor, Carter Page, traveled in his personal capacity to Moscow to deliver remarks. The campaign reportedly had then distanced itself from Page over his pro-Russian agenda.[39]

And then in August of 2016, Paul Manafort, who was chairman of the Trump's 2016 campaign, met with a Russian businessman and shared internal polling about the Trump campaign from midwestern voters.[40] But ultimately the criminal charges Manafort faced out of Mueller's investigation stemmed from personal financial frauds that were discovered—like tax evasion—not his actions linked to Trump, meeting with a Russian businessman, or the campaign.

Beyond Manafort, General Michael Flynn was the one most scrutinized in the aftermath of the 2016 federal spying revelations.

Shortly after the election victory, Trump named Flynn, a close ally of Trump's 2016 campaign, his incoming national security advisor. In that role, Flynn contacted his counterpart in Russia in December of 2016 to ask that they do not escalate conflict between the countries after the Obama administration issued sanctions against Russia for interfering in the 2016 election through cyber hacks.[41]

The scrutiny surrounding Flynn's phone call, which involved FBI agents coming to the White House to interview him, in part drove the Russian collusion narrative to a higher level. When news broke that a top-level advisor to Trump made contact with a Russian official, the Russian collusion narrative exploded. Flynn was thrust into the spotlight.

Flynn and Papadopoulos, the campaign's foreign policy advisor, both ended up pleading guilty to lying to the feds over

---

[39] Ibid.

[40] Ibid.

[41] Ibid.

their interactions with Russian personnel. Flynn, though, later moved to withdraw his guilty plea months before being pardoned by Trump in 2020.[42] But that was after he lost his coveted post as national security advisor and had been dragged in and out of courtrooms.

Quite possibly, the most important point to be made out of the lengthy Mueller report was that no one from the Trump campaign was ever charged with having unlawfully worked with Russia during the 2016 election.

Wasn't that the point of the investigation to begin with? At least, that's what the American voters had been led to believe.

Mueller, though, after coming up short on Russian collusion, did leave the door open for the Justice Department to charge Trump with the crime of obstruction of justice, citing the president's attempt to do away with the investigation altogether and his firing of Comey, the former FBI director.

"The evidence we obtained about the President's actions and intent presents difficult issues that prevent us from conclusively determining that no criminal conduct occurred. Accordingly, while this report does not conclude that the President committed a crime, it also does not exonerate him," he wrote.[43]

---

[42] Scott Neuman, "Flynn Asks To Withdraw Guilty Plea In Case Stemming From Mueller Probe," NPR, January 15, 2020, https://www.npr.org/2020/01/15/796524593/flynn-asks-to-withdraw-guilty-plea-in-case-stemming-from-mueller-probe

[43] John Durham, "Report on Matters Related to Intelligence Activities and Investigations Arising Out of the 2016 Presidential Campaigns," US Justice Department, May 12, 2023, https://www.justice.gov/storage/durhamreport.pdf

It was as if the Washington establishment realized it came up short on any criminal findings, and so it had to throw some suggestion out there as an alternative way to nab the president.

But Trump's Attorney General William Barr did not take the invitation to bring such a charge.

In public remarks in April 2019, Barr said that after evaluating Mueller's report and consulting with others in the Justice Department, he did not believe there were sufficient facts to connect Trump to the crime of obstructing justice.

"There is substantial evidence to show that the President was frustrated and angered by a sincere belief that the investigation was undermining his presidency, propelled by his political opponents, and fueled by illegal leaks," Barr said.[44]

> Nonetheless, the White House fully cooperated with the Special Counsel's investigation, providing unfettered access to campaign and White House documents, directing senior aides to testify freely, and asserting no privilege claims. And at the same time, the President took no act that in fact deprived the Special Counsel of the documents and witnesses necessary to complete his investigation.[45]

It is hard to suggest a president is obstructing justice when the probe was allowed to continue on for two years. And Trump's

---

[44] William Barr, "Attorney General William P. Barr Delivers Remarks on the Release of the Report on the Investigation into Russian Interference in the 2016 Presidential Election," US Justice Department, April 18, 2019, https://www.justice.gov/opa/speech/attorney-general-william-p-barr-delivers-remarks-release-report-investigation-russian

[45] Ibid.

firing of Comey is well within the president's authority and discretion. He was not the only president to terminate an FBI director; for example, there is precedent from more than two decades prior, when former President Bill Clinton fired his FBI director William Sessions in 1993.[46]

In 2022, nearly three years after Barr's decision not to go after Trump on obstruction, the public got a deeper glimpse into the reasoning behind the Justice Department's decision not to pursue Mueller's obstruction suggestion when a memo drafted by two top officials at the DOJ was made public. It noted that there was no similar precedent to bring such a prosecution under obstruction, and that Trump's firing of Comey, coupled with his attempts to end the probe, were due to him believing it was politically motivated.[47] The memo also noted that Trump never actually interfered with the investigation and Mueller was never fired, having had the ability to thoroughly complete his work.[48] The obstruction suggestion was yet another use of lawfare, an attempt to manipulate a criminal charge that lacked any veracity.

It took most of Trump's first term for the Justice Department to squash any potential of criminal charges coming down against the president related to Russia.

When I spoke to Stephen K. Bannon, who served as White House's chief strategist for Trump in his first administration,

---

46 Sarah Begley, "James Comey Is the Second FBI Director to Be Fired. Here's What Happened the Other Time," *Time*, May 20, 2017, https://time.com/4773774/fired-fbi-director-william-sessons/

47 Eric Tucker, "Memo sheds light on decision to clear Trump in Russia probe," Associated Press, August 24, 2022, https://apnews.com/article/russia-ukraine-donald-trump-obstruction-of-justice-899cb4d9c-b921e21440451f942608500

48 Ibid.

he told me the whole federal probe stymied the American First agenda.

"We never really got the American First policies implemented until essentially late in Trump's first term. The deep state, their number one objective is to make sure you begin no program of deconstructing the administrative state," Bannon said when we spoke about the MAGA lawfare and where it all began, amid his own legal battles.

"If you think about it, they did a pretty good job. They stopped us from any real deconstruction. We did some deregulation, but we really didn't get down to the heart of it. They definitely thwarted us on every element," he said.

Some on the right believe that is precisely what the Trump-and-MAGA-targeted lawfare was all about—halting Trump and his administration from cutting bureaucracy and chipping away at federal power.

Republicans on Capitol Hill have likewise chastised Mueller over his investigation and the final report.

In 2019, before becoming director of national intelligence, then Texas Representative John Ratcliffe, a Republican, grilled Mueller during a hearing before the House Judiciary Committee.

"Donald Trump is not above the law. He's not. But he damn sure shouldn't be below the law, which is where volume two of this report puts him," Ratcliffe said of the part of Mueller's report suggesting Trump obstructed justice.[49]

---

49 Kaitlan Collins, et al., "GOP congressman who defended Trump during Mueller hearing is up for administration job," CNN, July 24, 2019, https://www.cnn.com/2019/07/24/politics/john-ratcliffe-trump-administration-job-mueller-hearing/index.html

Ratcliffe has maintained his loyalty to Trump over the years and was made Trump's director of the Central Intelligence Agency in his second administration.

Before leaving the White House in 2020, Trump tried to right some of the wrongs committed against his staff, who had been stained by the Russian hoax. He pardoned Flynn and Papadopoulos.

Flynn has remained a loyal backer of the president, truly believing in and supporting his America First agenda.

Papadopoulos served twelve days behind bars and was placed on a supervised release for a period of twelve months.[50] The Trump White House said Papadopoulos was nabbed on "a process-related crime, one count of making false statements."[51] According to reports, Papadopoulos was not forthcoming with the FBI about being offered dirt about Hillary Clinton from Russian contacts.

"Today's pardon helps correct the wrong that Mueller's team inflicted on so many people," Trump's first White House said in a statement.[52]

Papadopoulos, in an interview with ABC 7 Chicago in 2023, said the Crossfire investigation should never have started.[53]

---

50 Steve Holland, "Trump grants full pardon to Russia probe figure George Papadopoulos," Reuters, December 22, 2020, https://www.reuters.com/article/world/us/trump-grants-full-pardon-to-russia-probe-figure-george-papadopoulos-idUSKBN28X00Q/

51 Ibid.

52 Ibid.

53 ABC 7 Chicago, "Exclusive: George Papadopoulos speaks with ABC7 about damning Durham report," YouTube, May, 15, 2023, https://www.youtube.com/watch?v=-ug8U3DkU2Y

"This was a dirty political trick," he said. "There were a lot of casualties in this. I was one of them."[54]

"The democratic process was tarnished," he added. "This is something that will take years to repair in this country."[55]

He spoke out about the special counsel's investigation following the release of Special Counsel John Durham's 316-page report, which found the FBI opened the Russia probe into Trump's campaign too quickly, without substantiated evidence. Durham's report, which was done to probe the origins of the FBI's Russia probe, also pointed out that when evaluating alleged foreign interference in Hillary Clinton's 2016 campaign, the FBI acted differently than it had towards Trump.

Law enforcement should treat political candidates the same, since all are said to be equal under the law. But the double standards by federal law enforcement in the treatment of Trump compared to his Democratic opponents would not stop with Russia collusion. It continued on in the form of an indictment, as we would later see in regard to Trump's handling of classified documents. He was charged for mishandling classified records while Biden, who also mishandled classified papers, was not.

But turning back to Durham: He noted that the FBI "swiftly opened the Crossfire Hurricane investigation."[56] However, it did so without justification. "The FBI had no information in its holdings indicating that at any time during the campaign anyone in the Trump campaign had been in contact with any Russian intelligence officials," his report read. "The speed and manner in which the FBI opened and investigated Crossfire Hurricane

---

54 Ibid.

55 Ibid.

56 Durham, "Report on Matters Related to Intelligence Activities and Investigations…," https://www.justice.gov/storage/durhamreport.pdf

during the presidential election season based on raw, unanalyzed, and uncorroborated intelligence also reflected a noticeable departure from how it approached prior matters involving possible attempted foreign election interference plans aimed at the Clinton campaign."[57]

Remarkably, out of the Durham review came criminal charges against an FBI official, who altered an email to obtain a surveillance warrant of Trump's campaign advisor, Page. That former agent did not serve jail time and instead was only given probation.

Who is John Durham, you may be asking?

He was a special counsel who had been tasked with evaluating whether there was political bias that had launched the initial Crossfire Hurricane investigation by the FBI into Trump's 2016 campaign, which led to the appointment of Mueller.

It was essentially a special counsel investigation into a special counsel investigation, something rather historic. It was a result of the unfair lawfare against Trump and his allies. And arguably it was a waste of tax dollars, because had the first probe never been opened, there would not have been a second one. The dueling probes yielded taxpayers a price tag of more than $38 million.

Feeling vindicated following Durham's report, Trump continued his pardons in November and December of 2020.

He also pardoned Manafort, his former campaign chairman, who was caught up in financial crimes, and Roger Stone, a close political advisor during the 2016 election, who was set to report to prison for interfering with the Mueller investigation. Trump's White

[57] Ibid.

House said there was "prosecutorial overreach" in Manafort's case, and said there were "potential political bias" with Stone's trial.[58]

Trump could issue more pardons throughout his new administration, especially for former aides like Bannon and Peter Navarro, who served as the director of Trump's White House National Trade Council. Both went to jail ahead of the 2024 election for rejecting a congressional subpoena pushed by Democrats in their probe of January 6, 2021. Bannon and Navarro refused to testify, claiming it would interfere with executive privilege.

Flynn, said he did not really need the pardon that Trump gave him years ago. It took nearly eight years for him to feel cleared, which he told me came after Trump's reelection in 2024.

"I feel very vindicated now that Trump won again," Flynn said when discussing the lawfare deployed against him and the president. "I feel like an incredible weight was lifted off my shoulders that night when he declared victory, and I felt like, 'Okay, this actually shows that the American people clearly understand what happened,' and they know how evil it is inside of our government and the corruption that is really deep inside our government. Particularly, at the Department of Justice."

Still, Flynn told me that he was one of the most searched names online for more than a year and that the fake Russia narrative at the start of Trump's first administration cost him his career.

He had spent more than three decades in the military and became the director of the Defense Intelligence Agency in 2012.

---

[58] Doha Madani, "Trump pardons Roger Stone, Paul Manafort, Charles Kushner and others," NBC News, December 23, 2020, https://www.nbcnews.com/politics/politics-news/trump-pardons-roger-stone-paul-manafort-charles-kushner-others-n1252307

Under Trump's first administration, he served as the US national security advisor for about three weeks...until his fateful phone call with his Russian counterpart. That occurred during the transition period between the Obama administration and the new Trump administration. The call, captured through the feds' surveillance, is what led to increasing FBI scrutiny.

"As much as I wanted to serve my country again, I was a little bit naive to the level and depth of corruption we were up against. It was so extreme," Flynn told me.

"I have tried to maintain my dignity throughout all of this. I rose to the highest levels of our government, highest levels of our military, led one of the largest intel agencies in the world, and how embarrassing was it for me to be so visible internationally, brutally attacked. Me, my family, my children—I have grandchildren. So, I have tried to maintain my dignity, and part of that is I want people to see you can beat these people, you can fight back. And that is why I say I feel very vindicated that Trump won."

Despite that feeling, Flynn does not want to go back into the government this time with Trump, partly because of the stress the Russiagate lawfare had on his family, and also since he feels he is in a good position to advise from the outside. But he did speak with Trump after his 2024 election landslide, telling me he told the president "thanks for running" and "don't get killed," referencing the two assassination attempts against Trump during the 2024 campaign. Trump was shot at—and one of his supporters killed—during a July 2024 rally in Butler, Pennsylvania. Shortly thereafter, a man was nabbed at Trump's Florida golf course attempting to lie in wait to take a shot at the president. That man is currently in custody.

Flynn's plea deal years ago, during the first Trump administration, over lying to the FBI was made in an effort to protect his son, who apparently law enforcement was looking to target for acting as an unregistered foreign agent.[59]

All of this, Flynn told me, was a deal cut between lawyers without the court's knowledge, and it was not formalized. Flynn saw the negotiations in an email between his former lawyer and the Justice Department's attorney, calling them shady and illegal.

But even as more exculpatory evidence comes forth, he says there will still be people who believe the Russia narrative and that he committed a crime.

"The media partners with lawfare. It is not just the lawfare side," Flynn said. "If you are the most googled name in the world, which I was for two years…when you googled me, they didn't have the truth. They had what they wanted people to believe—that Flynn is a traitor, that General Flynn is a puppet of Vladimir Putin, that General Flynn committed treason—that is what the narrative was for two years."

He said he still sees media reports that say he lied and that Trump had to pardon him. But that is not an accurate portrayal of what took place, Flynn insists.

"Actually, neither of those are true because I didn't need a pardon from Trump—that case was dismissed. And I didn't lie to the FBI, and that has been proven. Part of it was when my case was dismissed, they had to admit that," Flynn said. "People can question me all day long why I pled guilty, and I've been public about that. I have a movie out about that."

---

59 Andrew McCarthy, "Something seems rotten in Flynn's case—and maybe others, too," *The Hill*, April 30, 2020, https://thehill.com/opinion/judiciary/495366-something-seems-rotten-in-flynns-case-and-maybe-others-too/

The movie, *Flynn*, which came out in 2024 with Tucker Carlson, focuses on his life—from his rise in the military to the political prosecution.[60]

Sidney Powell, a pro-Trump lawyer who represented Flynn, argued in court filings that her client did not make materially false statements to the FBI—that he just had a failure of recollection, and that he had been forced into cooperation over threats of indicting his son.[61]

Flynn told me he viewed the side negotiations between the lawyers as being done "outside the law" in his case.

"These guys are going to find you guilty, and the judges are going to go right along with it, especially the Washington, DC, judges," he said.

What has also been uncovered in the years since Flynn's 2016 phone call is that the inspector general for the Justice Department—like Durham—also questioned whether there was adequate predicate even to have opened a probe into the Trump campaign.[62]

Flynn said the legal abuse within the intelligence community started against him and Trump during the Obama administration, under the forty-fourth president. He wants to see Trump and his new administration pursue the corrupt individuals that he said perpetrated the Russia collusion narrative.

---

60 *Flynn,* IMDb, 2024, https://www.imdb.com/title/tt30413525/

61 McCarthy, "Something seems rotten in Flynn's case," https://thehill.com/opinion/judiciary/495366-something-seems-rotten-in-flynns-case-and-maybe-others-too/

62 John Malcolm, "Michael Flynn Finally Seems to Be Getting the Justice He Deserves," The Heritage Foundation, May 11, 2020, https://www.heritage.org/crime-and-justice/commentary/michael-flynn-finally-seems-be-getting-the-justice-he-deserves

"People have to be held accountable for that," Flynn said. "It needs to happen. Trump is the poster child for judicial abuse—for lawfare. He is the poster child in history for the weaponization of government against a president, and it makes it almost feel like this is not even America."

"It is going to get worse until there are some scalps. These people won't stop," he added. "For the rest of my life, I am going to have to deal with the idiots that believe I am a traitor."

"Trump, to get to the victory line this time—to the end zone this last election—was hard. But the really hard part is just about to begin. And if he doesn't do it right, then I fear for the country," Flynn concluded.

One of the key players pushing the "Russia Russia Russia" narrative was Representative Adam Schiff, who was the top Democrat on the House Permanent Select Committee on Intelligence during the Mueller probe. From 2018 to 2019, he led the committee after Democrats took control of the House. In 2024, he was elected to the US Senate.

Schiff should be known as the boy who cried "Russia."

I remember it very clearly. In the basement of the US Capitol, I was staked out with fellow reporters pacing outside of a closed-door hearing with members of Schiff's committee, who were being briefed on details of Trump's 2016 campaign and alleged Russian contacts at the time.

Schiff would emerge to speak to reporters, affirming—repeatedly—that behind the closed doors he heard bombshell evidence of collusion. He'd field questions, convincingly make eye contact with all reporters, and leave journalists in suspense of what sort of troubling findings he had uncovered—and promised would surface.

Schiff was certain—and persuaded the mainstream media—that illegal conduct had taken place.

"There is already, in my view, ample evidence in the public domain on the issue of collusion if you're willing to see it," Schiff said in 2018, roughly a year after Mueller's appointment and as his committee was also probing the collusion theory.[63]

"We continue to learn things that take your breath away," Schiff told CNN in January of 2019.[64] "There is clear evidence on the issue of collusion...but whether it amounts to conspiracy beyond a reasonable doubt, we have to wait for Bob Mueller's work."

His assurance that there was criminal conduct—and his weekly appearances on cable news shows vowing that the public will soon see what he knew to have happened—became part of the foundation for Democrats in their attempt to entrap Trump in lawless activities with the initial allegations he "colluded" with Russia to win the 2016 campaign. The hook was their convincing media interviews insisting that because of Russia, Trump was in the White House.

Schiff overpromised and underdelivered.

Neither he nor Mueller came up with a smoking gun—or any evidence that would support his "take your breath away" claim.

But he was able to peddle the message with the help of the mainstream media, which became key in Democrats' lawfare

---

63 Erin Kelly, "Adam Schiff: There is 'ample evidence' of collusion between Trump campaign, Russians," *USA Today*, February 14, 2018, https://www.usatoday.com/story/news/politics/2018/02/14/adam-schiff-there-ample-evidence-collusion-between-trump-campaign-russians/336786002/

64 Adam Schiff, "Rep. Schiff on CNN: Evidence of Collusion Is Clear, Mueller Will Find Out If There's Been a Crime," YouTube, https://www.youtube.com/watch?v=3VKMhiWp5nc

tactics. They oversaturated the audience with their message, which created division and bias. Notably, it created fake news.

The First Amendment provides Americans with the freedom of speech, and politicians like Schiff are given even higher protections for political speech. However, the misinformation that is spread due to political bias and animus toward an opponent undermines the ability of voters to make educated decisions when their minds are clouded by this type of political propaganda. The way in which social media posts and news are spread at such a rapid speed in the digital world also creates a problem when a lie is told, as it spreads like wildfire before any misrepresentation can ever be corrected. It also tarnishes people's reputations—like Flynn's.

Brent Baker, an expert at Media Research Center, a press watchdog organization, told me the Russia narrative overshadowed everything else in Trump's first administration.

"It may not have mattered to his hardcore supporters, but to the whole political class and anybody who wasn't a committed Trump fan, it just gave them legitimacy to say 'we knew this guy was a fraud, we knew he was a phony, we knew he had to cheat,' and it confirmed this bias," Baker explained. He added that we still hear about Russia, and people believe that there was in fact collusion in 2016, though Mueller never suggested that was so.

"People assume it's true," Baker told me. "People just heard headlines. They heard those things, and therefore why would they not believe it, because there's no retraction with the media."

He said the same is true for the Hunter Biden laptop story, which emerged during the 2020 election. Intel officials said the salacious material found from President Biden's son's laptop was Russian disinformation, so the photographs and emails that suggested potential corruption within the Biden family were censored online.

"You had credible people who had real jobs in intelligence making up a false story," Baker said. "The media would follow what the political establishment would say, and the political establishment would say a lot of things that weren't true." Baker added, referencing the mainstream media: "They obviously were very happy and enjoyed doing this; they agreed with the premise."

The media could not get enough of Schiff, whom it gave a major platform to spread the real Russian disinformation. When Republicans later won back control of the House of Representatives, they censured Schiff in 2023 over his comments about Russian collusion. A censure is a form of public reprimand or humiliation.

Despite the recorded rebuke, the damage was done.

One important aspect to note in the Russian collusion story is that "collusion" is absent from the Federal Code. It is not actually a crime. Conspiracy is, but that was not the chosen lingo of the Washington establishment. But if you had asked the average American about "collusion," they would think it was something sinister, given its constant use in news coverage.

This deliberate choice in wording by Democrats signals they were muddying the waters from the very beginning by trying to make something sound unlawful that in reality lacks any criminality.

The other important wrinkle in the story is that it was actually Trump's rival, Hillary Clinton, who used a foreign operative to aid in the implementation of a Russia collusion narrative. Six years later, she, along with the Democratic National Committee, were fined $113,000 by the Federal Election Commission for funding the infamous dossier that started the whole Russia probe.[65] Specifically, they were fined for failing to disclose details surrounding campaign payments to Fusion GPS, a Washington research firm. Fusion GPS had hired Steele, the ex-British spy, to dig up opposition research and disseminate his unverified dossier. Steele's work, as I've referenced, arguably helped launch the whole Russian collusion narrative. Even before Trump took office in January of 2016, Steele's dossier—which was unverified—made headlines when *Buzzfeed* first published it. Reports also surfaced that Comey had even briefed Trump on it. Those reports were later confirmed by Trump's staff, who noted how unfair and ridiculous it was for the incoming president to come into office subject to a partisan "witch hunt."

The feds seemed caught up in trying to prove "Russian collusion" through the surveillance of Trump's 2016 campaign personnel and the unverified, salacious dossier, which in reality was opposition research from Trump's opponent.

Trump went on to fire Comey roughly four months after taking office, with critics suggesting the termination was due to the Russia probe.[66] In reality, Comey ran afoul of FBI practices. It is fair to reason he was fired for his actions taken as the leader of the FBI. One example was when he beat the Justice Department to the media microphones in July of 2016, holding a press conference to comment that there would be no recommendation of charges

---

65 Marshall Cohen, "FEC fines Hillary Clinton campaign and DNC over Trump-Russia dossier research," CNN, March 30, 2020, https://www.cnn.com/2022/03/30/politics/clinton-dnc-steele-dossier-fusion-gps/index.html

66 Patricia Zengerle and Susan Cornwell, "Comey says Trump fired him to undermine FBI Russia investigation," Reuters, June 8, 2017, https://www.reuters.com/article/world/comey-says-trump-fired-him-to-undermine-fbi-russia-investigation-idUSKBN18Z0HC/

against Hillary Clinton ahead of the 2016 election for her use of a private email server during her time as secretary of state. She had allegedly mishandled classified information. Typically, such an announcement would be reserved for the Justice Department, which is the agency tasked with actually announcing and issuing federal charges against people.

Comey even leaked his own notes to a friend about his meetings with Trump. In 2019, the inspector general said Comey violated department policy by the leak, but the Justice Department did not move to prosecute him.[67] When federal officials leak sensitive information, they usually do jail time. But not the former director of the nation's top law enforcement agency.

The American people saw the double standard—one of many—which in part is why they elected an outsider like Trump to fix the special treatment Washington insiders repeatedly receive.

The DNC, meanwhile, actually brought a lawsuit in 2018 against the Trump campaign, Russia, and Wikileaks, which reportedly had Russian hackers infiltrate Clinton's emails and disseminate them online during the campaign.[68] In the legal battle, they claimed that Trump willfully took help from Russia to

---

67 Allan Smith, "Inspector general says Comey violated policy by leaking memos, but DOJ declines to prosecute," NBC News, August 29, 2019, https://www.nbcnews.com/politics/justice-department/department-justice-declines-prosecute-comey-over-leaked-memos-n1047706

68 Cristiano Lima, "DNC sues Russian government, Trump campaign, WikiLeaks alleging 2016 conspiracy plot," *Politico*, April 20, 2018, https://www.politico.com/story/2018/04/20/dnc-sue-trump-campaign-russia-plot-539521

use the hacked emails against his political opponent. A federal judge, however, dismissed the case roughly a year later.[69]

Many Americans did not hear much from the media about Clinton's fine and her campaign paying the ex-British spy to dig up dirt on Trump, which helped cement the Russian collusion probe. Nor did they hear about the Democrats' dismissed, meritless lawsuit. That coverage was a drop in the bucket compared to the Russian collusion narrative, which had plagued Trump and his administration, and which had divided Americans for roughly two years.

In January of 2019, NBC News White House correspondent Kristen Welker asked Trump—the sitting president—if he worked for Russia.[70]

"Mr. President, yes or no. Have you or are you now—have you ever worked for Russia? Yes or no?" she asked, according to the Media Research Center.[71]

I do not recall mainstream media reporters ever asking former President Joe Biden if he ever worked on behalf of Ukraine officials, as his son pocketed millions from a top Ukrainian energy company.

---

69 Jan Wolfe, "U.S. judge tosses Democratic Party lawsuit against Trump campaign, Russia over election," Reuters, July 30, 2019, https://www.reuters.com/article/world/us-politics/us-judge-tosses-democratic-party-lawsuit-against-trump-campaign-russia-over-e-idUSKCN1UP2OH/

70 Geoffrey Dickens, "Flashback: The Worst Promoters of the Russia Collusion Hoax," The Media Research Center *NewsBusters*, February 15, 2022, https://www.newsbusters.org/blogs/nb/geoffrey-dickens/2022/02/15/flashback-worst-promoters-russia-collusion-hoax

71 Ibid.

Media Research Center's *NewsBusters*, a press watchdog, found that in 2019, after thirty-one months of Trump being in office, more than 2,600 minutes of evening broadcasts from ABC, NBC, and CBS were spent on covering the alleged Russia collusion.[72] That math came out to one-fifth of the major broadcasts focusing on the collusion narrative, which MRC noted was "a huge shadow on his presidency."[73]

The mainstream media, MRC found, did not shed light on some of the controversial bias within the probe itself, though. For example, there was a lack of coverage over politically biased texted messages shared between two FBI agents working the Russia probe—Peter Strzok and Lisa Page.[74] In one of their text exchanges, they vowed to stop Trump from being elected. The texts were included in just 1.5 percent of coverage, according to MRC's 2019 analysis.[75] And MRC also found only thirty-four minutes—a single night—of coverage was given to the fact that Hillary Clinton's campaign and Democrats had funded the controversial dossier.[76]

The American people—you—deserved to know the politically biased nature of those who were actually running the investigation of a sitting president at taxpayer expense.

The "Russia" gripes from Democrats tend to get louder and louder every four years as Election Day approaches.

---

72 Rich Noyes, "Study: TV Offered Deluge of Russia News, But Buried Anti-Trump Bias," Media Research Center *NewsBusters*, July 23, 2019, https://newsbusters.org/blogs/nb/rich-noyes/2019/07/23/study-tv-offered-deluge-russia-news-buried-anti-trump-bias

73 Ibid.

74 Ibid.

75 Ibid.

76 Ibid.

Peter Strzok was one of the agents on Mueller's team working the costly federal "Russia collusion" probe into Trump's 2016 campaign. In 2020, just two months before that election contest between Trump and former President Joe Biden, the fired FBI agent (terminated over his texts revealing anti-Trump bias) declared in a book that Trump "was compromised."[77] Never mind the two-year investigation's conclusion that there was no conspiracy or collusion or whatever you want to call it. Despite his continued insistence that Trump is compromised and a threat to democracy, Strzok himself admitted he was skeptical whether there was criminal conspiracy at issue.

"I was skeptical that all the different threads amounted to anything more than bumbling incompetence, a confederacy of dunces who were too dumb to collude," Strzok wrote, according to NBC News.[78] "In my view, they were most likely a collection of grifters pursuing individual personal interests: their own money- and power-driven agendas."

So he believes Trump is compromised, despite acknowledging the lack of evidence? It makes one wonder how Trump Derangement Syndrome can so cloud the judgment of federally trained law-enforcement personnel.

Nevertheless, the Russia narrative continues to tarnish not just Trump but his entire party. A *New York Magazine* columnist suggested in early 2024 that Trump had "remade Republicans

---

77 Ken Dilanian, "FBI agent who helped launch Russia investigation says Trump was 'compromised,'" NBC News, September 7, 2020, https://www.nbcnews.com/politics/donald-trump/fbi-agent-who-helped-launch-russia-investigation-says-trump-was-n1239442

78 Ibid.

into Putin's playthings."[79] And roughly a month later, *The Guardian* reported that intelligence officials were concerned over the "Putin bromance" for a second Trump presidency.[80]

But it's a fallacy to claim Trump would be weak in his diplomacy with Russia.

During his first administration, former President Obama's Secretary of Defense Robert Gates even acknowledged in 2019 to CBS's *Face the Nation* that Trump's administration had been the strictest in terms of imposing sanctions on Russia.[81]

"In terms of the magnitude of the sanctions that have been put on Russia, they are more significant than have been imposed in the past," he said.[82]

Any media outlets suggesting Trump and the GOP show weakness to Putin's Russia should also report about the ever-so-strong sanctions they had imposed. But balance, as we have seen in the Trump era, is never part of the mainstream media's work.

Trump was not quiet about his dissatisfaction with being tagged a Russian puppet. He complained about the ongoing probe during his first administration, saying the Russia web was interfering with his duties as president.

---

79 Jonathan Chait, "Russian Dolls—Trump has finally remade Republicans into Putin's playthings," *New York* magazine's *Intelligencer*, February 23, 2024, https://nymag.com/intelligencer/article/donald-trump-republicans-vladimir-putin-puppets.html

80 Peter Stone, "Putin bromance has US intelligence officials fearing second Trump term," *The Guardian*, March 18, 2024, https://www.theguardian.com/us-news/2024/mar/18/us-intelligence-trump-putin-threat

81 Trump War Room, "Watch: President Obama's Secretary of Defense Robert Gates says it's 'true' that President Trump's administration has been the toughest on Russia," X.com, May 13, 2019, https://x.com/TrumpWarRoom/status/1128032139570761729

82 Ibid.

"With North Korea, China, the Middle East and so much more, there is not much time to be thinking about this, especially since there was no Russian 'Collusion,'" he said in a 2018 tweet.[83]

Former Secretary of State Rex Tillerson said in 2018 that the Russia investigation did not actually hamper his diplomacy efforts around the world, but he did acknowledge there was tension between Moscow and the United States.[84]

"It has been a difficult year with Russia," said Tillerson, who was fired by Trump later that year.[85] "I've said clearly, the president stated clearly, our two nations should have a more productive relationship. Today it's very strained for all reasons that I think the American people well understand."

Retired Colonel John Mills, the author of *War Against the Deep State* and *The Nation Will Follow*, who has significant experience in the area of defense and cybersecurity, had a front-row perspective of the DC establishment's—and media's—obsession with Russia.

"I was ground zero in these matters and had colleagues directly involved," he told me. "I have a material-witness perspective. What I witnessed, starting in early 2016, was suddenly at these top-level, inter-agency meetings, we started getting this sudden 'Russia Russia Russia' chant—it was almost as if it was on

---

83 David Jackson, "Donald Trump claims Robert Mueller probe is interfering with his presidential duties," *USA Today*, May 2, 2018, https://www.usatoday.com/story/news/politics/2018/05/02/donald-trump-claims-robert-mueller-probe-interfering-presidential-duties/572068002/

84 Nicole Gaouette and Elise Labott, "Russia investigation a challenge for US-Moscow relations, Tillerson says," CNN, January 5, 2018, https://www.cnn.com/2018/01/05/politics/tillerson-russia-contradicts-trump/index.html

85 Ibid.

cue, given by someone. Folks were almost giddy with excitement. Something was going on."

Mills worked as a careerist in the federal government while also being active in the reserve military service.

"I wasn't really a Trump guy in early 2016 during the GOP primary. Personally, I was for Cruz, but I was a professional and took an oath of office to deal with matters agnostic of political leanings. But all of a sudden here it comes: The GOP primary is in full swing, and Russia is suddenly interested in Trump, according to the FBI and IC officials at these meetings," he recalled. "It was far more than just the Steele dossier. It was far more than that. That was just one part of a coordinated RICO operation."

Mills also gave information to Special Counsel John Durham.

"From the criminal referrals in the Durham report, I think there are potentially things out there that are ongoing or could be reenergized once Trump is in office. At least three of the criminal referrals in the report were likely about people I knew," Mills said. "We need federal intelligence and law enforcement, but we need to look in-depth at a reset of the culture at these organizations and hold personalities accountable through criminal investigations."

Van Hipp, chairman of the consulting firm American Defense International, Inc., said the Russian collusion probe was "terribly damaging" for Trump, and he echoed concerns about the intelligence community needing to clean house. Hipp has experience, having served as deputy assistant secretary in the Army and as the principal deputy general counsel for the Navy during the late President George H.W. Bush's administration.

"A president—no matter how good he or she is—when you're having to fight shenanigans like that in your own government, you start off with one hand tied behind your back," he told me of Trump up against the Mueller investigation.

He said Trump is not the first president to worry about reliable information from the intelligence community. The late President Dwight D. Eisenhower had similar concerns, so Hipp said Eisenhower started the Office of the National Security Advisor to the president.

"He also started the president's Intelligence Advisory Board. In the past, presidents haven't used it like they should," Hipp said, noting that Trump tapped Devin Nunes, a former California Republican lawmaker, to lead it during his second administration. Nunes was the top Republican lawmaker on the House Intelligence Committee during its time grappling with the Russia claims and investigation.

The board makes recommendations to the president on how to reform the intelligence community to make sure the intel it is gathering is accurate, and the board could address issues like the handling of classified documents, so that everyone knows the rules.

The Russia rants, meanwhile, continued during the latest campaign season. Even during Trump's 2024 run, we heard critics suggest he was propped up by the Kremlin.

A US intelligence official said in September, just two months before the November 2024 election, that RT—Russian state media—was trying to use American social media influencers to persuade voters to back the former president.[86]

"RT has built and used networks of U.S. and other Western personalities to create and disseminate Russia-friendly

---

[86] Jonathan Landay, et al., "Russia's RT seeking to push US voters toward Trump, US intelligence official says," Reuters, September 6, 2024, https://www.reuters.com/world/us/russia-china-iran-trying-influence-us-election-intelligence-official-says-2024-09-06/

narratives," the official told Reuters. "These actors among others are supporting Moscow's efforts to influence voter preferences in favor of the former president (Trump) and diminish the prospects of the vice president (Harris)."[87] The report was even shared internationally by the BBC[88] and *Le Monde*,[89] detailing Russia's alleged interference in the 2024 election.

And just fourteen days before the November 5 contest, an intelligence official said the Russian government was behind a fake video of Vice President Kamala Harris's running mate Tim Walz being accused of sexual misconduct by one of his former students.[90]

Here we go again, I thought. More disinformation.

But from whom? The Russians or the feds? Unfortunately, that's a question most Americans are asking themselves as they take in the news these days, especially around election time.

Remember, it was the federal government—specifically former intelligence officials[91]—who told the American people in

---

87 Ibid.

88 Sam Cabral, "US accuses Russia of 2024 election interference," BBC, September 4, 2024, https://www.bbc.com/news/articles/c8rx28v1vpro

89 *Le Monde* with AP and AFP, "US accuses Russia's RT news outlet of election interference," *Le Monde*, September 5, 2024, https://www.lemonde.fr/en/international/article/2024/09/05/us-accuses-russia-s-rt-news-outlet-of-election-interference_6724817_4.html

90 Dustin Volz, "U.S. Spy Agencies Say Russia Created Viral False Claims About Tim Walz," *The Wall Street Journal*, October 23, 2024, https://www.wsj.com/livecoverage/harris-trump-election-10-22-2024/card/u-s-spy-agencies-say-russia-created-viral-false-claims-about-tim-walz-hCvfQFTQpz9v7FS6wZag

91 Natasha Bertrand, "Hunter Biden story is Russian disinfo, dozens of former intel officials say," *Politico*, October, 19, 2020, https://www.politico.com/news/2020/10/19/hunter-biden-story-russian-disinfo-430276

2020 that the viral *New York Post* story on Hunter Biden's hacked laptop, full of salacious information, was Russian disinformation.

Emails from the laptop appeared to bolster Republicans' claims that the Biden family had profited from Hunter Biden's overseas dealings while his father was vice president.

Twitter and Facebook took the *Post*'s laptop story off their platforms, claiming it was Russian election interference. The *Post* was effectively censored, along with the revelations from the laptop. The mainstream, liberal-bent media made it taboo to even mention the laptop: They would accuse critics of peddling Russian propaganda.

Ironically, the same federal government that pushed to silence the laptop story, actually had its prosecutors later use that very laptop as evidence against Hunter Biden in his federal gun prosecution last year.[92]

It is as if the feds were saying, "Do as I say, not as I do."

Americans understand there is disinformation on the internet; they just are not quite confident about *who* exactly the real culprits are behind the false information. And rightfully so, based on the erroneous media reports that often led to reporters having to walk back stories of Kremlin collusion and misinformation.

After Trump's 2024 victory, Kellyanne Conway—who entered the first Trump administration as senior counselor to the president, after leading his 2016 campaign to victory—told Fox News that Trump had to begin his first presidency under investigation by the FBI over a bogus "pee tape" claim, recognizing the probe served as a blockade.

---

92 ABC News, "Prosecutors introduce Hunter Biden's infamous laptop as evidence," YouTube, June 4, 2024, https://www.youtube.com/watch?v=eGost-Df23w

"We were up against a wall," she said of the Mueller investigation during an interview November 13, 2024 with Fox News's *America's Newsroom.*

Under Trump's new administration, though, he's taken office free of any FBI scrutiny—that is, as far as we know.

The Russia collusion lawfare snowballed beyond the special counsel probe and has even grown ever more intense since Trump left office in 2020.

Lawfare mushroomed from executive buildings on Capitol Hill into federal and state courtrooms across the country. The American people have seen it play out as Trump campaigned for reelection on the campaign trail in 2023 and 2024, bouncing back and forth between campaign rally to courthouse, up and down the East Coast.

Even in 2025—nearly a decade past the 2016 election—a significant number of Americans are still convinced Trump was the "colluder," after being exposed to the wall-to-wall Russia coverage and claims that Trump defeated Clinton because of his faux foreign ties. Despite Mueller's report finding no evidence to support the charge, 48 percent of Americans said they still believed Trump or someone from his 2016 campaign colluded with Russia.[93]

Democrats, then and now, continuously suggest Putin has dirt on Trump, and that he could use the threat of blackmail as a quid pro quo against the president.

---

[93] Chris Kahn, "Despite report findings, almost half of Americans think Trump colluded with Russia: Reuters/Ipsos poll," Reuters, March 26, 2019, https://www.reuters.com/article/world/despite-report-findings-almost-half-of-americans-think-trump-colluded-with-russ-idUSKCN1R72SJ/

"I don't know what the Russians have on President Trump, whether it's personal, whether it's political, whether it's financial. I don't know what it is," House Speaker Nancy Pelosi, a California Democrat, said to CBS in 2021.[94] "But there's no other explaining why this President of the United States is such—a handmaiden of Putin."

That suggestion stuck.

Ferrechio, the veteran Washington reporter I previously noted, who has followed the Russian collusion story, said Pelosi even repeated the same allegation during the 2024 contest. Never mind the lack of charges, Ferrechio observed, noting the left continues to believe the Mueller report proved—somehow—Trump was colluding with Russia.

"Maybe the Russians were trying to influence the election, but Trump wasn't connected to collaborating with them," Ferrechio said. "The left is not giving up on Russian collusion."

The Democrats' quid pro quo accusation—that Russia had something on Trump and could blackmail him—would later return to bite Trump in the form of an impeachment trial over another alleged quid pro quo dealing. But that one was with Ukraine, as I visit in the next chapter. With the Russia probe failing to level any criminal charges, impeachment was the next tool in the Democrats' lawfare apparatus.

---

[94] Lesley Stahl, "Nancy Pelosi on the riot at the Capitol, Congress' mandate under Joe Biden and the youth in the Democratic party," CBS News, January 11, 2021, https://www.cbsnews.com/news/nancy-pelosi-interview-60-minutes-2021-01-10/

QUID PRO QUO

When the Russian collusion narrative failed to nab Trump, Democrats turned to impeachment as their mechanism for trying to out—or at the very least, tarnish—the former president. Impeachment was the next step forward in their march for lawfare.

On December 18, 2019, just nine months after Special Counsel Robert Mueller's report amounted to zero criminal charges, US House Speaker Nancy Pelosi's chamber voted to impeach President Trump for the first time. It made Trump the third president in US history ever to be impeached—but the first to bear that stain without any participation from his own party.

Despite lacking bipartisan support, Democrats thought they finally had enough evidence to charge the sitting president with abuse of power and obstruction of Congress. This time the alleged criminal behavior related to Trump's communications and dealings with Ukrainian officials, not Russians. Democrats had moved their scapegoat southwest of the Russian border.

They had claimed Trump committed an unlawful quid pro quo in his demands of the Ukrainian president to probe corruption, specifically within the Biden family. The Latin term, quid pro quo, means a transaction of "this for that." The Democrats charged that Trump illegally withheld financial assistance that was meant to go to Ukraine, and that his request of the Ukrainians to probe Joe Biden and his family was made for political purposes, as Biden was on his way to becoming the Democratic presidential nominee ahead of the 2020 election.

Robert C. Cahaly, chief pollster and strategist with The Trafalgar Group, said that of the two impeachments Trump faced, this one had the least amount of public support.

"The first impeachment had the most skepticism," he told me. "It just sounded like the Democrats had the House, and they didn't like him, and so they did this."

The partisan Ukrainian drama began around May of 2019, when the former president directed his staff to withhold roughly $400 million in military aid that Congress had authorized to go to the country that was awaiting Russian invasion.

That invasion eventually did become reality two years later under the watch of former President Biden—not President Trump. But while Trump was the commander in chief, he was troubled with allegations of corruption linked to Ukraine and the Biden family.

He—and fellow conservatives—have alleged wrongdoing on behalf of former President Joe Biden and his son Hunter Biden, who was paid $50,000 a month to sit on the board of Burisma, a Ukrainian energy company, despite having no specialized expertise on the subject matter.[95] While serving as vice president

---

95 S.A. Miller, et al., "Alexander Vindman shoots down Democrats' 'bribery,' cover-up claims," *The Washington Times*, November 19, 2019, https://www.washingtontimes.com/news/2019/nov/19/alexander-vindman-shoots-down-democrats-bribery-co/

under former President Barack Obama, Biden had successfully gotten the Ukrainian government to fire its top prosecutor, Viktor Shokin. Shokin was reportedly investigating Burisma, the company paying his son, and its owner.

Obama administration officials have pushed back on Republicans' claims by reasoning that there was an international push for Shokin's ouster. But a year before the firing, Biden had visited the country and said that $1 billion in loan guarantees would be withheld if Shokin was not removed.[96] Ukrainian government officials ultimately did vote to remove him the following year, and then the loan guarantees were approved just three months after that.[97]

Does that sound like a quid pro quo? Fire your top prosecutor investigating the company linked to my son, and then you'll get $1 billion in loan guarantees?

Of course it does. But never mind any quid pro quo allegations against Biden. Democrats can only be bothered with investigating such claims if they are linked to Trump.

Biden, as vice president, would have faced a partisan impeachment for that sort of pressure campaign if all things were equal. Republicans could have labeled it abuse of power, given the fact that his son was still connected to Burisma at the time of Biden's bartering with Ukraine.

Retired Colonel John Mills, an author and expert in foreign dealing, defense, and security matters, told me there is a legal

---

[96] Glenn Kessler, "Correcting a media error: Biden's Ukraine showdown was in December 2015," *The Washington Post*, October 2, 2019, https://www.washingtonpost.com/politics/2019/10/02/correcting-media-error-bidens-ukraine-showdown-was-december/

[97] Ibid.

debate about whether a president can put a hold on foreign-aid funds once they have been appropriated by Congress.

"My simple position is: yes," Mills told me. "The State Department has never made a compelling legal case about why it is unlawful for a president to withhold foreign aid once it is appropriated. But if matters change in the receiving nation, that raises reasonable questions on whether the aid should still flow to that nation."

He pointed to the prospect of America appropriating money to a country, but then that country declaring war against us before receiving any of the money.

"If we were at war with Germany, and before the war we appropriated foreign aid money, war breaks out—that means we still have to give money to them? Is that the logic?" Mills pushed back.

He also said that during his years working in government under the Obama administration, questions on using foreign aid as a tool for negotiations arose, but were always swatted down by the State Department without sufficient legal reasoning.

"One time, the Obama team was upset with organized cyber-attacks originating from and willfully enabled by an African nation that was acting as a proxy for Russia and China. One of the ideas was to place a hold on foreign aid from the US that amounted to like 13 percent of the GDP of this nation," Mills said, noting he could not disclose the country at issue for intelligence reasons. "State Department ferociously fought any hold, and won, but never proffered a statute-based legal argument on why a hold would be illegal. So we did nothing."

He added: "It depends on the degree of the condition and what was going on in the country. I think there is room for discussion on this issue. To just say 100 percent 'that's illegal,' I don't think that is correct."

Mills said he likewise questioned Biden's use of loan guarantees in the Obama administration's negotiations over alleged corruption in Ukraine in order to get Shokin fired.

"That doesn't sound like a policy issue or disagreement between the US government and Ukraine. That sounds like a very, very personal financial matter that is being used—being weaponized. I think that is far more egregious to say, 'hey, you fire this prosecutor.' That doesn't sound like it is within the boundaries of legal or policy matters. That sounds corrupt."

"The Trump-haters…don't care or ignore the gross Biden malfeasance.… Biden's actions had nothing to do with the national interest of the United States. Biden's actions were very related to personal matters."

But when it comes to Washington, without double standards, there would be no standards.

The US Constitution's Article II, Section 4 gives Congress the authority to impeach any president or vice president or federal officer for a high crime or misdemeanor. "High crime" was a term that some argue could equate to felonies today. Specifically, the clause lists treason and bribery.[98]

But never mind Biden's personal interest on behalf of and surrounding his son in dealings with Ukraine, and aid being handed over to the country in exchange for cooperation of his requests. Democrats were unburdened by that.

Their sole focus was—and is—Donald J. Trump.

---

[98] Article II, Section 4, US Constitution, https://constitution.congress.gov/browse/essay/artII-S4-1/ALDE_00000282/

You may be wondering how Democrats became aware of Trump's communications with the Ukrainian president. That all started when a whistleblower report was made public in the late summer of 2019, roughly six weeks after Trump spoke with Ukrainian President Volodymyr Zelenskyy on the phone in July.

The whistleblower had concerns over Trump relying on his personal attorney, Rudolph Giuliani, and Attorney General William Barr, who were working to track corruption in Ukraine linked to the Biden family.

After catching wind of the whistleblower report, House Democrats—who controlled Congress at the time—launched impeachment proceedings in September to review the allegations of a quid pro quo.

It was alleged Trump was conditioning the military aid, and a White House meeting with President Zelenskyy, on the Ukrainian leader making a public statement about a probe into the Biden family.

Trump also wanted an investigation examining a missing server that belonged to the Democratic National Committee, which was hacked by Russians during the 2016 campaign. The president believed that the server, which went missing before the FBI was able to examine it, had ended up in Ukraine.[99]

Democrats charged that this was illegal conduct by the president, having asked a foreign country to investigate a political rival.

"What President Trump has done on the record in terms of acting to advantage a foreign power to help him in his own election and the obstruction of information about that—the

---

[99] S.A. Miller and Alex Swoyer, "Chief justice, senators sworn in for Trump impeachment trial," *The Washington Times*, January 16, 2020, https://www.washingtontimes.com/news/2020/jan/16/senators-sworn-trump-impeachment-trial/

coverup—makes what Nixon did look almost small," said House Speaker Nancy Pelosi, calling it "bribery."[100]

Republicans defended Trump, saying federal law requires that foreign aid is not being used toward corruption.[101] They were not the only ones defending the phone call. Zelenskyy, in September, recalled the July phone call and said it was "good."

"We had I think good phone call. It was normal. We spoke about many things. So, I think, and you read it, that nobody pushed. Pushed me," Zelenskyy said while speaking at the United Nations alongside Trump on September 25.[102]

To be clear, nothing from my own review of the transcript of the phone call revealed any pointed conditions being discussed related to military aid or an unlawful quid pro quo.

"There's a lot of talk about Biden's son, that Biden stopped the prosecution and a lot of people want to find out about that so whatever you can do with the Attorney General would be great. Biden went around bragging that he stopped the prosecution so if you can look into it.... It sounds horrible to me," Trump said during the call.[103]

---

[100] Heather Caygle, "Pelosi says Trump committed 'bribery' in Ukraine scandal," *Politico*, November 14, 2019, https://www.politico.com/news/2019/11/14/pelosi-trump-bribery-impeachment-070914

[101] Miller et al., "Alexander Vindman shoots down...claims," https://www.washingtontimes.com/news/2019/nov/19/alexander-vindman-shoots-down-democrats-bribery-co/

[102] Tessa Stuart, "'No Pressure,' Trump Insists, While Sitting with Ukraine's Zelensky at U.N.," *Rolling Stone*, September 25, 2019, https://www.rollingstone.com/politics/politics-news/trump-sitting-ukraine-zelensky-united-nations-889491/

[103] "Read Trump's phone conversation with Volodymyr Zelensky," CNN, September 26, 2019, https://www.cnn.com/2019/09/25/politics/donald-trump-ukraine-transcript-call/index.html

"Whenever you would like to come to the White House, feel free to call. Give us a date and we'll work that out. I look forward to seeing you," he added.[104]

Meanwhile, Trump and his team insisted withholding military aid was not politically or personally motivated. The former president said his concerns were around corruption in Ukraine and that other European countries were not doing enough to help.[105]

After all, Trump often used funding as a way to negotiate and influence foreign relations during his first administration. He questioned funding to the United Nations and the World Health Organization, as well as the United States participating in trade and climate agreements, all concerning the increased burden and costs to US taxpayers.[106]

Trump was not alone in his manipulation of aid and foreign policy. Former US presidents often used it to influence diplomacy.

In 1991, the late President George H.W. Bush created tension with America's greatest ally, Israel, over refusing to deliver $10 billion in aid unless the Jewish state stopped settling in Palestinian land.[107] The loan guarantees were delayed 120 days,

---

[104] Ibid.

[105] Quint Forgey, "Trump changes story on withholding Ukraine aid," *Politico*, September 24, 2019, https://www.politico.com/story/2019/09/24/donald-trump-ukraine-military-aid-1509070

[106] Betsy Klein and Jennifer Hansler, "Trump halts World Health Organization funding over handling of coronavirus outbreak," CNN, April 15, 2020, https://www.cnn.com/2020/04/14/politics/donald-trump-world-health-organization-funding-coronavirus/index.html

[107] Alia Brahimi, "America Has Pressured Israel Before—and Can Do It Again," *Foreign Policy*, March 29, 2024, https://foreignpolicy.com/2024/03/29/biden-netanyahu-israel-gaza-aid-weapons-leverage-pressure-bush-baker/

longer than the time that Trump withheld the aid to Ukraine, which was roughly two to three months.[108]

The late President Ronald Reagan also withheld aid to Israel in 1981 for a couple of months over its bombing of an Iraqi nuclear reactor.[109]

But neither Bush nor Reagan was impeached.

Just Trump, as Democrats were laser-focused on waging political lawfare.

House Democrats, in their vitriol toward Trump, did not believe his reasoning for withholding the money to Ukraine. They saw it as a quid pro quo for a personal gain rather than negotiations meant to protect our country's interests.

The Democrats under Pelosi's leadership pursued a roughly two-month probe that ended in their partisan vote on December 18, 2019, impeaching Trump for abuse of power and obstruction of Congress, with no Republican lawmaker joining them in their majority vote.[110]

Instead of sending the articles of impeachment straight to the US Senate for a trial to begin, however, Pelosi withheld the charges for roughly one month—from December 19 to January

---

[108] Daniel Marans, "George H.W. Bush's Pressure On Israel Provides Model For Progressives," *HuffPost*, May 25, 2021, https://www.huffpost.com/entry/george-hw-bush-israel-palestinians-progressives_n_60a6d388e4b0a25683107530

[109] Ivan Pereiera, "Pausing military aid seen as key tool in a president's foreign policy toolbox," ABC News, May 11, 2024, https://abcnews.go.com/Politics/pausing-military-aid-key-tool-presidents-foreign-policy/story?id=110117137

[110] Philip Ewing, "President Trump Impeached By The House In Historic Rebuke," NPR, December 18, 2019, https://www.npr.org/2019/12/18/789020525/president-trump-impeached-by-the-house-in-historic-rebuke

16, when the Senate first kicked off Trump's impeachment trial. It became a waiting game for us in the press shop about when we would actually begin covering the second half of the impeachment proceedings. Pelosi said she wanted to see the terms of the trial in the GOP-controlled Senate before she released the House's articles of impeachment.

So much for a defendant's right to a speedy trial, right?

Those judicial protections do not apply in impeachment proceedings—nor to Trump in some Democratic-controlled courtrooms.

But as to impeachment 1.0, I remember sitting at my desk inside of the Senate Press Gallery thinking how historic it is for a president to be impeached, but then how unbelievably political it is for the leader of the Democratic Party to withhold the charging documents against the Republican president simply for political gain.

Little did I know I would be sitting at that same desk roughly a year later covering another Trump impeachment trial—one where the president had already actually left office.

After all, isn't impeachment meant as a tool for removal of a sitting official?

Democrats cannot seem to be bothered with those details when it comes to their mission to get Trump.

Pelosi's willful delay of the impeachment articles was calculated.

With 2020 being an election year, it appeared Pelosi, the leader of the Democrats on Capitol Hill, was determined to continuously keep Trump's impeachment in the news. And she likely saw the writing on the wall in the GOP-controlled Senate that Trump would be acquitted. He was, in fact, acquitted by the Senate on February 5, 2020.

But the withholding of the Articles of Impeachment for a political delay was one of several violations of due process during Trump's impeachment process. And it was potentially the Democrats' first lawfare episode to see a trial—though, it was held inside the US Capitol and not in a courtroom.

His next trial would be held in a Manhattan courtroom, years later, as Democrats' lawfare efforts grew.

Much of what was claimed about Trump and his allies' dealings when it came to Ukraine, though, would have amounted to hearsay under the rules of evidence, if the proceeding had taken place in an actual courthouse. And the president and his legal team did not have the ability to cross-examine the witnesses during the House proceedings, making it all the more one-sided.

As Jonathan Turley, a distinguished law professor at George Washington University, said during his testimony as an expert witness to House lawmakers, the legal case for impeachment was weak.[111]

"One can oppose President Trump's policies or actions but still conclude that the current legal case for impeachment is not just woefully inadequate, but in some respects, dangerous, as the basis for the impeachment of an American president," said Turley at the time.[112]

---

[111] David Morgan and Susan Cornwell, "Legal experts called by Democrats tell Congress that Trump's actions are impeachable," Reuters, December 4, 2019, https://www.reuters.com/article/world/legal-experts-called-by-democrats-tell-congress-that-trump-s-actions-are-impeach-idUSKBN1Y8151/

[112] Ibid.

Turley had previously testified over the impeachment of President Bill Clinton, too. He said he did not vote for Trump, but his legal views are irrelevant to the fact he voted against him.[113]

"I am concerned about lowering impeachment standards," he said. "It's a case of the peripheral...to impeach a president on this record would expose every future president to the same type of inchoate impeachment."[114]

Republican lawmakers, too, had noted it came down to policy over withholding of the aid.[115]

Impeachment is more of a political exercise than a legal one.

The way witnesses are handled and the manner in which evidence is presented is done under different rules and procedures than how courtrooms typically carry out a trial against a defendant.

White House counsel Pat Cipollone, who served in the first Trump administration, echoed that grievance in a letter to the top Democrat overseeing the House impeachment inquiry.[116]

"As you know, this baseless and highly partisan inquiry violates all past historical precedent, basic due process rights, and fundamental fairness," he wrote.

---

[113] Candace Norwood, "Watch: Jonathan Turley's full opening statement in Trump impeachment hearing," PBS, December 4, 2019, https://www.pbs.org/newshour/politics/watch-jonathan-turleys-full-opening-statement-in-trump-impeachment-hearing

[114] Ibid.

[115] Ibid.

[116] Tom Howell Jr. and Alex Swoyer, "Donald Trump will not participate in impeachment hearing by Judiciary Committee," *The Washington Times*, December 1, 2019, https://www.washingtontimes.com/news/2019/dec/1/trump-will-not-participate-impeachment-hearing-jud/

"You have afforded the president no scheduling input, no meaningful information, and so little time to prepare that you have effectively denied the administration a fair opportunity to participate. Although the hearing is set to occur in just three days, you still have not disclosed the identities of the witnesses who will appear."[117]

He also argued that Mr. Trump's impeachment process was different from past Presidents Richard Nixon and Bill Clinton.[118]

"Nothing in the procedures for those impeachment inquiries permitted the [Judiciary Committee] chairman to deny the president the ability to participate or to deny any other procedural rights as a punishment for asserting executive branch constitutional privileges," Cipollone wrote. "Both presidents in those proceedings had asserted numerous privileges, but it never even occurred to the Judiciary Committee that offering the opportunity to present a defense and to have a fair hearing should be conditioned on forcing the president to abandon the longstanding constitutional rights and privileges of the executive branch."[119]

Aside from a defendant's due process rights and the right to a fair trial, they also have a right to an unbiased jury. However, in an impeachment trial, the jury could not be more partisan, as it is composed of sitting senators. Lawyers also do not have the opportunity to strike any juror that they believe would pose a conflict or bias towards their client.

In the end, Trump did not testify in his own defense. A pattern we later saw during his criminal trial.

---

[117] Ibid.

[118] Ibid.

[119] Ibid.

The rules of his impeachment trial were simply set by a majority vote, making the process all the more political than at all judicial.[120]

David Schoen, an attorney who represented Trump during his second impeachment trial, said there is a big difference between impeachment trials and real trial courtroom procedures protected by judicial rules and decorum.

"The impeachment proceedings have no rules of evidence, no one can really interrupt the presentation. You can basically say whatever you want, whenever you want. The presiding officer doesn't really interrupt, and there are no hard-and-fast rules," Mr. Schoen told me, recalling the political nature of it all.

Schoen did not represent Trump in his Ukraine impeachment but later on, in the second Trump impeachment over January 6, 2021, and in the president's contest of the 2020 election results. By the time that impeachment trial began, Trump had left office.

"On the first day, we were supposed to just be talking about whether the Senate had jurisdiction to try an impeachment trial for the House to impeach a former president.... Instead, Jamie Raskin (one of the Democrats' impeachment prosecutors) came in and virtually ignored the jurisdictional question and instead made an emotional pitch, with stories about his family and videos," Schoen recalled. "It was completely inappropriate and against the ground rules; but the Democratic leadership and Senator Leahy as the presiding officer allowed it.

"I believe the impeachment proceedings and the more recent criminal prosecutions are all just tools in the basket of devices

---

120 S.A. Miller and Alex Swoyer, "Chief justice, senators sworn in for Trump impeachment trial," *The Washington Times*, January 16, 2020, https://www.washingtontimes.com/news/2020/jan/16/senators-sworn-trump-impeachment-trial/

that Congressman Jerry Nadler (the top Democrat on the House Judiciary Committee at the time) had in mind when he called for the first impeachment and said, in effect, we can't trust the voters to get rid of Donald Trump. That was about as anti-democratic a statement as I could ever imagine coming from a member of Congress."

Trump was the third president to ever be impeached—but the first to be impeached without a single vote from his own party. His impeachment scorecard would continue to set a record when, roughly a year later, he was impeached by Pelosi's Democratic-controlled House yet again.

Making history—as Trump often does—he became the first president to be impeached twice.

But impeachment was not the end for Democrats' lawfare. They soon sought a conviction, so they could label the president a convicted felon.

The impeachment coverage engulfed airwaves at the start of an election year, likely as Pelosi and her Democratic allies had planned.

Media Research Center's *NewsBusters* blog, a media watchdog firm, found that impeachment dominated mainstream-media coverage, with more than one thousand minutes of airtime—61 percent—of coverage focusing on the proceedings compared to other Trump administration coverage from September 2019 to January 2020.[121]

---

[121] Rich Noyes, "Rewind: The Media's Four-Year War Against the Trump Presidency," MRC *NewsBusters*, December 31, 2020, https://newsbusters.org/blogs/nb/rich-noyes/2020/12/31/rewind-medias-four-year-war-against-trump-presidency

By contrast, MRC noted that the media "deplored impeachment as the persecution of an elected President" during the Clinton years, the last time a president—Bill Clinton—had been impeached prior to Trump's Ukraine scandal.[122]

Boy, has the press's tone changed, however.

When it came to Trump, Americans read headlines like, "New revelations from first public hearings paint damning portrait of Trump"[123] and "Trump impeachment evidence overwhelming—House report."[124]

Little did I know at the time, Democrats were just warming up their impeachment lawfare efforts and would give it another try the following year.

---

[122] Ibid.

[123] Stephen Collinson, "New revelations from first public hearings paint damning portrait of Trump," CNN, November 14, 2019, https://www.cnn.com/2019/11/14/politics/donald-trump-impeachment-hearing/index.html

[124] "Trump impeachment evidence overwhelming—House report," BBC, December 3, 2019, https://www.bbc.com/news/world-us-canada-50650216

INSURRECTION, WITHOUT DIRECTION

President Trump is the forty-seventh president of the United States because Democrats were unsuccessful in their first—and second—try at impeaching and convicting him during his first term. Had Trump been convicted in one of the impeachment trials, there would have been a bar on him holding elected office in the future.

Perhaps, the president should thank former Senate Majority Leader Mitch McConnell for that. It was because of the Kentucky Republican lawmaker that he escaped enough GOP support for conviction during his second impeachment trial over his contest of the 2020 election results.

McConnell declared that it was unconstitutional to impeach a president who had left office, which swayed members of his party from voting to convict Trump over the January 6, 2021 riot at the US Capitol.

In a historic moment, McConnell who often sparred with the former president, took to the chamber floor and defended his vote to acquit Trump. He said the January 6 rioters "had been fed wild falsehoods by the most powerful man on earth because he was angry he lost an election."[125]

"If President Trump were still in office I would have carefully considered if House managers proved their specific charge," McConnell said.[126]

"By the strict criminal standard, the president's speech was probably not incitement. However, in the context of impeachment, the Senate might have decided this was acceptable shorthand for the reckless actions that proceeded the riot, but in this case, the question is moot because former President Trump is constitutionally not eligible for conviction."[127]

McConnell and others who had voted to acquit Trump reasoned that impeachment is used as a tool to remove an officeholder, but Trump by that time had already left office. That didn't, however, stop House Democrats' lawfare crusade from moving forward—despite knowing he was exiting the White House.

David Schoen, the lawyer who represented Trump at this second impeachment trial over January 6, told me the Democrats' motives were obvious.

"The Democrats' clearly stated goal in bringing the second impeachment after Trump was already out of office was to try to bar him from ever again being able to hold public office. His acquittal is how he was able to run again this time," Schoen explained to me.

---

125 CBS News, "Full speech: McConnell denounces Trump's conduct after voting to acquit at impeachment trial," YouTube, February 13, 2021, https://www.youtube.com/watch?v=kj5pvgXAgMs

126 Ibid.

127 Ibid.

> Their brief makes the argument explicitly that any former president can be impeached. So, today you can impeach Thomas Jefferson, George Washington, Barack Obama, or Joe Biden for conduct while in office. It's a very dangerous road to go down, and I believe they are wrong.

Building upon impeachment 1.0, House Democrats had launched and conducted impeachment 2.0 of Trump over January 6, where he contested the 2020 results. They blamed him for the lawless acts of the rioters, though the legal threshold of actually inciting violence was never met by Trump, nor did he have intent for brute force to take place.

To incite violence, the legal threshold demands a high standard to overcome the protection of the First Amendment's right to free speech. There's even more protection afforded to political speech. That's because there's an interest in promoting the exchange of ideas and debate in our country.

To incite violence, one must say or do something that poses an immediate risk of harm. Trump's rhetoric—if put before a fair and impartial jury—likely fell below that standard.

"We have come to demand that Congress do the right thing and only count the electors who have been lawfully slated, lawfully slated. I know that everyone here will soon be marching over to the Capitol building to peacefully and patriotically make your voices heard," he told the January 6 supporters before the riot broke out down the National Mall from the Ellipse where he spoke outside the White House.[128] "We fight like hell. And if you don't fight like hell, you're not going to have a country anymore," he also said.[129]

"Peacefully and patriotically" were the words he used.

He did not tell the crowd to go attack police officers and lawmakers. He also has a right as an individual—and as president—to express his viewpoint, which was that there had been a fraudulent election in 2020. Democrats pounced on his choice of the word "fight," but that's a word other politicians have frequently used; however, they did not face impeachment. For example, in August, just before the November election, Vice President Kamala Harris rallied supporters by using the word "fight." "Let us fight," she told her supporters. "When we fight, we win."[130] No one called her out or shamed her for using that lingo.

Trump has also proffered that in the days leading up to his January 6 rally and protest of the election results, he said the Pentagon should ready ten thousand national guardsmen. That move alone suggests he did not want violence to take place or intend for the protest to get out of hand.[131]

---

[128] Brian Naylor, "Read Trump's January 6 Speech, A Key Part Of Impeachment Trial," NPR, February 10, 2021, https://www.npr.org/2021/02/10/966396848/read-trumps-jan-6-speech-a-key-part-of-impeachment-trial

[129] Ibid.

[130] Kamala Harris, "When we fight, we win | Harris-Walz 2024," Facebook, August 20, 2024, https://www.facebook.com/watch/?v=462987713229725

[131] Jamie McIntyre, "Trump says he told the Pentagon 10,000 National Guard troops would be needed January 6 but was ignored," *Washington Examiner*, March 2, 2021, https://www.washingtonexaminer.com/policy/national-security/2638362/trump-says-he-told-the-pentagon-10000-national-guard-troops-would-be-needed-jan-6-but-was-ignored

Congressional leaders did later discover that his requests to the Pentagon were ignored.[132]

Moreover, my colleagues, who were both inside the US Capitol during the riot—one in an undisclosed safe room with the lawmakers who had been swept away by security, and the other outside the chamber interviewing protesters—said the historic event did not unfold the way it was portrayed by Democratic lawmakers and the mainstream media.

My colleague who was actually in hiding with the lawmakers noted they saw none of the protesters, although they could hear them. She said any fear portrayed by Democratic lawmakers of the "insurrection" was essentially fear of the unknown, not knowing what was happening outside their safe space.

Kerry Picket, a *Washington Times* colleague of mine, was in the US Capitol on January 6, 2021. At the time, she was reporting for another news outlet. She said she recalls Representative Paul Gosar, Arizona Republican, debating Democrats over Arizona's electors when there was a loud banging on the outside of the main doors. At first, she said, people just ignored it.

"Everyone was kind of concerned that there was stuff going on outside," she recalled. "No one actually thought they were going to be coming inside the Capitol."

Security then began shouting to lock the doors and barricade the press, staff, and lawmakers inside the chamber. She said cops drew their guns.

---

[132] Committee on House Administration, "Transcripts Show President Trump's Directives to Pentagon Leadership to 'Keep January 6 Safe' Were Deliberately Ignored," US House of Representatives, September 20, 2024, https://cha.house.gov/2024/9/transcripts-show-president-trump-s-directives-to-pentagon-leadership-to-keep-january-6-safe-were-deliberately-ignored

"I was concerned. I wasn't terrified because I've covered scary things in the field, like Ferguson, Missouri, where there were gunshots going on all over the place. So I looked at it from different perspectives," she said. "Based on everyone's personal experiences, you pretty much reacted to the circumstances going around."

She was instructed by staff to use the gas hoods, and they were all escorted out with lawmakers through secret staircases down to the basement hallways under the Capitol, and to their office buildings, to remain on lockdown.

"As far as being scared, I wouldn't say terrified. It was more just concerned, alert."

She said there had been buzz something could happen on January 6, 2021, so it was curious why there was not more law enforcement or security on hand.

"This was being reported all over the place. People were concerned something was going to happen; but for some reason, why was it that the cops were not properly geared up for it? Why didn't they have enough cops?" she said, questioning why the leadership at the time—the Democrats—did not beef up security. "Why wasn't it that we didn't have national guards all over the place? You didn't have the Capitol perimeter that was all fenced up. It was just bizarre."

I spent nearly every workday for four years or so inside the US Capitol at my desk within the Senate Press Gallery, but ironically, on January 6, 2021, I was not there.

Roads had already been blocked off, and I could not get to the designated parking area outside the Senate. I turned around to head home, and my plan was to take an Uber back to Capitol Hill. But when I got home after my short half-hour drive and phoned my editor, we realized there was no way I would be able to access the building. My editor said to turn on the television and see what was happening.

Once I did, I recall that the first images of the January 6 riot I had seen were not of violence, but rather of January 6 protesters strolling through the federal building, taking a look at the artifacts. It looked to me as though people were giving themselves a tour through Statuary Hall, a room in the Capitol where states display statues of legendary residents. Initially, the idea of protesters giving themselves a tour of the Capitol—which are usually scheduled and guided—brought out a chuckle.

Along with the rest of the nation, I began tracking the happenings on television. As the violence started to unfold in real time, I was perplexed—like my colleague Kerry—to think that protesters got past at least three different security checks to reach the second floor of the Capitol, where both chambers meet.

It falls on the Capitol Police Board, which includes offices within the Capitol like the Senate and House Sergeant at Arms, to phone in for national guard troops.[133] They did not do so in preparation for January 6, but waited until the riot was already underway. The security failures were rampant, but Democrats only wanted to blame Trump.

My colleague Susan Ferrechio, a veteran Washington reporter who has covered politics for more than three decades, was also there at the US Capitol on January 6, 2021. But unlike Kerry, she was on the outside of the lockdown and able to chat with protesters.

She said a lack of signage confused some of the protesters, and that visitors often do not realize they are not permitted inside

---

[133] Arijeta Lajka, "Pelosi did not block the National Guard from the Capitol on January 6," Associated Press, July 23, 2021, https://apnews.com/article/fact-checking-235651652542

the building, but think they should be able to access it since it is a public building.

"There were different groups of people," she told me of the protesters. "There were a lot of people there who actually had no idea what was going on inside the building. They were there earlier at the march, and they thought everything went well, and they were all behind Trump, and they were just wandering around in the streets around the Capitol."

She said one group of people told her the police let them into the Capitol, and then later told them to leave, and they left.

"They didn't think there was anything really wrong with their actions," she said. "People work up there—including reporters—and see it as a secure space closed to the public. But the Capitol used to be wide open to the public not too long ago."

"To this day, people come up to the building and say, 'can I come in?' That happens on a daily basis because people think the nation's Capitol is an open building," she said, though she acknowledged some of the male protesters said things got out of hand. "The perspective of the people who pushed their way in is, 'this is my Capitol, why can't I walk in there?' They said they felt they had a right to be there and the police shouldn't stand in their way."

"It was a relatively small group," she said of the January 6 protesters who actually committed violence. "A lot of people were just standing there, milling around or walking through the building."

House Democrats, meanwhile, charged Trump in his second impeachment with inciting an insurrection for the damage caused at the Capitol on that day.

The legal standard of incitement, as I have mentioned, is a high bar.

The Democrats claimed their investigatory panel was bipartisan because it included two Never-Trump Republicans, Representatives Adam Kinzinger of Ohio and Liz Cheney of Wyoming. Both are now former representatives, unable to win reelection.

They accused Trump of inciting the riot that resulted in the deaths of four of his own supporters and a Capitol Police officer. Two other police officers later committed suicide. Roughly 140 officers sustained injuries during the attack.[134]

Two of Trump's supporters suffered heart attacks while another one died of an overdose. Ashli Babbitt, an Air Force veteran, was shot by a police officer when she attempted to crawl through a window inside the federal building.[135] An officer later died after the riot. Initial reports suggested he had suffered blunt force trauma trying to defend the building, but it was later revealed he passed from suffering two strokes, though it was noted the experience of January 6 contributed to his condition.[136]

From a legal perspective, incitement as a charge in the Articles of Impeachment was a complete stretch against Trump, since he had repeatedly told his supporters to "peacefully and patriotically" protest the certification of the 2020 election, as his legal challenges in swing states were still pending.

---

[134] David Boyer and Alex Swoyer, "Democrats in impeachment trial say Trump didn't stop riot," *The Washington Times*, February 10, 2021, https://www.washingtontimes.com/news/2021/feb/10/democrats-impeachment-trial-say-trump-didnt-stop-r/

[135] Robert Farley, "How Many Died as a Result of Capitol Riot?," FactCheck.org, November 1, 2021, https://www.factcheck.org/2021/11/how-many-died-as-a-result-of-capitol-riot/

[136] Ibid.

"Stay peaceful!" read part of Trump's tweets roughly twenty minutes after violence erupted.[137]

Trump's defenders, his legal team, hit the nail on the head when they said Democrats' real motive for the impeachment trial was to try to get a conviction, so that Trump could never hold office again.[138] It was a strategic way to eliminate a political opponent.

David Schoen, who I mentioned earlier, and Bruce Castor, who also represented Trump in the impeachment trial, said Democrats were merely putting on a political show, because Trump had already left office.[139]

"This was only ever a selfish attempt by Democratic leadership in the House to prey upon the feelings of horror and confusion that fell upon all Americans across the entire political spectrum upon seeing the destruction at the Capitol on January 6 by a few hundred people," they said. "Instead of acting to heal the nation, or at the very least focusing on prosecuting the lawbreakers who stormed the Capitol, the Speaker of the House and her allies have tried to callously harness the chaos of the moment for their own political gain."[140]

---

[137] Jim Acosta, "Trump did not want to tweet 'stay peaceful' during January 6 riot, key former aide says," CNN, January 6, 2022, https://www.cnn.com/2022/01/06/politics/trump-tweet-january-6/index.html

[138] Dave Boyer and Alex Swoyer, "Senate approves Trump impeachment trial; six Republicans join Democrats," *The Washington Times*, February 9, 2021, https://www.washingtontimes.com/news/2021/feb/9/senate-approves-trump-impeachment-trial-six-republ/

[139] Dave Boyer and Alex Swoyer, "David Schoen, Bruce Castor say Trump impeachment could lead to Republican retaliation," *The Washington Times*, February 8, 2021, https://www.washingtontimes.com/news/2021/feb/8/trumps-lawyers-say-impeachment-political-theater-e/

[140] Ibid.

Trump's lawyers noted the impeachment trial now involved a private citizen since Trump was out of office, adding that it is "nothing less than the political weaponization of the impeachment process—pure, raw sport fueled by the misguided idea of party over country."[141]

In fact, before the trial began, forty-four senators had voted that even to hold a trial would be unconstitutional, since Trump had already left office.[142]

Trump's defense team blamed the rioters for their own actions and said those "who criminally breached the Capitol did so of their own accord and for their own reasons, and they are being criminally prosecuted."

They defended Trump's use of the word "fight" as being only used figuratively.[143] The legal team showed a video montage of elected leaders like Biden, Kamala Harris, Chuck Schumer, and Nancy Pelosi all using the word "fight." It was intended to show that the word is not meant to inspire supporters to throw punches but instead to stand up for their convictions.

"A simple timeline of events demonstrates conclusively that the riots were not inspired by the president's speech at the Ellipse," they said.[144]

---

[141] Boyer and Swoyer, "Senate approves Trump impeachment trial," https://www.washingtontimes.com/news/2021/feb/9/senate-approves-trump-impeachment-trial-six-republ/

[142] Dave Boyer and Alex Swoyer, "Senate acquits Trump in second impeachment trial on charge of inciting Capitol riot," *The Washington Times*, February 13, 2021, https://www.washingtontimes.com/news/2021/feb/13/senate-acquits-trump-second-impeachment-trial-char/

[143] Boyer and Swoyer, "David Schoen, Bruce Castor say Trump impeachment...," https://www.washingtontimes.com/news/2021/feb/8/trumps-lawyers-say-impeachment-political-theater-e/

[144] Ibid.

And there was evidence those who intended to commit violence planned to do so ahead of the former president's remarks.

Conservatives had argued there had been pre-planning for the violence, noting that there were pipe bombs discovered on Capitol Hill prior to the former president's speech. The individual who placed the pipe bombs is still unknown four years later, despite thorough FBI probes to identify thousands of January 6 rioters.[145]

Two people armed with explosives and tactical gear that had arrived in the Capitol area on or before January 6 were nabbed by police, according to court documents. The FBI was also aware of plans for a "war," *The Washington Post* had reported.[146]

Still, though, security was lax despite warnings ahead of time about how big January 6 could—and did—become.

Trump also moved to calm the violence that had erupted.

"Upon hearing of the reports of violence, he tweeted, pleading with the crowd to be 'peaceful,' followed by a tweeted video urging people to 'go home' and to do so in 'peace,'" his attorneys wrote in a filing ahead of the impeachment trial.

> He and the White House further took immediate steps to coordinate with authorities to provide whatever was necessary to counteract the rioters. There was a flurry of activity inside the

---

[145] "$500,000 Reward Remains in Effect for Information About Capitol Hill Pipe Bomber," FBI, January 4, 2024, https://www.fbi.gov/contact-us/field-offices/washingtondc/news/500000-reward-remains-in-effect-for-information-about-capitol-hill-pipe-bomber

[146] Alex Swoyer, "Democrats: Donald Trump still to blame if Capitol attack pre-planned," *The Washington Times*, January 17, 2021, https://www.washingtontimes.com/news/2021/jan/17/democrats-donald-trump-still-to-blame-if-capitol-a/

> White House working to mobilize assets. There is no legitimate proof, nor can there ever be, that President Trump was "delighted" by the events at the capital. He, like the rest of the country, was horrified at the violence.[147]

Just like in the first impeachment proceedings, evidence that was used against Trump would have amounted to hearsay if the trial had actually taken place in a court of law—not a showroom for political grandstanding.

Cassidy Hutchinson, a former White House aide, testified that Trump became irate when he could not go to the Capitol to support the January 6 protesters and even tried to jerk the steering wheel of the vehicle taking him back to the White House after his speech.[148]

Other top personnel, though, disputed her account and said it was not true.

Hutchinson's story, whether true or not, was hearsay and would have never been admissible if this type of prosecution were taking place inside a courthouse. When the person being quoted in court is not present to testify to the truth or falsity of the statement or dispute it, it is considered hearsay and generally not admitted under the rules of evidence against a defendant. The basic idea is a defendant should be able to cross-examine and

---

147 Boyer and Swoyer, "David Schoen, Bruce Castor say Trump impeachment…," https://www.washingtontimes.com/news/2021/feb/8/trumps-lawyers-say-impeachment-political-theater-e/

148 Allan Smith and Peter Alexander, "Former Meadows aide: Trump lunged at Secret Service agent, tried to grab steering wheel on Jan. 6," NBC News, June 28, 2022, https://www.nbcnews.com/politics/donald-trump/cassidy-hutchinson-trump-lunged-secret-service-agent-tried-grab-steeri-rcna35775

confront the accusers. This level of fairness and attempt to avoid prejudice is not enshrined in impeachment proceedings.

Despite Trump leaving office in just days following the January 6 riot, the House went ahead and impeached him with hopes it would leave a political stain on his legacy.

The House impeachment vote in Trump's second impeachment saw bipartisan support, unlike the first. Ten Republicans voted with Democrats to impeach Trump for inciting an insurrection.[149] Senators meanwhile voted 57–43 to acquit Trump after his trial, which was ten votes shy of what was needed for a conviction and thus removal—or bar—from holding office in the future.[150]

It would have taken the Senate a two-thirds vote to convict Trump, but the lawmakers fell significantly shy. Seven Republicans joined Democrats in voting to convict.[151] Two of them are now former senators having since left politics.

If they had reached the two-thirds vote, then another vote would have been taken. If a majority had been met, then that would have barred Trump from running for office again.[152]

It was a waste of time—and tax dollars—for the Senate to hold an impeachment trial for a former president who had already

---

149 "Roll Call 17 | Bill Number: H. Res. 24," United States House of Representatives, January 13, 2021, https://clerk.house.gov/Votes/202117

150 Boyer and Swoyer, "Senate acquits Trump…," https://www.washingtontimes.com/news/2021/feb/13/senate-acquits-trump-second-impeachment-trial-char/

151 Ibid.

152 Swoyer, "Democrats: Donald Trump still to blame…," https://www.washingtontimes.com/news/2021/jan/17/democrats-donald-trump-still-to-blame-if-capitol-a/

left office. Impeachment is used to remove someone from office under Article II, Section 4 of the US Constitution:

> The President, Vice President and all civil Officers of the United States, shall be removed from Office on Impeachment for, and Conviction of, Treason, Bribery, or other high Crimes and Misdemeanors.[153]

But it was all part of Democrat's lawfare against Trump, where they've been able to use the "insurrection" narrative in subsequent legal challenges, hoping to keep the former president from ever being reelected.

Robert C. Cahaly, the chief pollster and strategist for The Trafalgar Group, told me that unlike the first impeachment over Ukraine, Trump did not have public support behind him with this one—at least, early on.

"It was just seen as a tactic to wound his presidency," Cahaly told me of the Ukraine impeachment. "Now the second one, that was still on the cusp of January sixth, so he did not have the level of public or even Republican support at the time of that impeachment."

"Of course, both groups' opinions of January sixth have changed great deal by the start of the 2024 campaign," he added.

Trump, after the acquittal of his second impeachment trial, foreshadowed his own return. He said in a statement that the trial was "yet another phase of the greatest witch hunt in the history of our country."

---

153 "ArtII.S4.1 Overview of Impeachment Clause," Constitution Annotated, https://constitution.congress.gov/browse/essay/artII-S4-1/ALDE_00000282/

He thanked his supporters and told them they had not seen the last of him.

"Our historic, patriotic and beautiful movement to Make America Great Again has only just begun," Trump said. "In the months ahead I have much to share with you, and I look forward to continuing our incredible journey together to achieve American greatness for all of our people."[154]

Trump was not the only one to suffer legal and political consequences from January 6.

Rioters also had the book thrown at them in a disproportionate administration of justice.

I reported alongside my *Washington Times* colleague Stephen Dinan that protesters who assaulted federal officers at a courthouse in Portland, Oregon, in 2020 had charges dismissed, while the feds largely refused to negotiate charges down against January 6 rioters.

Justice Department records in 2023 showed that not one January 6 defendant had been offered a diversion agreement by attorneys, in which cases are dismissed if a defendant meets terms such as performing community service.[155]

Federal attorneys have defended the disparate treatment, suggesting those that attacked the Portland courthouse did so at night when no hearings were happening, while the Capitol riot was done while Congress was in session.

---

[154] Boyer and Swoyer, "Senate acquits Trump…," https://www.washingtontimes.com/news/2021/feb/13/senate-acquits-trump-second-impeachment-trial-char/

[155] Stephen Dinan and Alex Swoyer, "Riot act: Feds go hard on January 6 defendants but dismissed most Portland riot cases," *The Washington Times*, January 5, 2024, https://www.washingtontimes.com/news/2024/jan/5/riot-act-feds-go-hard-on-jan-6-defendants-but-dism/

In the Portland debacle, the longest sentences went to Dakotah Horton. He bashed a US marshal with a baseball bat and received a two-year sentence. Jacob Michael Gaines used a hammer on a federal officer and got four years.[156]

Meanwhile, Hunter Seefried got two years for the January 6 riot, since he was one of the first to breach the Capitol after brushing away shattered glass from a window of the Capitol, in a move that aided others to gain entry. He was in the building for only about fifteen minutes. Prosecutors had sought more than five years for his involvement in the Capitol riot.[157]

Curt Levey, president of the Committee for Justice, told me that January 6 protesters were treated more harshly than others who participated in political protests that turned violent.

"The most obvious comparison is to the Black Lives Matter riots, in which violence was taken far less seriously and even condoned. Many of the BLM rioters broke into buildings, set fire to buildings and police cars, and threw things at police officers—wrongdoing that went on for months rather than a few hours. However, unlike the January 6 protesters, they were not hunted down to the ends of the earth by law enforcement nor given prison sentences for non-violent offenses," Levey said.

The harsh treatment of the January 6 defendants was to teach them a lesson, according to Levey, "for what was deemed 'election denial' and its effort to portray the January 6 riot as an insurrection and grave threat to democracy."

"The harsh treatment was enabled by the mainstream media's vilification of the January 6 protesters, as compared to its virtual adoration of the BLM protesters and other left-leaning rioters," he said.

---

[156] Ibid.

[157] Ibid.

Levey observed that it appears violent political protests on the left seem to help progressive causes while they backfire on conservatives.

"To the extent that January 6 may have helped to galvanize Trump supporters, it is the political and legal overreaction to the riots rather than the violence that had that effect. Consider that the January 6 rioters had few friends, even within conservative circles, following the incident," he said.

INCITEMENT EXCITEMENT

Landmark legal precedent weighing the incitement of violence versus free speech rights dates back more than six decades.

Clarence Brandenburg was convicted under a criminal statute in Ohio that prohibited his advocacy of violence at a Ku Klux Klan rally where he spoke to a group about taking the country back. He was advocating brutality against blacks and Jews. It was 1964.

His comments were captured on film by a news reporter, which was later used as evidence against him at trial.

"If our president, our Congress, our Supreme Court, continues to suppress the white, Caucasian race, it's possible that there might have to be some revengeance [sic] taken," Brandenburg said. "We are marching on Congress July the Fourth, four hundred thousand strong. From there, we are dividing into two groups, one group to march on St. Augustine, Florida, the other group to march into Mississippi," he said. "Personally, I believe the nigger should be returned to Africa, the Jew returned to Israel."

"Bury the niggers," Brandenburg was also heard saying.

Brandenburg was convicted of violating Ohio's Criminal Syndicalism Statute, which made it unlawful to advocate for others to commit "crime, sabotage, violence, or unlawful methods of terrorism as a means of accomplishing industrial or political reform."[158] He was fined $1,000 and sentenced to one-to-ten years behind bars. He appealed his conviction, and the American Civil Liberties Union funded his Supreme Court fight.

Can you imagine the American Civil Liberties Union—which often has a very liberal bent—defending Brandenburg nowadays? Times have certainly changed.

Race relations were different at that time compared to how they are now. In the '60s, there were laws treating races unequally, despite the high court having ruled separate is not equal. There was inconsistency. For example, schools were to be integrated, but interracial marriage was still outlawed in some states.

Brandenburg, who advocated for violence against minorities, challenged his conviction, arguing that mere advocacy—speech—cannot be criminalized. His words and actions, although repugnant, have become part of the bedrock of First Amendment jurisprudence, giving heightened protection to speech.

Brandenburg's 1969 case resulted in the Supreme Court unanimously ruling that a law regarding the right to assemble and speak freely must have "distinctions between mere advocacy and incitement to imminent lawless action."[159]

The key is that for any speech to be unlawful, it has to imminently incite violence.

To put it as directly as a law school professor would, someone has to say "go do this," and a mob or group has to immediately go and do that, for the "incitement" charge to stick to a defendant.

---

[158] ACLU Ohio, *Brandenburg v. Ohio*, 395 U.S. 444 (1969), https://www.acluohio.org/en/cases/brandenburg-v-ohio-395-us-444-1969

[159] Justia US Supreme Court, *Bradenburg v. Ohio*, 395 U.S. 444 (1969), https://perma.cc/9HER-ZTHD

The justices at the time issued their per curium opinion, where the court speaks in one voice, reasoning that precedent had supported "the principle that the constitutional guarantees of free speech and free press do not permit a State to forbid or proscribe advocacy of the use of force or of law violation except where such advocacy is directed to inciting or producing imminent lawless action and is likely to incite or produce such action."[160]

The opinion went on to say that abstract teaching is "not the same as preparing a group for violent action."[161]

The same could be said for Trump's January 6 speech.

From the Brandenburg precedent, courts have analyzed whether speech is inciting imminent lawless action, or if it is likely to do so, in order to permit speech to be punished. An individual cannot be prosecuted for advocating violence in the future—it must to be direct and imminent.[162]

Legal scholars have recognized that the Brandenburg analysis "can be a high bar."[163]

On January 6, 2021, Trump was accused of inciting an insurrection when hundreds of his supporters journeyed from his rally—of thousands—at the White House down to the US Capitol, where they committed violence against police to enter the building unlawfully.

---

[160] Ibid.

[161] Ibid.

[162] Joseph Fawbush, "*Brandenburg v. Ohio*: Permissible Restrictions on Violent Speech," *FindLaw*, May 5, 2022, https://supreme.findlaw.com/supreme-court-insights/brandenburg-v--ohio--permissible-restrictions-on-violent-speech.html

[163] Ibid.

Five days after the riot, Pelosi said Trump "has done something so serious—that there should be prosecution against him."[164]

"This president is guilty of inciting insurrection. He has to pay a price for that," she told CBS.[165]

But under the Supreme Court's 1969 standard, Trump's words during his speech ahead of the riot were not enough to incite violence, let alone an insurrection. In his remarks, he said, "peacefully and patriotically make your voices heard" and "we're going to cheer on our brave senators and congressmen" in protest of certifying the 2020 election results.[166]

"By the strict criminal standard, the president's speech was probably not incitement," Senator Mitch McConnell, who is no Trump fan, had acknowledged.[167]

Jeffrey Scott Shapiro, who served as a Washington prosecutor and worked as a colleague of mine at *The Washington Times*, wrote in the *Wall Street Journal* that Trump's rhetoric and speech at his January 6 rally fell short of any criminality.[168]

---

164 Lesley Stahl, "Nancy Pelosi on the riot at the Capitol, Congress' mandate under Joe Biden and the youth in the Democratic party," CBS News, January 11, 2021, https://www.cbsnews.com/news/nancy-pelosi-interview-60-minutes-2021-01-10/

165 Ibid.

166 Brian Naylor, "Read Trump's January 6 Speech, A Key Part Of Impeachment Trial," NPR, February 10, 2021, https://www.npr.org/2021/02/10/966396848/read-trumps-jan-6-speech-a-key-part-of-impeachment-trial

167 CBS News, "Full speech: McConnell denounces Trump's conduct after voting to acquit at impeachment trial," YouTube, February 13, 2021, https://www.youtube.com/watch?v=kj5pvgXAgMs

168 Jeffrey Scott Shapiro, "WSJ: No, Trump Isn't Guilty of Incitement," July 29, 2023, https://www.donaldjtrump.com/news/no-trump-isnt-guilty-of-incitement

"The president's critics want him charged for inflaming the emotions of angry Americans. That alone does not satisfy the elements of any criminal offense, and therefore his speech is protected by the Constitution that members of Congress are sworn to support and defend," Mr. Shapiro wrote.[169]

David Schoen, the lawyer who represented Trump in his second impeachment, said this type of lawfare against Trump has a risk of chilling political speech, which could lead to totalitarianism.

"These have been very scary times in this regard," he said when asked about lawfare's impact on the First Amendment.

> It extended outside just the prosecutions. There were calls to blacklist anyone who worked for or supported Trump. There were credible stories about staffs at leading newspapers like *The New York Times* and *Washington Post* demanding editorial positions and news stories that targeted Trump, abandoning the simple reporting of the news in favor of coloring it against Trump.

It tends to be Trump's words—generally protected by the First Amendment—that get him into many of his legal woes, as they trigger, or incite, Democrats into waging lawfare.

The First Amendment—specifically, the freedom to speak and to associate—has been at the heart of the weaponized litigation by politically motivated lawyers. Through their targeting of Trump, his inner circle, and his supporters, the challengers have sought to silence and shame the Make America Great Again movement.

---

169 Ibid.

Jerad Najvar knows this all too well as a First Amendment attorney located in Houston, Texas.

He spent more than a year representing a couple from New Braunfels, Texas, outside of San Antonio. They were sued for participating in a Trump Train protest that went viral in Texas back during the 2020 campaign. Trump Trains, Najvar explained, were big in the era of COVID, when people wanted to show their support, but in a way to avoid getting the virus.

The couple, Joeylynn and Robert Mesaros, spent more than $80,000 defending themselves against the claim that they violated the Ku Klux Klan Act of 1871, the *Epoch Times* reported in 2022.[170] Since the case continued on for another two years, I am sure that financial tally climbed immensely.

The incident in October of 2020 stemmed from the couple joining a group of Trump supporters who drove along Interstate 35 outside of Austin, Texas, displaying their Trump flags and others while following a Biden campaign bus.

The FBI investigated the mobile protest when a Biden supporter's vehicle collided with a Trump supporter's vehicle amid a lane change, but no charges were ultimately filed.[171]

Democrats seized on the collision, casting the incident as intimidation and harassment designed to suppress voters' rights. It made news, with CNN portraying the Trump supporters in a "swarm" around the Biden bus.[172]

---

[170] Darlene Sanchez, "Legal Fees Mount for Trump Train Couple Who 'Escorted' Biden Bus," *The Epoch Times*, July 14, 2022, https://www.theepochtimes.com/us/legal-fees-mount-for-trump-train-couple-who-escorted-biden-bus-4597966

[171] Ibid.

[172] "Video shows 'Trump Train' swarm Biden-Harris campaign bus," CNN, June 24, 2021, https://www.cnn.com/videos/politics/2021/06/24/trump-train-swarms-biden-bus-new-video-mh-orig.cnn

Backed by staff from the Biden campaign and Wendy Davis, a former Texas Democratic senator, Democrats enlisted Big Law to sue the Trump supporters in federal court in July of 2021. They alleged a conspiracy to violate civil rights.

Najvar told me that the claim focused on part of 42 U.S.C. § 1985(3), referred to as the "Ku Klux Klan Act" of 1871. The law, he says, protects the right to vote. But in his view, the Democrat-funded lawyers were using it in a novel way to silence counter-protesters, threatening to chill constitutionally protected speech.

Najvar said that the Democrats' claims were an "imaginary conspiracy" and that his clients had the same right to show their support for Trump that Biden supporters had to show their support for their chosen candidate.

He pointed to a 1983 Supreme Court case, *United Brotherhood of Carpenters v. Scott*, that dealt with the federal law pertaining to a conspiracy to violate civil rights, 42 U.S.C. § 1985(3). In that dispute, which involved an assault at a protest of a union-labor issue, the high court reasoned that to have the conspiracy claim be viable, a government actor must be involved with the interference of First Amendment rights. Najvar said his clients were not government actors, thus the claim against them failed.

He said the high court warned against using the law to support "the claim that a political party has interfered with the freedom of speech of another political party by encouraging the heckling of its rival's speakers and the disruption of the rival's meetings," reasoning that judges and courts cannot be "monitors of campaign tactics."

The Mesaros were cleared of any liability when they went to trial with about half a dozen other defendants. Only one—who was not represented by Najvar—was not acquitted, but that could likely be overturned on appeal due to problematic jury instructions, Najvar noted.

He said that there should be consequences for frivolous lawsuits like the one involving his clients, the Mesaros, where they should be able to recover attorneys' fees or sanctions.

"It is not going to stop the Trump supporters. I don't think they thought we would ever fight back," Najvar said. "We have to decide what our next move is going to be, but there is a really dangerous trend right now. We have to stand up against this. Lawfare is a real thing—this lawsuit, it is hard to describe the chilling effect it has on anybody who was sued here."

He said the lawsuit made it so people were scared to speak out, which flies in the face of free speech rights and liberties.

"The jury saw through it when they finally had the opportunity," Najvar said. "Be loud and proud. We have to stand up to this kind of trash because it is not going to stop, otherwise."

Joeylynn, from her own perspective, said the whole thing was crazy, explaining to me that the couple had been new to the world of politics and were not even sure whom they would vote for in 2020. But after researching the issues, they ultimately decided to vote for and support Trump. As a result, she said, they lost friends.

"They called us racists, bigots. It really surprised us," Joeylynn told me of the lawfare experience, speaking to me alongside her attorney, Najvar.

Joeylynn and her husband found new friends in a group of people who put on Trump trains to show political support.

Although the Biden campaign bus event made headlines in October of 2020 when mainstream-media outlets painted the Trump supporters as having intimidated the Biden bus, Joeylynn said they never heard about any lawsuit against them for eight months. It had died down somewhat, and she forgot about the whole media narrative until the following summer. She got a call while at the pool with her son from a friend who told her that CNN was reporting Trump Train drivers were being sued.

"We had to learn about nearly everything from the national press release before court paperwork was actually served," she told me.

The cost of their lawfare fight is not even known, with Joeylynn saying she cannot put an exact price on it just yet, but it is well beyond $300,000. She said the threat of losing their First Amendment rights was far greater.

"I went from being a mild, meek, timid, people-pleasing, afraid-to-rock-the-boat, quiet, kept-my-opinions-to-myself individual, to being loud, outspoken, speaking for those who are afraid to speak for themselves, standing up for what is right no matter the cost, and refusing to quit," she told me.

"Emotionally, we have gone up on the frontlines in the lawfare battle to do that for our fellow Americans," she added. "The price that was on the line was the freedom of speech and the infringement on the First Amendment right and our constitutional rights."

Big Law, Democrats, and the Biden administration did not just weaponize Trump supporters' First Amendment rights against them, but they also targeted those with religious and ideological beliefs that conflict with their progressive agenda.

For example, the Biden Justice Department targeted pro-life activists, but the feds turned a blind eye to the destruction and vandalization of pro-life pregnancy clinics in the wake of the Supreme Court overturning *Roe v. Wade*, the 1973 landmark Supreme Court decision that gave women a national right to abortion. The 2022 ruling in Dobbs v. Jackson Women's Health Organization sent the abortion issue back to the states to regulate.

Not all pro-life activists, to be fair, are Trump supporters. But because of their anti-abortion beliefs, they became a target of Biden's Democratic administration through the use of lawfare. Valerie Richardson, my colleague at *The Washington Times*, noted that at least thirty pro-life advocates had been charged with violating the Freedom of Access to Clinic Entrances (FACE) Act.[173]

The pro-life protesters come from various jurisdictions, with some having been nabbed for praying and singing hymns outside of a Tennessee clinic and then others outside a Washington, DC, clinic. The DC activists actually did barricade the entry of an abortion facility under the belief that late-term abortions were occurring there, where they thought that babies were born alive but left untreated.[174] The jury, though, never heard that part of the pro-life advocates' defense to the charges, which their lawyers noted in a plea to Trump for pardons.[175]

Trump did issue pardons to twenty-three of the pro-life activists on his third day in office.

Some of them even had their homes raided at gunpoint by the Biden administration.[176]

---

[173] Valerie Richardson, "Paul Vaughn sentenced to supervised release for breaking federal law on blocking clinic access," *The Washington Times*, July 2, 2024, https://www.washingtontimes.com/news/2024/jul/2/paul-vaughn-pro-life-activist-avoids-prison-time-a/

[174] Joe Barnas, "Thomas More Society Petitions President Trump to Pardon 21 Pro-Lifers Targeted by Biden DOJ," Thomas More Society, January 15, 2025, https://www.thomasmoresociety.org/news/thomas-more-society-petitions-president-trump-to-pardon-21-pro-lifers-targeted-by-biden-doj

[175] Ibid.

[176] Ibid.

Mark Houck of Pennsylvania was one of them to be targeted at his home. In 2021, he pushed an abortion clinic worker who was harassing his son.[177] Local law enforcement brushed off the incident. But not Biden's Justice Department.[178] The feds arrested him in front of his seven children and his wife at his house at gunpoint, charging him in 2022 with violating the Freedom of Access to Clinic Entrances Act, which makes it a federal crime to obstruct the entrance to an abortion facility.[179]

Houck, though, was later acquitted by a jury.[180]

"My family was raided," he told me.[181] "I don't want any other American citizen to have to experience that."

---

[177] Alex Swoyer, "Pro-life activist targeted by Biden's DOJ now running for Congress in Pennsylvania," *The Washington Times*, August 4, 2023, https://www.washingtontimes.com/news/2023/aug/4/pro-life-activist-targeted-bidens-doj-now-running-/

[178] Ibid.

[179] Ibid.

[180] Ibid.

[181] Ibid.

DEFENSE V. DEFAMATION

"I've never met this person in my life. She is trying to sell a new book; that should indicate her motivation. It should be sold in the fiction section."
—President Trump

Trump was talking in 2019 about E. Jean Carroll, a New York advice columnist and writer, who claimed he had raped her more than two decades prior in a department store dressing room.[182]

If you were accused of committing a crime, would you deny it? What if that denial cost you nearly $90 million?

That's the standard that was set in E. Jean Carroll's defamation cases against Trump, all centering on his denial of her rape allegation.

"Shame on those who make up false stories of assault to try to get publicity for themselves or sell a book or carry out a political

[182] Alex Swoyer, "Trump's lawyer on E. Jean Carroll defamation appeal: 'Quintessential he said, she said case,'" *The Washington Times*, September 6, 2024, https://www.washingtontimes.com/news/2024/sep/6/donald-trumps-lawyer-on-e-jean-carroll-defamation-/

agenda," the president added in his official White House statement denying Carroll's accusation.[183]

Trump was asked about Carroll's book *What Do We Need Men For?: A Modest Proposal*, which came out in 2019, and which accused him of rape. The story was also reprinted in a *New York Magazine* article.

At the time of the story becoming public, Trump was commander in chief during his first administration. With the sitting president being accused of violently assaulting a woman, it's no surprise that the long-running advice columnist's accusations made headlines.

But the president's ability to defend himself and respond to what was in the news was labeled by a New York court as defamation. It was legal gymnastics and another example of lawfare lodged against him.

Never mind Trump's right to deny brutal, felony allegations against himself—or any protection of political speech; a judge decided that he had damaged Carroll's reputation by pushing back on her allegations, to the tune of more than $83 million.

The defamation battle began when Carroll first alleged that, in either 1995 or 1996, she ran into Trump in a Bergdorf Goodman's department store in New York City. He allegedly told her he needed help buying a gift for a woman, and the two ended up joking around the lingerie section about trying some on for each other. They found their way into a fitting room where she claims he raped her. He's repeatedly denied the allegation, lending all

---

[183] Donald J. Trump, "Statement on the Assault Allegation by E. Jean Carroll," June 21, 2019, https://www.presidency.ucsb.edu/documents/statement-the-assault-allegation-e-jean-carroll

the more fodder for her legal complaints and claims of repeated defamation.

Trump has said Carroll's allegation of rape was an attempt to profit from her book. It came out around the time she had just lost her advice column in *Elle Magazine* that had run for more than two decades.[184] She, though, claimed she had lost her advice column as a result of her story about Trump's assault going public and his damage to her reputation.

The whole thing was—and still is—a typical he said, she said.

Carroll sued him for defamation in 2019 while he was president, alleging he damaged her reputation. The first lawsuit was launched just months after he made the press statements in the summer of 2019 denying her claim that he had raped her. In fact, he said he had never met her.

But that lawsuit was left in limbo as the former president argued the Justice Department should take over the case, given he was commander in chief.

Judge Lewis Kaplan, a Clinton appointee, repeatedly ruled against Trump's legal team throughout the litigation—even when Trump's team had asked for a few days' delay in proceedings so Trump could attend his late mother-in-law's funeral.

Trump's lawyers appealed to the Second US Circuit Court of Appeals over the issue as to whether the Justice Department should step in to defend Trump since he was president. That question was sent over to the DC Circuit Court of Appeals. The Biden Justice Department, after the 2021 transition following Trump's 2020 election loss, took over the case and relented on

---

[184] Gwen Aviles, "E. Jean Carroll fired from ELLE magazine following Trump rape allegation," NBC News, February 19, 2020, https://www.nbcnews.com/news/us-news/e-jean-carroll-fired-elle-magazine-following-trump-rape-allegation-n1138591

its position to defend Trump. Unsurprisingly, the Biden Justice Department did not want to take over a case defending former President Trump—it was focused on prosecuting him, as we'll explore in later chapters.

But back during the months-long legal fight over whether the Justice Department had authority to take on the case, New York had passed the Adult Survivors Act, which gave victims a one-year period to come forward and sue any alleged attackers in sexual assault cases. Carroll then used that new law to launch a new defamation lawsuit, where she also added the battery claim. So, Carroll had two defamation cases pending simultaneously.

Trump repeatedly defended himself throughout the litigation and trials, posting, for example, in 2022 on social media: "For the record, E. Jean Carroll is not telling the truth, is a woman who I had nothing to do with, didn't know, and would have no interest in knowing her if I ever had the chance."

That denial, according to the judgment, was repeated defamation.

What was the president supposed to say at the time? "I don't *think* I raped her.... Maybe she's mistaken?"

Those responses fall short of the right to vehemently defend oneself when accused of a heinous crime.

In the subsequent lawsuit, the jury—which was anonymous—found Trump liable for sexual abuse but not rape. The damages awarded to Carroll amounted to $5 million.[185]

The fact that the judge reportedly had the jury stay anonymous—even to the lawyers—potentially prejudiced Trump's

---

[185] Kara Scannell, "Judge affirms $83.3 million verdict against Donald Trump in E. Jean Carroll defamation case," CNN, February, 8, 2024, https://www.cnn.com/2024/02/08/politics/e-jean-carroll-judge-affirms-verdict/index.html

team, in that they could not weed out jurors with potential bias towards their client.[186]

The jury in the second defamation trial was also an anonymous jury. Compounding that difficulty was the fact that the judge said Trump's team was not allowed to deny the allegations as part of their defense.[187]

Sounds crazy that a defendant is unable to deny allegations of rape, right?

Anonymous juries are a relatively new phenomenon, coming into play in the 1970s.[188] In some cases, jurors' identities are just withheld from the public, but lawyers involved in the legal battle have the ability to know who they are and more about them. In Trump's defamation case, though, the lawyers did not. This could have limited their ability to research a potential juror and comb through the juror's digital footprint in order to eliminate anyone with obvious political bias towards the president, who has become one of the most polarizing figures in recent American political history.

Anonymous juries also raise issues with the freedom of the press, as they do away with a reporter's ability to scrutinize

---

[186] Adam Klasfeld, "Citing Trump's attacks on 'hush money' judge, court keeps E. Jean Carroll rape jury completely anonymous," *Law & Crime*, April 10, 2023, https://lawandcrime.com/live-trials/e-jean-carroll-rape-suit/citing-trumps-attacks-on-hush-money-judge-court-keeps-e-jean-carroll-rape-jury-completely-anonymous/

[187] Larry Neumeister, "Judge, citing Trump's 'repeated public statements,' orders anonymous jury in defamation suit trial," Associated Press, November 3, 2023, https://apnews.com/article/trump-carroll-rape-lawsuit-defamation-trial-748d205569b0e90d79826cf9477ad67e

[188] Stephen Carter, "Should jury in Trump's case really remain anonymous?," *Las Vegas Sun*, April 25, 2024, https://lasvegassun.com/news/2024/apr/25/should-jury-in-trumps-case-really-remain-anonymous/

jurors and thoroughly report on the trial. It also raises questions over a defendant's right to a fair trial, guaranteed by the Sixth Amendment.[189]

The judge, though, was worried that Trump's rhetoric would threaten juror safety, as he was known to be critical of the cases and courtroom proceedings against him.

The same judge oversaw both defamation cases.

The judge went ahead and sidestepped the jury's finding that Trump did not rape Carroll.

In a later order, Judge Kaplan stated that Trump did in fact rape her under the common meaning. In rejecting Trump's attempt to countersue Carroll, he substituted his own opinion over what the jury had found.

Trump had launched his own defamation lawsuit, over the rape allegation, after the jury had returned a verdict that he did not rape her.[190] His countersuit was also handled by Judge Kaplan.

Unsurprisingly, based on how Judge Kaplan handled Carroll's cases against Trump, he brushed off Trump's counter-defamation claim. He said that "Trump 'raped her,' albeit digitally rather than with his penis."[191]

"In fact, both acts constitute 'rape' in common parlance, its definition in some dictionaries, in some federal and state

---

[189] Christopher Keleher, "The Repercussions of Anonymous Juries," US Scholarship Repository, https://repository.usfca.edu/cgi/viewcontent.cgi?article=1225&context=usflawreview

[190] Jaclyn Diaz, "A judge tossed out Trump's countersuit to E. Jean Carroll. What does this mean?," NPR, August 7, 2023, https://www.npr.org/2023/08/07/1192526887/e-jean-carroll-trump-defamation-lawsuit-dismissed

[191] Ibid.

criminal statutes, and elsewhere," the judge wrote.[192] But New York law at the time required that it be proven the penis penetrated the vagina.[193]

The jury did not think Carroll's attorney proved that a rape—under that legal standard—occurred, but Judge Kaplan stepped in and did away with the actual text of the law and the jurors' final determination.

Meanwhile, after the first verdict against Trump, the judge did not allow the defamation issue to be re-litigated by Trump's team in Carroll's other pending defamation case. Remember, she had two. That verdict landed Trump another $83.3 million. The breakdown of the enormous reward was derived from emotional and reputational damages, as well as punitive damages worth a whopping $65 million.

The $65 million in punitive damages is meant to punish Trump and prevent him from further defaming others. He's appealing both verdicts.[194]

Defamation is a difficult claim to win successfully, especially when it involves public figures—or even semi-public figures.

To prove defamation, a person has to show by a preponderance of the evidence that someone said or wrote something about him or her that was false to another individual. They also have

---

[192] Ibid.

[193] "New York State Assembly Passes Rape is Rape Act, Clearing the Way for Governor Hochul's Signature," New York State Assembly, January 29, 2024, https://nyassembly.gov/Press/?sec=story&story=108933

[194] Erica Orden, "Appeals court seems skeptical of Trump's bid to overturn sexual abuse verdict in E. Jean Carroll case," *Politico*, September 6, 2024, https://www.politico.com/news/2024/09/06/trump-carroll-appeals-court-arguments-00177766

to show that the false statement resulted in harm to his or her reputation. That can be showing the loss of a job, for example.[195]

The standard becomes higher when it involves a public official, or even a semi-public official, where the statements involve matters related to the person's publicity or work.[196]

The Supreme Court ruled in *New York Times v. Sullivan*, a landmark 1964 decision, that to have a successful defamation claim involving a public official, the claimant must show the false statement was made with knowledge that it was false or with total reckless disregard for the truth of the matter asserted.

The 1964 decision heightened First Amendment protections, requiring the additional showing of actual malice.[197]

But the heightened standard of Carroll being a well-known figure, given her lengthy and successful writing career, did not matter. The juries still came out against Trump.

Judge Kaplan had ordered the second jury trial to decide just how much Trump should have to pay her.

For anyone like myself who studied defamation in law school, it was a shock that the justice system would come out the way it had. It seemed to me that a New York judge deemed it fair to put Trump's constitutional rights aside in another abuse of lawfare.

We've learned in recent months that Trump does not come out on top in New York courtrooms.

---

195 Legal Information Institute, "Defamation," Cornell Law School, https://www.law.cornell.edu/wex/defamation

196 "Defamation of a Public Figure vs. Private Figure," Buckingham, Doolittle & Burroughs, LLC, December 14, 2023, https://www.bdblaw.com/defamation-of-public-figure-vs-private-figure/

197 Justia US Supreme Court, *New York Times Co. v. Sullivan*, 376 U.S. 254 (1964), https://supreme.justia.com/cases/federal/us/376/254/#tab-opinion-1944787

As of Trump's swearing in on January 20, 2025, both E. Jean Carroll appeals were still pending.

In September of 2024, Trump's attorney representing him at the time, Dean John Sauer—whom he later appointed as US solicitor general—said that the *Access Hollywood* tape being allowed into evidence was prejudicial in the defamation trial.[198] In that tape, Trump is heard saying that women allow celebrities to grab their private parts. The tape leaked during Trump's 2016 presidential campaign.

Sauer told the Second US Circuit Court of Appeals that the defamation battle was a "quintessential he said, she said case." He said the tape was improperly used to try to establish a standard operating procedure for Trump.[199]

The oral arguments before the federal appeals court were over the $5 million judgment, and came before a three-judge panel of all Democratic appointees.[200] Unsurprisingly, the panel ruled against Trump on his appeal in December of 2024, less than a month before his second Inauguration Day.[201] Roughly two weeks after that decision, Trump appealed to the full Second Circuit for reconsideration. His next step on appeal would be to the US Supreme Court.

---

198 Alex Swoyer, "Trump's lawyer on E. Jean Carroll defamation appeal: 'Quintessential he said, she said case,'" *The Washington Times*, September 6, 2024, https://www.washingtontimes.com/news/2024/sep/6/donald-trumps-lawyer-on-e-jean-carroll-defamation-/

199 Ibid.

200 Ibid.

201 Kyle Cheney, "Appeals court upholds $5 million verdict against Trump for sexual abuse and defamation of E. Jean Carroll," *Politico*, December 30, 2024, https://www.politico.com/news/2024/12/30/appeals-court-upholds-verdict-against-trump-in-e-jean-carroll-sexual-abuse-case-00196116

In Trump's other judgment, reaching more than $83 million, Sauer was also representing him. No oral argument date had occurred for that dispute in 2024, but Sauer did submit a brief in September of 2024 on behalf of Trump, arguing that the Supreme Court's July 2024 ruling that a president is immune from prosecution for core presidential functions, presumed immune for others, and not immune from conduct unrelated to the presidency, should end the dispute.[202]

Sauer also said that the judge limited Trump's testimony in his own defense and did not allow the president's legal team to present evidence of Carroll's alleged political motives.[203] That move, Sauer's filing said, was prejudicial.[204] Also amounting to error, Sauer continued to argue, was the judge's use of the first defamation verdict to supplement the second defamation trial, and his instructions related to New York law.[205]

"This case...represents a miscarriage of justice against President Donald J. Trump, perpetrated for political purposes and in seeking unjust pecuniary gain," Trump's brief read.[206]

> Driven by political motivation and funded by President Trump's die-hard enemies, Carroll's unbelievable claims involve a series of coincidences that Carroll herself admits are "astonishing," "amazing," and "inconceivable"—such as the fact that her story is virtually identical to

---

202 Donald Trump, Appellate brief, September 2024.

203 Ibid.

204 Ibid.

205 Ibid.

206 Ibid.

> a plotline in a 2012 episode of *Law & Order*, a favorite fictional program of the Plaintiff.[207]

On top of all of that, Carroll's legal fees were paid by a billionaire Democratic donor, but the trial judge did not permit the paperwork tracing the payments to be entered into evidence.[208]

Legal experts, though, warn an overall appeal being overturned in a defamation case may be an uphill climb for the president. However, it is possible that the large amount of damages—more than $80 million—could be reduced.[209]

There's also the potential for the two parties—Carroll and Trump—to substantially negotiate the damages down and to agree to dismiss the appeals, especially given the fact that Trump was reelected and will be serving a four-year term as president.

It's unclear how his changing status during the years-long litigation fights—from being president, to then a private citizen in 2020, then back to being president in 2025—could impact any legal arguments or potential delay in Carroll receiving any payments.

The president's legal team could also argue the damages were erroneously motivated by passion and that the amount is

---

[207] Ibid.

[208] Aaron Kliegman, "Billionaire Dem donor defends bankrolling Trump accuser's rape lawsuit as judge seals funding docs," Fox News, April 22, 2023, https://www.foxnews.com/politics/billionaire-dem-donor-defends-bankrolling-trump-accusers-rape-lawsuit-judge-seals-funding-docs

[209] Alex Swoyer, "E. Jean Carroll's $83.3 million verdict in Trump defamation case could be reduced, experts say," *The Washington Times*, February 8, 2024, https://www.washingtontimes.com/news/2024/feb/8/e-jean-carrolls-833-million-verdict-in-trump-defam/

unconstitutional; however, given that Trump is a billionaire, that argument may fall flat.[210]

The composition of the appeals court also matters.

Given the heightened politics surrounding the dispute and a majority of Democratic appointees on the Second Circuit, Trump may have to take the defamation fight all the way to the Supreme Court before finding any success or relief on appeal.

David Schoen, the lawyer who represented Trump during his January 6 impeachment, foresees the Carroll judgment will be overturned.

"I am 100 percent convinced if the lawyering is any good in this, the judgment will be reversed," Schoen told me.

> I have never seen anything like what the judge did in the second phase of the case. The jury found in Trump's favor on the allegation of rape; but the judge directed the jury that it didn't matter what [the] jury found with respect to rape versus assault. Trump was barred from arguing that he did not rape Carroll, because in the judge's views, the inquiry should not just stop and start with how New York law defines rape. This is unheard of, and, while there are several issues that could well constitute reversible error, that is a leading one that everyone who cares about the right to a fair jury trial should hope leads to a reversal.

With rape allegations, two impeachments, and the unsuccessful Mueller probe not booting Trump from the White House,

[210] Ibid.

Democrats—and their aligned advocacy groups—escalated their lawfare fight against the president.

One of their next moves was to try to use the US Constitution to bar Trump from running for reelection, arguing states should not put his name on the ballot for the 2024 election because he allegedly incited an insurrection.

COLORADO CHAOS

It was a crisp December day in Colorado when a group of Democratic-appointed judges issued a chilling decision, giving lawfare a temporary win.

On December 19, 2023, in an unprecedented move, the majority of justices on Colorado's Supreme Court—all appointed by a Democratic governor—kicked Trump off the GOP primary ballot. In the 4–3 ruling, the court recognized that it found itself in "unchartered territory," but nonetheless, the judges said Trump had to be disqualified from the state Republican ticket.

"We do not reach these conclusions lightly. We are mindful of the magnitude and weight of the questions now before us. We are likewise mindful of our solemn duty to apply the law, without fear or favor, and without being swayed by public reaction to the decisions that the law mandates we reach," the decision read, which was unsigned.[211]

---

[211] CNN staff, "Read: Colorado Supreme Court ruling removing Trump from 2024 ballot," CNN, December 19, 2023, https://www.cnn.com/2023/12/19/politics/read-colorado-supreme-court-ruling-trump-2024-ballot-14th-amendment/index.html

The three dissenting judges all warned that the court went beyond its judicial authority. In their estimation, a court did not have the power to remove a candidate based on Section 3 of the Fourteenth Amendment, which was at the heart of the legal battle.

The court case had been brought by a group of Colorado voters represented by the left-leaning Citizens for Responsibility and Ethics (CREW) in Washington. They had sued the Colorado secretary of state, arguing she could not print Trump's name on the state ballot ahead of the GOP primary because Section 3 of the Fourteenth Amendment of the US Constitution—known as the Insurrection or Disqualification clause—bars anyone who participated in a rebellion from serving in office. This section, which had been used in the wake of the Civil War to keep Confederates out of office, reads:

> No person shall be a Senator or Representative in Congress, or elector of President and Vice-President, or hold any office, civil or military, under the United States, or under any State, who, having previously taken an oath, as a member of Congress, or as an officer of the United States, or as a member of any State legislature, or as an executive or judicial officer of any State, to support the Constitution of the United States, shall have engaged in insurrection or rebellion against the same, or given aid or comfort to the enemies thereof. But Congress may by a

> vote of two-thirds of each House, remove such disability.[212]

The former president described the Colorado court decision as "A sad day for America!!!" on social media and fundraised off the setback.[213] Trump has been able to successfully fundraise off of Democrats' lawfare in the past. Prior to the Colorado ruling, he brought in $3.9 million in the day he was arraigned in Manhattan court for felony charges over hush money payments to porn actress Stormy Daniels.[214]

As the Colorado ballot case made its way to the nation's highest court, Trump's name was already printed on the ballots that were expected to be cast in the March primary. But it was the justices who were set to determine whether or not the state could count those cast in his favor.[215] The dispute stemmed from a Colorado law that allows voters to challenge a candidate's

---

212 Section 3 Disqualification from Holding Office, Fourteenth Amendment Equal Protection and Other Rights, Constitution.congress.gov, https://constitution.congress.gov/browse/amendment-14/section-3/

213 Lauren Aratani and Martin Pengelly, "Trump lashes out after Colorado ruling removing him from ballot," *The Guardian*, December 20, 2023, https://www.theguardian.com/us-news/2023/dec/20/trump-response-colorado-disqualified-2024-ballot

214 Bridget Bowman, "Trump fundraises off of Colorado decision, after past legal clashes boosted donations," NBC News, December 20, 2023, https://www.nbcnews.com/meet-the-press/ meetthepressblog/trump-fundraises-colorado-decision-legal-clashes-boosted-donations-rcna130651

215 Marshall Zelinger, "Norma Anderson, leader of effort to get Trump off Colorado's primary ballot, prepares for Supreme Court," 9 News, February 7, 2024, https://www.9news.com/article/news/local/local-politics/norma-anderson-effort-to-get-trump-off-colorado-primary-ballot-supremecourt/73-166f5f83-eb40-498e-8988-19187f3eaf0f

qualifications in an effort to keep the Colorado secretary of state from placing the candidate's name on the ballot.[216]

Republicans viewed the Colorado Supreme Court's decision to boot Trump as a full-throated embrace of activists' lawfare against the former president. The decision gave Democrats a green light to keep pushing the outlandish ballot challenges in various states, all based on a centuries-old section of the Constitution rarely used. Colorado's radical legal precedent subsequently bolstered other activist election officials to reason that they, too, had the unilateral authority to remove Trump from their state's ballot. Maine's secretary of state tried to keep him from its ballot while the litigation was pending before the justices. She did not even rely on a court to make the call. She did it herself.

Since I was covering the ballot battles for *The Washington Times*, I had to drop everything and write up the breaking news after the Colorado decision, as it was the first time a court went so far as to say Trump's name could not appear on the 2024 ticket. I thought, "Here we go, a state finally has gone and done it."

Having covered the Supreme Court for seven years, I knew this was more of a political show than an actual legal dispute—and it would have little success being tolerated by the nation's highest court. Chief Justice John G. Roberts Jr., a Bush appointee and moderate on the bench, shies away from political lawsuits as much as the court can. And with this type of ruling, had the Supreme Court affirmed Colorado's judgment, it would have completely taken Trump off of all fifty states' ballots. It is impossible to fathom the outrage that would have ensued from more than 74 million people, who had previously voted for Trump and likely would do so again, if a group of judges decided the former

[216] Ibid.

president could not run for reelection. More so, it was unthinkable that the nine justices—especially with the 6–3 conservative majority—would rule in favor of the liberal challengers.

Nonetheless, too much media coverage, time, and attention was focused on this use of Democrats' lawfare, which was dressed up as yet another court case. The coverage breathed life into the far-fetched claims attempting to utilize a Civil War-era amendment against Trump. *Slate* categorized the chances of Trump's arguments against kicking him from the ballot as dim, based on legal choices made by his team, writing in one of its published critiques ahead of the Supreme Court's arguments, "Trump's Lawyers Made Some Very Odd Strategic Choices."[217] Similarly, *Vox* published an article days before the hearing titled, "Trump's legal arguments for staying on the ballot are embarrassingly weak."[218] Of course, he went on to win at the Supreme Court, but the media coverage led voters to believe it was Trump—not the liberal challengers—who had the uphill legal row to hoe.

Not only was Democrats' use of lawfare arguably legal malpractice, but the media not calling it straight was a perfect example of journalistic malpractice. It was the American voters who were the victims. A *Politico* | *Morning Consult* poll in September of 2023—before the Colorado Supreme Court even acted—showed a majority of voters believed Trump engaged in an insurrection

---

[217] Richard Hasen, "Trump's Lawyers Made Some Very Odd Strategic Choices in the Supreme Court Ballot Case," *Slate*, January 29, 2024, https://slate.com/news-and-politics/2024/01/trump-lawyers-strategy-supreme-court-ballot.html

[218] Ian Millhiser, "Trump's legal arguments for staying on the ballot are embarrassingly weak," *Vox*, February 6, 2024, https://www.vox.com/scotus/2024/2/6/24054902/supreme-court-trump-anderson-disqualification-insurrection-fourteenth-amendment

and could be taken off the ballot.[219] And just one month before the court heard oral arguments on the case, an ABC News/Ipsos survey showed that 56 percent thought the high court should disqualify Trump from the ballot or leave it to the states, which would mean a ruling in favor of Colorado.[220]

The scarcely credible legal challenges from the numerous state battles—including Colorado—gave Democratic activists earned media in the daily news coverage that all centered around January 6, 2021, and the riot at the US Capitol. Every media report had to reference the riot—which Democrats had labeled as an "insurrection" and part of Trump's "big lie" over losing the 2020 election. "Earned media" is a term used by campaigns when a candidate or political party gets favorable news coverage on an issue without having to pay for it.

And the litigation also caused Trump to spend more on his legal fees, which were ever-accumulating as he had been forced to defend himself in courtrooms across the country. More money going towards Trump's legal bills meant less he could spend toward his own reelection. And more time he had to spend in courtrooms meant less time he could spend on the campaign trail.

Other states, aside from Colorado, had grappled with the ballot litigation, as liberal advocates launched these long-shot bids in dozens of states hoping to end Trump's campaign once and for all. At one point, thirty-seven states had pending lawsuits over

---

[219] Zach Montellaro, "Poll: Majority of voters would support disqualifying Trump under 14th Amendment," *Politico*, September 29, 2023, https://www.politico.com/news/2023/09/29/poll-trump-disqualified-14th-amendment-00118980

[220] Lauren Irwin, "56 percent in new poll willing to see Trump disqualified from ballots in all or some states," *The Hill*, January 12, 2024, https://thehill.com/homenews/campaign/4405201-56-in-new-poll-willing-to-see-trump-disqualified-from-ballots-in-all-or-some-states/

the ballot contest.[221] Maine's Secretary of State Shenna Bellows, following Colorado's lead, bucked Trump from her state ballot, too, though that unilateral move was put on hold by the courts. Michigan's Supreme Court had sidestepped the issue of Section 3 of the Fourteenth Amendment, saying the case was not ripe for consideration during a primary. The court's reason was that it is a private party's (the GOP's) decision whether to keep Trump on its primary ticket. It was a way to temporarily avoid deciding the thorny issue, but it left the decision for a later date—one that would have come closer to the general election in November.

If a court had eventually sided with the challengers, that would have disenfranchised the Republican Party, since it would have had its chosen party nominee removed from appearing on state ballots shortly before Election Day. And the Republican Party would have had to grapple with how to replace a nominee following its convention. Luckily, though, none of those unpleasant hypotheticals was realized, as the Supreme Court stepped in to avoid last-minute mayhem.

As of that December, no state court had gone so far in ruling Trump was banned from a ballot. That is, until Colorado. The reaction in the Centennial State was mixed. A Trump supporter, Patty McCoy of Northglenn, Colorado, told Colorado Public Radio that the state's ruling was evidence that Democrats were trying to stop Trump's campaign.[222] "They're trying this against Trump because they know that he has the wherewithal (and) the

---

[221] Hyemin Han and Caleb Benjamin, "The Trump Disqualification Tracker," *Lawfare*, October 30, 2023, https://www.lawfaremedia.org/current-projects/the-trump-trials/section-3-litigation-tracker

[222] Bente Birkeland, "Colorado voters weigh in on Trump ballot ruling as experts closely follow a rare legal journey," *CPR News*, December 20, 2023, https://www.cpr.org/2023/12/20/trump-colorado-ballot-ruling-voters-experts-reaction/

smarts to get things done that they don't want done, which means they don't want Washington disturbed from the way it used to be," McCoy told CPR. Trump's campaign agreed.

"Democrat Party leaders are in a state of paranoia over the growing, dominant lead President Trump has amassed in the polls. They have lost faith in the failed Biden presidency and are now doing everything they can to stop the American voters from throwing them out of office next November," the former president's campaign said in reaction to the decision.[223]

The ballot drama first began when a Colorado state court ruled Trump—despite not being federally charged with leading an insurrection—did engage in one on January 6, 2021. The lower-court judge, though, did not initially remove his name from the ticket. It was the state's highest court that did so as the issue climbed its way up the court system.

The Disqualification Clause has been "seldom used," according to a Congressional Research Service report in 2022.[224] "The few times it has been used in the past mainly arose out of the Civil War—a very different context from the events of January 6," the report read. It was employed to keep Confederates out of office and later deployed in 1919 to keep a socialist from becoming a member of Congress after he was accused of aiding Germany during World War I.[225] From 1919 to January 6, 2021, it had not

---

[223] News 4 Tuscan, "Trump Campaign responds to The Colorado Supreme Court Ruling," KVOA, January 26, 2024, https://www.kvoa.com/news/top-stories/trump-campaign-responds-to-the-colorado-supreme-court-ruling/article_1da21c6e-9ec7-11ee-9a07-0fe4b625e3a1.html

[224] "The Insurrection Bar to Office: Section 3 of the Fourteenth Amendment," Congressional Research Service, September 7, 2022, https://crsreports.congress.gov/product/pdf/LSB/LSB10569

[225] Ibid.

been tapped. A New Mexico court, though, did resort to it in the aftermath of January 6, 2021, to remove a county commissioner from office who had participated in the January 6 riot. That man's appeal was rejected by the Supreme Court, which refused to hear the issue just two weeks after having decided in favor of Trump in his Section 3 challenge. The high court reasoned different rules can apply to state office holders compared to federal candidates.

The Supreme Court case out of Colorado, *Trump v. Anderson*, originated by a ninety-one-year-old Republican politician.[226] Norma Anderson had served as majority leader in both Colorado's House and Senate during her political career, according to CNN, which also noted that she said CREW, the liberal legal advocacy group, had sought her out to pursue the lawsuit against Trump. She was joined by other Republican and unaffiliated voters, but all were represented under her name by CREW. "They came to me and asked if I would be interested," Anderson told CNN of the liberal advocacy group. "And I said absolutely."

Although I, as both a lawyer and a reporter, disagreed with the reasoning and the subsequent fallout from Colorado's initial ruling against Trump—which relied on Section 3—it became the stepping stone to "one of the most important arguments in decades"[227] at the Supreme Court that I've had the opportunity to cover during my time in Washington. While Democrats' lawfare got an enormous amount of coverage, a counter-effort

---

226 Marshall Cohen, "Who is Norma Anderson? The Colorado Republican leading the 14th Amendment challenge against Trump," CNN, February 8, 2024, https://www.cnn.com/2024/02/08/politics/norma-anderson-trump-colorado-ballot/index.html

227 Marcia Coyle, "Tune into one of the most important arguments in decades: Trump v. Anderson," National Constitution Center, February 6, 2024, https://constitutioncenter.org/blog/tune-into-one-of-the-most-important-arguments-in-decades-trump-v-anderson

by Republican states did not get as much traction in the media. Texas, Missouri, and Florida officials suggested President Joe Biden should be removed from their state ballots over his failed duties at the southern border, where an estimated eight million illegal aliens had crossed during his administration.[228] That response from red states was highlighted during the Supreme Court's hearing.

On February 8, 2024, the justices heard oral arguments over whether Section 3 of the Fourteenth Amendment barred Trump from running for office. The Supreme Court quickly took up the state case. Arguments before the justices usually take months to get scheduled once an appeal is granted, but with the pressing nature of Colorado's primary quickly approaching, the justices scheduled oral arguments in under two months following the Colorado Supreme Court's ruling. The arguments lasted more than two hours, even though the justices had originally allotted only eighty minutes for the hearing.

The disputed section of the US Constitution says anyone who participated in a rebellion cannot hold office. That was a point stressed by the justices during oral arguments, as the court referenced that there seemed to be a bar on *holding* office, not necessarily *running* for office. In a politically charged case, there were definitely lines of questioning that suggested there was agreement across the ideological wings of the court.

Even after dozens of times inside the beautiful marble and mahogany courtroom, lined with red velvet curtains, it is cases like this one that still give me chills and keep me in awe of the nation's historic, revered judicial process. There's such history,

---

[228] Andrew Stanton, "Full List of States Wanting to Kick Biden Off the Ballot," *Newsweek*, January 9, 2024, https://www.newsweek.com/states-wanting-kick-joe-biden-ballot-full-list-1859028

legacy, and precedent that is being made inside the very walls where I get to sit and report on the nation's most pressing legal battles. To watch the arguments unfold, I sit in the press section. It is to the left of the lawyers as they argue before the justices, who sit side by side along a long bench just a few feet in front of them. Chief Justice Roberts sits in the middle, and the associate justices, from the most senior to least, flank his sides. For every case, I tend to jot down by hand (as computers are not allowed in the courtroom) key quotes from the justices. Based on their questioning during the arguments, I also maintain a running tally of who I think will rule a certain way. It gives me an idea of how the court may rule on any given dispute as I exit the courtroom to report to my editors. In this ballot case, I left the courtroom knowing Trump had a great day in court, and the arguments reaffirmed my belief that the Supreme Court would never tolerate the Colorado Supreme Court's decision.

As I wrote in my headline that day, the justices were "skeptical" of the state's decision to boot Trump.[229] I had hoped to spot the former president in the courtroom for the arguments, but he did not appear. My take on Trump having the better day in court over the liberal challengers was shared by fellow reporters, too. NBC News cast the arguments with the headline: "Supreme Court signals unlikely to let Colorado kick Trump off ballot."[230]

---

[229] Alex Swoyer and Stephen Dinan, "Supreme Court skeptical of Colorado kicking Trump off ballot: 'Just doesn't seem like a state call,'" *The Washington Times*, February 8, 2024, https://www.washingtontimes.com/news/2024/feb/8/supreme-court-skeptical-colorado-kicking-trump-bal/

[230] Lawrence Hurley and Dareh Gregorian, "Supreme Court signals unlikely to let Colorado kick Trump off ballot," NBC News, February 8, 2024, https://www.nbcnews.com/politics/2024-election/supreme-court-weighs-trumps-bid-stay-colorado-ballot-rcna136557

The *Washington Post*'s headline was "Supreme Court poised to allow Trump to remain on Colorado ballot."[231]

Jonathan Mitchell, who argued on behalf of Trump, told the justices that Congress is able—by a two-thirds vote in the House[232]—to restore someone for office after a Section 3 disqualification. He argued that means a state does not have authority to exercise a Section 3 disqualification on a federal candidate—only Congress would have that power. "A state cannot exclude any candidate for federal office from the ballot on account of Section 3," he said, "and any state that does so is violating the holding of Term Limits by altering the Constitution's qualifications for federal office."[233] "And in this situation, a ruling from this Court that affirms the decision below would not only violate Term Limits but take away the votes of potentially tens of millions of Americans."[234]

Opposing counsel argued Trump's protest of the 2020 election results on January 6, 2021, and the riot at the US Capitol that followed his speech, was an insurrection that barred Trump from reelection. "We are here because, for the first time since the War of 1812, our nation's capitol came under violent assault. For the first time in history, the attack was incited by a sitting president of the United States to disrupt the peaceful transfer of presidential

---

[231] Ann Marimow and Patrick Marley, "Supreme Court poised to allow Trump to remain on Colorado ballot," *The Washington Post*, February 8, 2024, https://www.washingtonpost.com/politics/2024/02/08/supreme-court-oral-arguments-trump-colorado-ballot/

[232] Congressional Research Service, "The Insurrection Bar to Office: Section 3 of the Fourteenth Amendment," September 7, 2022, p. 1, https://www.congress.gov/crs-product/LSB10569?s=1&r=2

[233] *Trump v. Anderson*, Supreme Court of the United States, February 8, 2024, https://www.supremecourt.gov/oral_arguments/argument_transcripts/2023/23-719_2jf3.pdf

[234] Ibid.

power," said Jason Murray, who represented the Colorado voters and liberal advocacy group that aimed to axe Trump from the ballot.[235]

"There's a reason Section 3 has been dormant for 150 years, and it's because we haven't seen anything like January 6th since Reconstruction. Insurrection against the Constitution is something extraordinary," Murray added.[236] Murray had clerked for Justice Elena Kagan on the Supreme Court and for Justice Neil Gorsuch on the Tenth US Circuit Court of Appeals, where Justice Gorsuch was a judge prior to being appointed to the Supreme Court by Trump. Murray's insurrection arguments met pushback—by both of his former bosses, among the other justices left chilled by his position. "Other states may have different views about what constitutes insurrection," Chief Justice Roberts said, his voice booming from the middle of the bench as he sat directly in front of the attorney.[237] The high court did not rule on whether or not January 6 constituted an actual insurrection. The justices did not even set out guidelines for lower courts to weigh when deciding whether to categorize January 6 as an insurrection. Instead, the justices decided to shut down the ballot challenges altogether by rejecting Colorado's argument. As I reported, the Supreme Court seemed highly skeptical that a Civil War-era amendment applied to Trump.

"Why should a single state have the ability to make this determination, not only for their own citizens but for the rest of the nation?" Justice Kagan, an Obama appointee, asked. Justice Amy Coney Barrett, a Trump appointee, echoed her liberal-leaning colleague. "It just doesn't seem like a state call," she said.

---

[235] Ibid.

[236] Ibid.

[237] Ibid.

The Supreme Court ruled unanimously that states could not remove Trump's name, sending the decision back to Colorado to fix ahead of its primary. The unanimous ruling definitively ended dozens of Section 3 challenges across the country in various states. It was a nail in the coffin for this episode of Democrats' lawfare. Although polls heading into the court's arguments showed that a majority of Americans would have backed a decision cutting Trump from the ballot, that tide shifted with the unanimous ruling. It revealed that by speaking in one voice, the high court can influence the American public. A Marquette Law School survey released about a month after the 9–0 opinion showed that 58 percent of respondents agreed with the justices ruling that a state could not remove a federal candidate from its ticket.[238] In the high court's opinion, the justices reasoned that Congress has the ability to remove any disqualification, so Section 3 should be enforced by it rather than by individual states.

"Because the Constitution makes Congress, rather than the States, responsible for enforcing Section 3 against federal officeholders and candidates, we reverse," the court's per curiam opinion read.[239] A per curiam opinion is when a ruling is issued that is unsigned, but from the full court. There were no noted dissents, meaning even the court's three liberal justices were in agreement with the conservative majority. Trump, pleased with the high

---

[238] James Lynch, "Majority of Americans Support SCOTUS Decision Barring States from Taking Trump off the Ballot: Poll," *National Review*, April 3, 2024, https://www.nationalreview.com/news/majority-of-americans-support-scotus-decision-barring-states-from-taking-trump-off-the-ballot-poll/

[239] *Trump v. Anderson*, March 4, 2024, https://www.supremecourt.gov/opinions/23pdf/23-719_19m2.pdf

court's decision, took to social media reacting with a four-word post (in all caps): "BIG WIN FOR AMERICA!!!"[240]

The 9–0 ruling, too, was not only a major victory for the former president as he fought to stay on the 2024 ballot, but it was also a slam dunk against the Democrats' lawfare, as it terminated a liberal advocacy group's judicial activism in a bipartisan manner from the nation's highest court. It was as if the justices—from various ideological wings—spoke in unity against the political weaponization of the courts. *The New York Post* ran the article, "A 9–0 Supreme Court ruling on Trump shows that democracy isn't partisan."[241] But *The Wall Street Journal* may have put it the best with its headline: "Supreme Court 9, Lawfare 0 in the Trump Ballot Case."[242]

---

[240] Nick Mordowanec, "Donald Trump's Four Word Reaction After Supreme Court Ruling," *Newsweek*, March 4, 2024, https://www.newsweek.com/donald-trump-reaction-after-supreme-courtruling-colorado-ballot-1875655

[241] Editorial Board, "A 9–0 Supreme Court ruling on Trump shows that democracy isn't partisan," *New York Post*, March 4, 2024, https://nypost.com/2024/03/04/us-news/a-9-0-supreme-court-ruling-on-trump-shows-that-democracy-isnt-partisan/

[242] Editorial Board, "Supreme Court 9, Lawfare 0 in the Trump Ballot Case," *The Wall Street Journal*, March 4, 2024, https://www.wsj.com/articles/donald-trump-v-anderson-supreme-court-opinion-9-0-colorado-ballot-presidential-election-7486b815

TOP PRESIDENTIAL CONTENDER GAGGED

Gag orders issued by a court are meant to protect First Amendment rights and the defendant's constitutional right to a fair trial under the Sixth Amendment. The accused—and the public, through media coverage—are expected to have free-speech rights and access to information that should not be infringed.

But that standard changed with President Trump's criminal cases in Manhattan and Washington, DC, where two trial judges attempted to silence the defendant—all while some witnesses were making public, disparaging remarks about him ahead of, during, and after the proceedings. Trump was also subject to gag orders in other disputes; but the Manhattan hush-money proceeding was the first criminal case to see an indictment, let alone a trial where the former president remained gagged for most of the pendency of the case.

When it came to the Trump gag orders and free-speech interests at stake, the courts' moves appeared to be a strange manipulation of Supreme Court precedent. And it was yet another form of Democrats' lawfare against their chief political opponent. If they could not jail him during the 2024 campaign, they would move to silence him. And they did, to an extent.

In April of 2023, Manhattan District Attorney Alvin Bragg, an elected Democrat, won an indictment against Trump over allegedly falsifying business records in his state.

The state had charged that Trump tried to cover up a crime by characterizing payments to Michael Cohen, his former attorney, as "legal fees"—when they were actually part of repayment for "hush money" that Cohen paid porn actress Stormy Daniels during the 2016 campaign, to keep her quiet about claims she had an affair with Trump in 2006. Although paying hush money is not a crime, prosecutors suggested Trump did it either to cover up a campaign finance issue, or for unlawful tax purposes.

Trial Judge Juan Merchan placed a gag order on Trump during the criminal proceedings, forbidding the defendant, former president, and leading presidential candidate from speaking out about counsel, the court staff, their families, witnesses, or jurors.[243]

Trump was not allowed to comment about Judge Merchan's daughter, Loren, working for a marketing firm that represented Democratic lawmakers and that fundraised off of Trump's trial. That created quite a conflict of interest for the judge, which a defendant would normally want to shed light on.[244] New York's judicial guidelines state that a judge must recuse if a family member has a financial interest in the outcome of a case before

[243] Michael Sisak, "Appeals court upholds Donald Trump's gag order as he again presses judge to exit hush money case," Associated Press, August 1, 2024, https://apnews.com/article/trump-gag-order-hush-money-02ed921ed04264766b53e64308d38847

[244] Ibid.

that judge.[245] Judge Merchan refused to comply. But California Democrat Rep. Adam Schiff and Senate Majority PAC took in $93 million from fundraising through Loren Merchan's progressive marketing company that had raised funds off of the Trump prosecution, according to House Republican lawmakers.[246] The direct financial interest for the judge's family member in the trial raises issues of Due Process that Trump should have been able to opine on during his reelection bid and trial.

House Judiciary Committee Chairman Jim Jordan told me that Judge Merchan "definitely should have recused." Jordan noted that Brad Smith, a campaign finance expert, had come to his committee and testified. Smith could have testified at trial to the alleged campaign finance violation in defense of Trump, but that was not allowed by the judge. "It was so many things he did in the course of the trial itself—the gag order on President Trump, the prohibiting Brad Smith from even testifying, was just ridiculous."

"There were all kinds of problems there," Jordan added of Judge Merchan's handling of the trial and Alvin Bragg's trumped-up charges. "They took a bookkeeping entry and turned it into some kind of campaign finance [issue], and wouldn't let the expert on campaign finance talk, and put a gag order on the defendant himself, with the judge whose daughter made it so he should have recused. That was just, like, so political that I think the country was able to figure all that out."

---

245 Harmeet Dhillon, X.com, April 15, 2024, https://x.com/pnjaban/status/1779890598251520329

246 Alex Swoyer, "House GOP targets daughter of Trump hush money judge in conflict of interest probe," *The Washington Times*, August 1, 2024, https://www.washingtontimes.com/news/2024/aug/1/loren-merchan-justice-juan-merchans-daughter-targe/

Jordan told me that his committee is mulling legislation to allow federal officials to move local prosecutions to federal court in hopes to help quell lawfare. "We think, at least in fairness, that if they want to remove those cases to federal court, the defendant should be able to do that," he said.

If the Supreme Court, for decades, has protected the press's right to disseminate key information about criminal trials to the public, surely so too should a court protect a defendant's (and top presidential candidate's) right to speak to the public on matters related to his own prosecution.

But New York's court system did not.

Shockingly, an appeals court left the gag order in effect.[247] It reasoned there were "significant and imminent" threats against prosecutors, and the fear was that Trump's supporters would lash out based on Trump's comments surrounding the proceedings, since the president had a history of being critical of lawyers and judges.[248]

Even after Trump was convicted by the Manhattan jury in May of 2024, his gag order stayed in place. It was later limited to an extent where he was able to comment on witnesses and jurors. He was also free to comment on Judge Merchan and Bragg, the Democrat-elected prosecutor bringing the case.

---

247 Michael Sisak, "Appeals court upholds Donald Trump's gag order as he again presses judge to exit hush money case," Associated Press, August 1, 2024, https://apnews.com/article/trump-gag-order-hush-money-02ed921ed04264766b53e64308d38847

248 Erik Uebelacker, "New York appeals court won't lift Trump gag order pending hush-money sentence," Courthouse News Service, August 1, 2024, https://www.courthousenews.com/new-york-appeals-court-wont-lift-trump-gag-order-pending-hush-money-sentence/

But even after winning the election, and his sentencing remaining in limbo for months, the president-elect was still unable to comment freely on the proceedings.

It's unlikely a gag order of this magnitude would have been upheld by the Supreme Court, should the justices have evaluated this matter. At the very least, in the interest of justice, Judge Merchan should have also gagged the witnesses from commenting publicly about Trump. If Trump was unable to speak out against Cohen and Daniels, they too should not have been able to bad-mouth the president—and defendant—to the press, as they took the stand against him before a jury that was not sequestered and was able to see and hear all news reports.

Separately, Trump was indicted again. This one came four months after his initial Manhattan indictment. In Washington, DC, Trump faced an indictment from charges brought by Special Counsel Jack Smith over alleged election fraud related to Trump's contesting of the 2020 election and his actions on January 6, 2021.

Two months later, the DC trial court—led by Judge Tanya Chutkan, an Obama appointee—issued a gag order restricting the president from making statements about the prosecutors, court staff, defense counsel, or witnesses.[249]

Even the American Civil Liberties Union, not a fan of Trump, submitted a brief arguing the gag order was vague and overboard, raising First Amendment concerns.[250]

---

[249] ACLU District of Columbia, "*United States v. Trump* (Challenging Vague and Broad Gag Order Against Criminal Defendant)," https://www.acludc.org/en/cases/united-states-v-trump-challenging-vague-and-broad-gag-order-against-criminal-defendant

[250] Ibid.

The DC Circuit Court of Appeals later limited Judge Chutkan's gag order on Trump, and applied it evenly to all parties involved, not just singling him out, as the New York order did.[251] However, Trump's right to defend himself and speak freely on matters of public concern was still curtailed.

Some of the leading Supreme Court precedents related to gag orders date back to the 1960s.

In *Sheppard v. Maxwell*, the high court ruled in 1966 that a court must balance First Amendment rights with safeguarding the judicial process.[252] The case involved Samuel Sheppard, who was accused of killing his pregnant wife. Sheppard maintained his innocence, although he was quickly suspected to be the killer by police. He was criticized in the media ahead of trial for not cooperating with law enforcement. During the trial, the judge allowed dozens of newsmen in and out of the courthouse and did not sequester or protect jurors or the defendant from the intense scrutiny and coverage.[253]

The high court overturned the conviction of Sheppard, reasoning his right to a fair trial was infringed. In its opinion, the justices said the trial court should have instituted stricter rules for the press, witnesses, and counsel.[254]

"Freedom of discussion should be given the widest range compatible with the essential requirement of the fair and orderly administration of justice," the opinion read.[255] "The theory of

---

[251] Ibid.

[252] Justia US Supreme Court, "*Sheppard v. Maxwell*, 384 U.S. 333 (1966)," https://supreme.justia.com/cases/federal/us/384/333/#tab-opinion-1946115

[253] Ibid.

[254] Ibid.

[255] Ibid.

our system is that the conclusions to be reached in a case will be induced only by evidence and argument in open court, and not by any outside influence, whether of private talk or public print."

Sheppard went on to have his conviction overturned and later be acquitted.[256] According to a University of Missouri-Kansas City legal blog, the press had called Sheppard a "liar" during the coverage and demanded his arrest.[257]

Does that sound at all similar to mainstream media's characterization of Trump during his judicial proceedings?

One notable difference between the First Amendment interests in Sheppard's trial versus Trump's Manhattan hush-money trial was that Trump, the defendant, was silenced while the state's key witnesses against him, Michael Cohen and Stormy Daniels, were not. They were free to communicate with the public—and did so—during the defendant's proceedings.

Trump was even fined $9,000 for violating the gag order, by commenting on social media about witnesses ahead of the trial, and Judge Merchan said if he continued, the president could be locked up.[258]

While Trump was subject to the gag order from the Manhattan legal proceeding, Cohen did interviews, sharing them on his social media, saying Trump was not a generous or kind

[256] "Fair Trial Issues," *Exploring Constitutional Conflicts*, http://law2.umkc.edu/faculty/projects/ftrials/conlaw/fairtrialissues.htm

[257] Ibid.

[258] Kara Scannell et al., "Donald Trump fined $9,000 for violating gag order in hush money case," CNN, April 30, 2024, https://www.cnn.com/2024/04/30/politics/donald-trump-fined-usd9-000-for-violating-gag-order-in-hush-money-case/index.html

person, attempting to disparage the character of the defendant that he was about to testify against.[259]

Daniels, meanwhile, debuted a documentary where she detailed her experience with Trump and claimed she was scared over being silenced—all while Trump was unable to respond, due to the gag order. The documentary debuted the same month Trump was put under the gag order.[260]

Between Daniels's documentary and Cohen's podcast and book deals, it is unclear exactly how much the two have profited off of their quarrels with the president. According to *Forbes*, Cohen made roughly $4.4 million from turning on Trump, which is double what he was making working for the Trump Organization as the president's attorney.[261] *Forbes*, meanwhile, also reported Daniels profited more than $100,000 from her tiff with Trump, through strip shows, a book deal, and her documentary—but she owes him significant legal fees after losing to him in a defamation lawsuit.[262] Although her notoriety skyrocketed, she has not seen the payday that Cohen has from his falling out with Trump.

Meanwhile, campaigning across the nation during the judicial proceedings, Trump was not permitted to respond to the state's

---

259 MichaelCohen2.0, Instagram Reels, https://www.instagram.com/reel/C5BQJSTOvxh/?igsh=MXcyMnl1Y2JkNjg1ZQ==

260 Kara Scannell, "Stormy Daniels says she was scared for her life after hush money deal with Trump went public," CNN, March 18, 2024, https://www.cnn.com/2024/03/18/politics/stormy-daniels-trump-allegations-peacock-movie/index.html

261 *Forbes* Breaking News, "Here's How Much Michael Cohen Has Made Off Trump and What He Could Do Next | NYC Hush Money Trial," YouTube, May 29, 2024, https://www.youtube.com/watch?v=it5xP5q8Gp0

262 *Forbes,* "How Much Is Stormy Daniels Making Off Donald Trump?," YouTube, May 14, 2024, https://www.youtube.com/watch?v=rZHlV1dYzFA

key witnesses. The gag order stayed in effect even after he won the election and was readying to enter the White House.

Another noteworthy Supreme Court precedent came in 1976, in the case of *Nebraska Press Assn. v. Stuart*, when the Court recognized the high burden one must meet to interfere with First Amendment rights. That case dealt with the high-court ruling against a trial judge's gag order on the press, restricting coverage of a six-person homicide.[263]

"The authors of the Bill of Rights did not undertake to assign priorities as between First Amendment and Sixth Amendment rights, ranking one as superior to the other," the justices' recognized.[264]

But what about when the defendant's First and Sixth Amendment rights are both at stake, with a gag order like that impeding Trump's ability to speak out against the government's prosecution against him, and thus his ability to receive a fair trial? It seems both of those constitutionally protected rights outweigh worries about judicial efficiency and the speculated safety concerns of those involved in the proceedings.

Remember, at no time did Trump call on his supporters to commit violence against the prosecutors, judges, witnesses, or jury members.

It was yet another unparalleled turn of events, which seem to happen reliably when it comes to Trump. Not only did two trial judges decide to silence a defendant, disregarding his constitutional rights. It also was the first time a former president and major party's presidential nominee was sitting in a defendant's chair

---

263 Justia US Supreme Court, *Nebraska Press Assn. v. Stuart*, 427 U.S. 539 (1976), https://supreme.justia.com/cases/federal/us/427/539/

264 Ibid.

under historic gag orders while trying to run a campaign. While his opponents—first President Joe Biden and then Vice President Kamala Harris—were eventually able to label him a criminal and convicted felon, Trump was unable to adequately respond.

No defendant—even one as polarizing as Trump—should be unable to defend himself publicly against criminal charges. That's antithetical to judicial protections enshrined since our nation's founding. Just as a defendant has the right to remain silent before the court, so too should the defendant have the right to vehemently defend himself in the court of public opinion. That right was taken away from Trump. His First Amendment rights, and that of the public to hear from the top presidential candidate, were infringed when he was silenced by courts.

And his Sixth Amendment right to a fair trial was damaged when prosecutors and state witnesses were able to disparage the president and comment on the proceedings while he was not. The tilted media coverage favoring the witnesses' comments without Trump's response tainted the jury pool.

Never before—and still to this day—has the high court seen such a consequential legal battle over the First and Sixth Amendment rights of a former president, who also happened to be the Republican Party's presumed presidential nominee. One wonders how the justices would grapple with not only the protections of the First Amendment for Trump as a defendant, but also with the even-more-protected status of one's political speech.

Political speech is a form of speech given heightened First Amendment protections. The Supreme Court for decades has recognized political speech—the free exchange of ideas over policy, candidates, and campaigns—as being integral to the democratic system.[265]

For example, lawmakers are immune from liability for speeches they give on the chamber floor due to the desire to protect the free exchange of ideas in a political setting, which is enshrined in the Constitution's Speech and Debate Clause.[266]

So too is political speech considered sacred at political rallies.[267]

Trump, though, had to carry out roughly ninety campaign rallies while being under the gag order from his criminal proceedings during his 2024 campaign.[268] His opponents—President Joe Biden and Vice President Kamala Harris—were able to campaign freely without having their speech subjected to censorship by a court or being under the threat of being jailed.

Missouri, along with a handful of other red states, tried to sue New York over the gag order issued out of the Manhattan court, reasoning it infringed on their residents' ability to hear from the top presidential candidate.[269] The case was filed before

---

[265] "Protection of Core Political Speech," US Legal.com, https://civilrights.uslegal.com/freedom-of-speech-and-expression/protection-of-core-political-speech/

[266] John R. Vile, "Speech and Debate Clause," Free Speech Center, July 30 2023, https://firstamendment.mtsu.edu/article/speech-and-debate-clause/

[267] "Protection of Core Political Speech," US Legal.com, https://civilrights.uslegal.com/freedom-of-speech-and-expression/protection-of-core-political-speech/

[268] "List of rallies for the 2024 Donald Trump presidential campaign," Wikipedia, https://en.wikipedia.org/wiki/List_of_rallies_for_the_2024_Donald_Trump_presidential_campaign

[269] Alex Swoyer, "Missouri takes Trump's New York gag order, sentencing to Supreme Court," *The Washington Times*, July 25, 2024, https://www.washingtontimes.com/news/2024/jul/25/missouri-takes-donald-trumps-new-york-gag-order-se/

the Supreme Court, but the justices, with the exception of Justice Clarence Thomas and Justice Samuel A. Alito Jr., rejected Missouri's move.[270]

Separately, the justices declined to take up a request from a New York podcaster challenging the gag order as infringing the First Amendment and the freedom of the press.[271]

It is unfortunate that only a podcaster—and no legacy media outlet—attempted to challenge the Trump gag orders in court. It suggests the mainstream media was not interested in hearing fully the defenses from the former president and top presidential candidate against the criminal charges he faced in multiple venues. I suppose the lack of First Amendment defense from the press when it came to Trump should not be all that surprising, given their mostly hostile treatment of him during his first administration.

Lara Trump, the president's daughter-in-law, who led the Republican National Committee during the 2024 election, said the gag orders were horrible for him during the campaign.

"It was very challenging. How it is you are able to go out and actually talk to the public and defend your reputation in the midst of what is a character assassination—and that is what that whole thing was about," she told me.

---

[270] Alex Swoyer, "Supreme Court rejects Missouri's move to sue New York over Trump's hush money conviction," *The Washington Times*, August 7, 2024, https://www.washingtontimes.com/news/2024/aug/7/supreme-court-rejects-missouris-move-to-sue-new-yo/

[271] Alex Swoyer, "Supreme Court rejects podcaster's request to lift Trump's hush money case gag order," *The Washington Times*, October 8, 2024, https://www.washingtontimes.com/news/2024/oct/8/supreme-court-rejects-joseph-niermans-request-to-l/

BUSINESS RECORD$

Manhattan District Attorney Alvin Bragg's criminal prosecution of President Trump was cast by the media as having "perceived weakness" and "flimsiness" when the indictment was first launched. Many Democrats thought other criminal investigations against the former president at the time—like those being handled by the feds—had more legs.[272]

But to be fair to Bragg, his April 4, 2023 criminal indictment of Trump was the first formal document charging the president with criminal wrongdoing, and it is the only one out of four criminal indictments during a four-month period that resulted in a conviction. Albeit, a conviction that would likely never have happened if the case had been brought in a more neutral and fairer forum.

The rest of the Democrats' lawfare episodes so far have been dropped—or at the very least, paused.

---

[272] Niall Stanage, "The Memo: Will Flimsiness of Bragg case taint other Trump legal probes?," *The Hill*, April 7, 2023, https://thehill.com/homenews/campaign/3938498-the-memo-critics-worry-braggs-case-against-trump-is-too-flimsy/

The Manhattan madness, though, first began for Trump when Bragg issued an indictment that charged him with thirty-four felony counts of falsifying business records with the intent to cover up another crime between 2015 to 2017. The indictment never mentions what the underlying crime was, but it did charge him for violating New York's Penal Law §175.10, a misdemeanor with a two-year statute of limitations—or window—for prosecutors to bring the charge.[273] Bragg's way around that time limit was to bump the misdemeanor charge up to a felony, by claiming that the false business entry was done with the intent to conceal another illegal activity.[274] In his press release, Bragg suggested that activity could have been violation of campaign finance laws, or for tax-evasion purposes.[275] The formal charging document, though, is mum on that point—a fact that spells a lack of Sixth Amendment fairness, specifically, the right of a defendant to know the charges he or she faces.

By elevating the misdemeanor to a felony, the statute of limitations increased to a three-to-five-year window, and prosecutors could make the argument that for some crimes in New York, the statute of limitations began to toll when the allegedly false entries were discovered, rather than when they actually took place.

---

[273] Gregory Germain, "Law Professor: The Manhattan District Attorney's Convoluted Legal Case Against Donald Trump Gets More Convoluted," *Syracuse University News*, May 7, 2024, https://news.syr.edu/blog/2024/05/07/law-professor-the-manhattan-district-attorneys-convoluted-legal-case-against-donald-trump-gets-more-convoluted/

[274] Ibid.

[275] Press release, "District Attorney Bragg Announces 34-Count Felony Indictment of Former President Donald J. Trump," Manhattan District Attorney, April 4, 2023, https://manhattanda.org/district-attorney-bragg-announces-34-count-felony-indictment-of-former-president-donald-j-trump/

Bragg's justification for bringing the unprecedented criminal case against Trump was that he allegedly hid crimes from the voting public.[276]

"Manhattan is home to the country's most significant business market. We cannot allow New York businesses to manipulate their records to cover up criminal conduct," Bragg said in a press release.[277] "As this office has done time and time again, we today uphold our solemn responsibility to ensure that everyone stands equal before the law."

The problem, though, is that Trump was not treated equally before the law.

I argue that his underlying crime was running for reelection, putting him in the crosshairs of Democratic district attorneys and prosecutors.

Bragg's team alleged Trump illegally paid Michael Cohen, his former personal lawyer (who went by the nickname "the fixer"), over $130,000 in hush money that Cohen had given to porn actress Stormy Daniels to keep her quiet during Trump's 2016 campaign.[278] She claims that she had sexual relations with him in 2006 and stayed in touch with Trump years earlier, while Melania Trump was pregnant with their son Barron.

Trump paid Cohen back for the $130,000, and fraudulently labeled the payments as "legal fees." Bragg's team also said Trump had American Media Inc., which owned the National Enquirer, pay others with salacious allegations to stay mum.[279]

---

276 Ibid.
277 Ibid.
278 Ibid.
279 Ibid.

Trump denies having the affair or committing any criminal wrongdoing.

Aside from the manipulation of a misdemeanor into a felony, the nature of how the jury was handled is suspect.

Dozens of prospective jurors admitted that they could not be impartial during the selection process, and that is no surprise at all since the New York City jury pool was more than 80 percent anti-Trump.[280] (Roughly 80 percent of New York City residents voted against Trump for president in both 2016 and 2020.) On top of those unattractive odds for the Manhattan venue, Trump's lawyers also ran out of strikes to remove some jurors who had expressed negative opinions of Trump, but suggested they could still be fair.[281] The defense attorneys only had ten peremptory strikes under state law.[282] Peremptory strikes allow lawyers to remove a juror without giving a reason.[283] The only bar on the strike is that it cannot be for discriminatory reasons, such as striking a juror based on his or her race or sex.[284]

Mike Davis, president of the Article III Project and a former clerk to Supreme Court Justice Neil M. Gorsuch, posted on his

---

280 Fox News, "Mike Davis: Trump is not going to get a fair trial in the New York hush money case," YouTube, April 17, 2024, https://www.youtube.com/watch?v=FrOdH1BgaFo

281 Jeremy Herb, et al., "Here's how the Trump hush money trial unfolded, from jury selection to conviction," CNN, May 31, 2024, https://www.cnn.com/politics/donald-trump-hush-money-trial-dg/index.html

282 Kevin Breuninger, "Trump gripes he can't reject 'unlimited' jurors in New York hush money trial," CNBC, April 17, 2024, https://www.nbcnewyork.com/news/business/money-report/trump-gripes-he-cant-reject-unlimited-jurors-in-new-york-hush-money-trial/5329544

283 "Peremptory challenge," Legal Information Institute, Cornell Law School, https://www.law.cornell.edu/wex/peremptory_challenge

284 Ibid.

social media that the juror questionnaire posed a question about their support of Trump, but did not ask prospective jurors about whether or not they support Joe Biden.[285]

"Judge Merchan rigged the jury questionnaire so people who support Trump have to state that, so they can get struck through the process, so the people who support Biden don't," Davis said.[286]

The selection process took just four days to pick a jury. Jury selection can range from one day to a few days to even weeks in complex cases. It is fair to argue the criminal case of a former president—the first of its kind—made Trump's hush money trial a complex dispute. It also involved potential campaign finance issues or tax issues in a felony trial, which added to the complexity.

It was justified for Trump to question the quick speed at which his jury was selected, given the historic nature of the legal battle. He had accused the judge of "rushing" the trial.[287]

The judge also failed to sequester the jury. Sequestration happens when a court finds it necessary to isolate members of a jury to keep them free from outside influences that could damage their thoughts and sway their decision during the proceedings. With the press covering the trial 24/7, it could have benefited the defendant if the jury had been sequestered.

The trial even took a break for Memorial Day weekend, where the judge did not keep the jury separate from family, friends, and the news. The lack of sequestration was a matter that Alina

---

[285] Mike Davis @Mrddmia, Instagram, April 18, 2024, https://www.instagram.com/reel/C56IL4uvOn6/

[286] Ibid.

[287] Michael Sisak, et al., "First 7 jurors are chosen for Trump's hush money criminal trial, with 11 more still needed," Associated Press, April 17, 2024, https://apnews.com/article/trump-hush-money-criminal-trial-new-york-dd1a8dcc063b7ad0fbe14af6e8724c2f

Habba, Trump's legal spokesperson at the time, took issue with during the trial.

"They should have been sequestered, because, in my opinion, these jurors are handling something that is completely unprecedented and unwarranted in America," Habba said during an appearance on Fox News.[288] "And for them to be able to be out and about on a holiday weekend with friends and families who have opinions, who are watching the news, TVs in the background at the pool party, I have serious concerns. If they're left-wing and they're watching MSDNC, as my client calls it, [MSNBC] or CNN, they're not going to get fair news."[289]

Trump's lawyers brought forth claims that there was juror misconduct that called into question the fairness of the result, in filings that were unsealed in December of 2024, more than six months after the guilty verdict—but the specific details were redacted.[290]

It is no surprise there would be questions of juror misconduct, given the highly biased venue and lack of jury sequestration. And a change of venue is warranted when a defendant cannot receive a fair and impartial trial in a jurisdiction, given the

---

[288] Miranda Nazzaro, "Alina Habba says Trump's hush-money jury should have been sequestered over holiday weekend," *The Hill*, May 26, 2024, https://thehill.com/regulation/court-battles/4687092-alina-habba-says-trumps-hush-money-jury-should-have-been-sequestered-over-holiday-weekend/

[289] Ibid.

[290] Katherine Faulders, et al., "Trump claims jury misconduct in latest attempt to discredit hush money conviction," ABC News, December 17, 2024, https://abcnews.go.com/US/trump-claims-jury-misconduct-latest-attempt-discredit-hush/story?id=116866642

notoriety of the defendant and the media coverage he received related to the charges.[291]

In Manhattan specifically, Bragg had campaigned on getting elected to hold Trump accountable. It is justified to argue that Bragg's constituents—Trump's jury pool—voted to give Bragg the opportunity to charge the president, and thus had bias against Trump from the outset of the criminal proceeding.

"I have investigated Trump and his children and held them accountable for their misconduct with the Trump Foundation," Mr. Bragg said during one debate in his crusade to get elected Manhattan District Attorney.[292] "I know how to follow the facts and hold people in power accountable."

The judge could have considered moving the trial to nearby Nassau or Suffolk Counties, where the voting pool was fairer to Trump. Nassau saw Biden win 54 percent of the vote in 2020 to Trump's near 45 percent, while Suffolk saw the two candidates in a dead tie at 49 percent—making it the most purple venue in the area, where Trump may have been given a fairer trial.[293]

John Edwards, a former senator who ran a failed 2008 presidential bid, faced his jury in the purple state of North Carolina, which delivered an acquittal and mistrial on charges that were far more spelled out than what Bragg brought forward against Trump. Edwards was indicted by the federal government for

---

291 "What Are the 5 Factors the Judge Considers to Change Venue?," Greg Hill & Associates, https://www.greghillassociates.com/what-are-the-5-factors-the-judge-considers-to-change-venue.html

292 Byron York, "Bragg's Trump indictment is a campaign promise kept," *Orlean Times Herald*, April 5, 2023, https://www.oleantimesherald.com/opinion/braggs-trump-indictment-is-a-campaign-promise-kept/article_e7f11833-3c5b-52b7-9c5b-a1018943c3cf.html

293 Election results; "President: New York," CNN Politics, https://www.cnn.com/election/2020/results/state/new-york

allegedly giving $1 million in campaign money to his mistress and their child. It was a similar hush-money allegation wrapped into a federal campaign finance issue. But Edwards case had a different result than Trump's. The difference in venues—Trump's being deep blue and Edwards's being purple—likely attributed to the conflicting verdicts.

Media Research Center's *NewsBusters* uncovered in April of 2024—at the start of the Manhattan hush-money trial—that the mainstream media's major evening newscasts failed to mention Bragg's Democrat affiliation.[294]

According to the press watchdog's research, ABC's World News Tonight only once mentioned Bragg being a Democrat out of fifty-six stories it had aired on the upcoming trial.[295] CBS Evening News did even worse, covering the proceedings in forty-eight stories, but with none identifying Bragg as a Democrat.[296] NBC News mentioned that Bragg was a Democrat in 27 percent of its coverage, roughly one-fourth of the time.[297]

What's more, MRC's May 2024 analysis also showed that the major media outlets' hundreds of hours of coverage of Trump's Manhattan proceedings, up to jury deliberations, used the word "criminal" 111 times, which came out to more than once per

---

[294] Rich Noyes, "Study: At Least 90% of TV News Fails to Call Trump Prosecutors 'Democrats,'" MRC *NewsBusters*, April 15, 2024, https://www.newsbusters.org/blogs/nb/rich-noyes/2024/04/15/study-least-90-tv-news-fails-call-trump-prosecutors-democrats

[295] Ibid.

[296] Ibid.

[297] Ibid.

story.[298] And while the government's key witness was Michael Cohen, who had pled guilty to a number of crimes, including perjury, the mainstream outlets failed to note the perjury charge 96 percent of the time over the six-week trial.[299] MRC also found that the press largely failed to tell viewers of Judge Merchan's political conflicts of interest, in particular a donation he made to Joe Biden and to a group named "Stop Republicans."[300]

Trump did not testify at the trial. Don Jr. said his father's testimony would be in a kangaroo court, which was his take on the proceedings.[301] Others, too, have suggested Judge Merchan ran an unfair, one-sided trial.

The judge limited Trump's witness list, barring his lawyers' ability to bring in an expert on campaign finance, former Federal Election Commission Chairman Bradley Smith, to rebut suggestions from the prosecutors that the hush-money payment was illegal and was done to cover up any underlying crime.[302] In the end, the judge said the testimony could confuse jurors.[303] But his

---

298 Rich Noyes and Curtis Houck, "Wrap-Up: TV's Negative, Nasty, Lurid & Obsessive Coverage of Trump's Trial," MRC *NewsBusters*, May 30, 2024, https://www.newsbusters.org/blogs/nb/rich-noyes/curtis-houck/2024/05/30/wrap-tvs-negative-nasty-lurid-obsessive-coverage-trumps-trial

299 Ibid.

300 Ibid.

301 Victoria Bekiempis, "'Mr Trump, why won't you testify?': hush-money trial nears end with a fizzle, not a bang," *The Guardian*, May 21, 2024, https://www.theguardian.com/us-news/article/2024/may/21/trump-hush-money-trial-defense-final-stretch

302 Josh Gerstein, "Judge limits scope of testimony from Trump's planned expert witness," *Politico*, May 20, 2024, https://www.politico.com/live-updates/2024/05/20/trump-hush-money-criminal-trial/judge-limits-trumps-expert-00158857

303 Ibid.

decision limited Trump in being able to fully defend himself from the alleged crime(s).

Like the questionable nature in Trump's Fulton County, Georgia, prosecution (which I will detail later, where the local special prosecutor traveled to Washington, DC, and met with Biden's White House counsel), the Bragg case similarly had assistance from a top Washington, DC, lawyer inside the Biden administration.

Matthew Colangelo, who worked in the Biden Justice Department and probed the Trump Organization, joined Bragg's team to help prosecute the case. The move caught the attention of GOP lawmakers on Capitol Hill, who have sought communications concerning Colangelo between Bragg and New York Attorney General Leticia James, who prosecuted Trump on civil fraud charges related to his family business organization.[304]

Bragg's victory marked the first time a former president was ever prosecuted and found guilty of committing a crime. The jury found Trump guilty on all thirty-four felony counts related to falsifying business records in connection with his 2016 campaign—seven years later, and during his 2024 campaign. The jury deliberated for less than ten hours when the verdict was read, sparking cheers from outside the courtroom, making the scene all the more political.[305]

---

[304] Press release, "Chairman Jordan Demands Documents about Bragg Prosecutor Matthew Colangelo from Letitia James," US House Committee on the Judiciary, May 15, 2024, https://judiciary.house.gov/media/press-releases/chairman-jordan-demands-documents-about-bragg-prosecutor-matthew-colangelo

[305] Michael Sisak, et al., "Guilty: Trump becomes first former U.S. president convicted of felony crimes," Associated Press, May 30, 2024, https://whyy.org/articles/trump-hush-money-trial-jury-deliberations-testimony-verdict/

Even before the verdict was returned, a contact I have within the press, who had spent much of the trial covering it from inside the courthouse, had accurately predicted the jury would return a finding of guilt. My contact said that the prosecution appeared more organized, which in the eyes of the jury carries a lot of weight. When the prosecution has a more organized presentation of the facts and receives more favorable rulings from the judge—who jurors look to as a referee between the two sides—that leaves an impression in the jurors' minds. They may not understand the complexities of the law, but they observe how the case is put on by the two sides and how the judge treats the various parties.

It's unlikely, though, that the conviction against Trump will stand on appeal for several reasons, ranging from constitutional errors to procedural challenges.

As I reported in *The Washington Times* following the guilty verdict, legal experts spotted three flaws in how the judge ran the hush-money trial against the former president. The issues spark concerns over Due Process and the right to a fair trial protected by the Sixth Amendment of the US Constitution.[306] The legal scholars say the pitfalls created by the judge's treatment of Trump and his legal team likely equate to the conviction being overturned as the appeal works its way up the chain. But a victory at the appeals court did not occur before the 2024 election, which may have been the whole point of this lawfare exercise.

Bragg alleged Trump committed thirty-four false entries on business records by classifying hush-money payments as legal

---

[306] Alex Swoyer, "Here are Trump's top three arguments for appeal after guilty verdict in hush money trial," *The Washington Times*, May 30, 2024, https://www.washingtontimes.com/news/2024/may/30/here-are-donald-trumps-top-three-arguments-for-app/

fees to his personal lawyer. In reality, he was paying his lawyer back for paying the hush money. The business records charge was a misdemeanor, but because the statute of limitations of two years had passed, Bragg was able to resurrect the charge as a felony only by claiming the false entries were done with the intent of covering up another crime.[307]

The constitutional problem with that allegation and strategy is that the second crime was never clearly identified, but it trumped up the charges to felonies—pun intended. Onlookers were led to believe that it could have been a campaign finance violation, which is a federal offense and not within Bragg's state court jurisdiction to prosecute. The other theory was it may have been a tax issue. The judge instructed jurors that they would have to find only that Trump committed bookkeeping infractions to conceal a campaign finance violation, tax law infraction, *or* falsification of business records. They did not even have to *agree* on the underlying crime to find the former president guilty. Legal experts say the fact that Bragg never identified the crime that transformed a lapsed misdemeanor into a felony will create a problem for the prosecution on appeal, as it runs afoul of the Sixth Amendment guarantee for a defendant to know the charges for which he or she is accused.[308] Understanding the specific charges allows a defendant to properly mount a defense. That opportunity was denied to Trump.

---

[307] Gregory L. Germain, "Law Professor: The Manhattan District Attorney's Convoluted Legal Case Against Donald Trump Gets More Convoluted," *Syracuse University News*, May 7, 2024, https://news.syr.edu/blog/2024/05/07/law-professor-the-manhattan-district-attorneys-convoluted-legal-case-against-donald-trump-gets-more-convoluted/

[308] Swoyer, "Here are Trump's top three arguments for appeal…," https://www.washingtontimes.com/news/ 2024/may/30/here-are-donald-trumps-top-three-arguments-for-app/

It is possible an appeals court also casts a skeptical eye on Trump's conviction due to prejudicial testimony that was allowed to be entered by Judge Merchan, such as details of his alleged sexual encounter with porn actress Stormy Daniels, and whether he wore a condom, what physical position he was in, and so on.[309] None of that testimony had anything to do with classifying hush-money payments as legal fees—or whether a campaign finance violation occurred—which was what the prosecution had suggested in its opening statement and filings. Daniels' detailed testimony about sexual intercourse was unrelated to the actual crime charged: falsifying business records.[310] The inflammatory nature of her testimony that the judge green-lighted could be seen on appeal as too prejudicial against the defendant.

Other problematic testimony that was used against Trump included allegations of another alleged affair with former *Playboy* model Karen McDougal, who was paid by one of Trump's allies to not publish her story about their relationship.[311] Prosecutors also used testimony about the infamous *Access Hollywood* tape against Trump, where the former president is heard discussing grabbing women's private parts.[312] That inflammatory tape, which made headlines during Trump's 2016 campaign, is also unrelated to the hush-money allegations, so it could also be viewed on appeal as too prejudicial to the defense.[313]

Trump, meanwhile, has continued to deny any affairs and illegal activity.

---

[309] Ibid.
[310] Ibid.
[311] Ibid.
[312] Ibid.
[313] Ibid.

Another issue that might cause an appeals court to cast a skeptical eye on this conviction is the handling of the legal battle by Judge Merchan.

He gagged Trump—the defendant in the case—in a way that was over broad, jeopardizing Trump's First and Sixth Amendment rights.

There should not have been a gag order imposed—and if there was, it should not have been one-sided. And when Trump did try to defend himself by posting comments on social media, Judge Merchan imposed a $9,000 penalty against him for violating the gag order and threatened to jail him if it happened again.[314]

Davis—the pro-Trump attorney I referenced earlier, who leads the Article III Project—said the censorship was "an illegal, unconstitutional gag order."[315] "We have gag orders to protect criminal defendants who are going through the process," he told Fox News.[316] "If there is anyone on the planet who must have the constitutional right to speak out about the judge, the prosecutor, the staff, the witnesses, the bias, it has to be a criminal defendant going through a criminal process."

On top of unfairly gagging the former president during his criminal trial, the judge refused to recuse himself despite questionable conflicts of interest.

Under New York's Judiciary Law, Judge Merchan had a financial interest in the legal battle through a relative. Under

---

[314] Michael Sisak, et al., "Hush money trial judge raises threat of jail as he finds Trump violated gag order, fines him $9K," Associated Press, April 30, 2024, https://apnews.com/article/trump-stormy-daniels-hush-money-election-2024-d2f9badee0b28a60d32bc98c0d4e783f

[315] Fox News, "Mike Davis: Trump is not going to get a fair trial in the New York hush money case," YouTube, April 17, 2024, https://www.youtube.com/watch?v=FrOdH1BgaFo

[316] Ibid.

one of the state's laws, a judge must recuse if he has a relative connected to a case within the sixth degree.[317] Judge Merchan's daughter worked for a Democratic-aligned marketing firm that was taking in millions for Democratic candidates and fundraising on Trump's prosecution to help her clients.

On top of that, it was also reported that Judge Merchan had donated money to Democrats—including Trump's political rival at the time, President Joe Biden, in 2020. He donated $35 to Democrats and $15 to Biden, and although those are small dollar amounts, it still presents a perception of bias that suggests Biden's political opponent as a defendant would not get a fair trial in Judge Merchan's courtroom.[318]

In September of 2024, former Congresswoman Elise Stefanik, a Trump defender, told the New York State Commission on Judicial Conduct that even more information had come forward about Judge Merchan's daughter's financial dealings. When Vice President Kamala Harris took over the Democratic presidential campaign from Biden in August of 2024, she hired Loren Merchan's marketing firm, Authentic.[319] This move presented more evidence of an illegal financial connection to Judge Merchan and his family, at the time when Judge Merchan was still handling Trump's sentencing.

---

317 Harmeet Dhillon, X.com, April 15, 2024, https://x.com/pnjaban/status/1779890598251520329

318 Jeremy Herb, et al., "$35 political contribution to Democrats raises fresh scrutiny of Judge Merchan," CNN, April 6, 2023, https://www.cnn.com/2023/04/06/politics/judge-merchan-trump-biden-contribution/index.html

319 Elise Stefanik, Letter to New York State Commission on Judicial Conduct, September 6, 2024, https://eliseforcongress.com/wp-content/uploads/2024/09/NYSCOJC-complaint-Merchan-New-Evidence.pdf

"The Code of Conduct, specifically § 100.3(E)(1)(d)(iii), dictates that a judge must recuse from a case where a relative up to and including the sixth degree has a financial interest in the outcome of the case. Ms. Merchan is related to Justice Merchan in the first degree," Stefanik said in the complaint.[320]

David Schoen, who served as Trump's impeachment lawyer, suggested to me that Judge Merchan was "hand-picked" for the case instead of being randomly selected for it.

"It certainly was not because he was particularly qualified," Schoen said. "His conflicts of interests were, in my view, overwhelming and absolutely disqualifying and, again, the integrity of the system and the public's confidence that justice will be done through its system suffers terribly from this kind of brazen ignoring of real conflicts.

"If you're going after the president of the United States or a former president in a criminal case, or even a major civil case, you need to be aboveboard and holier than the pope in the way you proceed, if you want the American public to believe in it," he added.

Judge Merchan may have seen the writing on the wall with Trump's massive election landslide. He had delayed Trump's sentencing repeatedly as he mulled how to handle the situation he had allowed to snowball out of hand. Ultimately, Judge Merchan sentenced Trump to no jail time or penalty, just days before he entered the White House in January of 2025.

Bragg, meanwhile, made dubious arguments to try to make the conviction stick, as Trump fought for months to toss the verdict.

In an eighty-two-page filing just weeks before Trump was to be sworn in as the forty-seventh president of the United States,

---

[320] Ibid.

Bragg urged the judge to postpone the criminal proceedings until the president exits the White House in January of 2029.[321] At the time, Judge Merchan had still not made public his sentencing decision. Bragg suggested it would be too extreme to discard his jury's unanimous guilty verdict.[322]

"At most, defendant should receive temporary accommodations during his presidency to prevent this criminal case from meaningfully interfering with his official decision-making," Bragg wrote.[323] "Courts routinely approve of yearslong delays in sentencings when the delay is attributable to the defendant's own conduct, or when it is attributable to factors outside of the People or the Court's control."

Of course, it does not take a learned legal scholar to understand that having a president serve the nation for four years and make negotiations with our country's adversaries, all while awaiting a criminal sentence that is hanging over his head, would be less than ideal. A president is supposed to—and is expected to—fully focus on serving the country's best interests. That requires his undivided attention.

In fact, Bragg recognized that New York's criminal procedure law, specifically CPL § 210.40, provides guidance when an indictment should be dismissed "in the interest of justice."[324] The law requires the court to consider dismissal when there's a

---

[321] Alvin Bragg, "People's Memorandum of Law in Opposition to Defendant's Motion to Dismiss," *The People of the State of New York v. Donald J. Trump*, December 9, 2024, https://www.documentcloud.org/documents/25451173-2024-12-09-peoples-mem-opp-mot-to-dismiss-filed/

[322] Ibid., p. 4.

[323] Ibid.

[324] Ibid., p. 8.

"compelling factor."[325] I would argue the presidency is a pretty compelling reason. Bragg, though, does not believe the defendant becoming president of the United States would count towards "the interest of justice."[326]

Bragg also rejected the Justice Department's Office of Legal Counsel's guidance that a sitting president cannot be prosecuted. Ultimately, that guidance eventually prompted Special Counsel Jack Smith—who we will get more into in the next two chapters—to suspend his two criminal prosecutions against Trump—even though the indictments were issued when he was a former president and not currently in office.

Bragg said the "limited remaining steps" in sentencing Trump would not "obstruct the federal government in any event."[327]

"Trial ended more than six months ago with the jury's guilty verdict on May 30, 2024, so there is no risk that a time-consuming trial would require defendant's full-time presence in court and unduly burden the presidential transition process," he wrote.[328] "Those interests do not require the extraordinary step of abating post-trial motion practice in a pre-existing criminal case."

What's even more ridiculous to any lawyer—or a first-year law student, for that matter—was Bragg's next option for the judge, should he decide not to stay Trump's sentencing until Trump left the White House in 2029. Bragg said Judge Merchan

---

325 *FindLaw* Staff, "New York Consolidated Laws, Criminal Procedure Law - CPL § 210.40 Motion to dismiss indictment; in furtherance of justice," *FindLaw*, January 1, 2024, https://codes.findlaw.com/ny/criminal-procedure-law/cpl-sect-210-40/

326 Bragg, "People's Memorandum...," https://www.documentcloud.org/documents/25451173-2024-12-09-peoples-mem-opp-mot-to-dismiss-filed/

327 Ibid., p. 13.

328 Ibid.

could use the process of abatement to make sure the jury's hush-money conviction sticks to Trump.[329] That process would mean treating Trump as though he had died.[330]

Trump, of course, did not die. He was very much alive and very much winning.

The "abatement-by-death" theory would be an end to the proceedings, not allowing for any sentencing or appeal to take place.[331]

"Under the abatement doctrine, courts have considered an analogous question of what to do with a jury verdict and indictment when further criminal proceedings are no longer possible because of the defendant's death," the prosecutor wrote.[332]

Other than Trump being alive and not dead, there was yet another problem with this suggestion from Bragg: New York's abatement-by-death standard would vacate the conviction and have dismissed the indictment, something Bragg adamantly did not want to have happen.[333]

Instead, Bragg suggested the judge should not follow New York's rule—which is the very jurisdiction for which he and the judge have authority—but instead, adopt Alabama's rule that allows the conviction to be noted after a defendant dies.[334]

Most attorneys would be laughed out of the courthouse and legal field altogether if they entered a courtroom and told a judge

---

[329] Alex Swoyer, "D.A. Alvin Bragg urges N.Y. judge to treat Trump as if he died, not dismiss hush-money conviction," *The Washington Times*, December 15, 2024, https://www.washingtontimes.com/news/2024/dec/15/alvin-bragg-manhattan-district-attorney-suggests-n/

[330] Ibid.

[331] Ibid.

[332] Ibid.

[333] Ibid.

[334] Ibid.

to follow another state's law. Courts are bound by their own jurisdiction's precedent.

The whole suggestion of an abatement by death was not only legally unsound, it was absent any common sense. Trump's attorneys said it was "absurd" and that Bragg was trying to "pretend as if one of the assassination attempts against President Trump had been successful."[335]

But Democrats got what they wanted with this use of lawfare. They're able to label Trump a convicted felon, which we heard President Joe Biden do during his July debate with his political opponent. And since that time, we saw Vice President Kamala Harris—after she became the Democratic nominee for president—as well as her running mate, Minnesota Governor Tim Walz, echo that "convicted felon" label.

Despite Democrats getting what they ultimately wanted in their lawfare efforts—to mark Trump a convict or felon during the 2024 campaign—Robert C. Cahaly, chief pollster and strategist at The Trafalgar Group, said the conviction did not really sway public opinion away from Trump.

"Our polling found that the majority of people thought Trump was guilty of simply paying hush money, but it did not change the fact they would vote for him," Cahaly told me. "To them, it was a trial about hush money. It was like—yeah, but celebrities and big powerful people do it all the time, so fine, whatever."

---

[335] Rachel Dobkin, "Trump's Lawyers Slam Alvin Bragg's Recent Hush Money Case Idea: 'Absurd,'" *Newsweek*, December 13, 2024, https://www.newsweek.com/donald-trump-hush-money-alvin-bragg-dismissal-2000728

DOCUMENT DOUBLE STANDARDS

Was former President Joe Biden criminally charged with keeping classified documents in his Delaware garage? No.

Was former Vice President Mike Pence criminally charged with keeping classified documents from his time in the administration at his home in Indiana? No.

Was former Secretary of State Hillary Clinton criminally charged with using a personal email server, kept at her New York home, for classified electronic communications? No.

Notice a pattern?

Political leaders, through the course of recent history, were not nabbed by the feds for their improper retention of classified documents detailing the nation's military, foreign, and national-security interests. That is, until President Donald Trump.

Mark Bradley, the director of the National Archive's Information Security Oversight Office, told House lawmakers that his office "has found boxes of classified information in unclassified containers from every administration since the

Reagan Administration."[336] His remarks came in 2023, while both former President Biden and President Trump were under scrutiny for their handling of classified documents.

But it was only President Trump whom the feds charged criminally for retaining classified material at his home at Mar-a-Lago after he left the White House.

Trump, according to court documents, left the White House with dozens of cardboard boxes. During his time there, he had filled those boxes with newspapers, photographs, letters, notes, documents, and other materials.[337] The boxes were transported to Mar-a-Lago, Trump's personal residence, and placed in a ballroom and in a bathroom.[338] In total, they contained about three hundred classified documents.[339] Trump uncovered 197 of them about a year after leaving office, upon demands from the National Archives and Records Administration.[340]

In Democrats' lawfare against Trump, even the National Archives got involved. The department, known most famously for displaying the Declaration of Independence and housing the nation's historic records, got aggressive.

---

[336] Brian Bushard, "Not Just Trump and Biden: Every Administration Since Reagan Mishandled Classified Records, National Archives Finds," *Forbes*, May 17, 2023, https://www.forbes.com/sites/brianbushard/2023/05/17/not-just-trump-and-biden-every-administration-since-reagan-mishandled-classified-records-national-archives-finds/

[337] *United States of America v. Donald J. Trump and Waltine Nauta*, Indictment, June, 8, 2023, https://d3i6fh83elv35t.cloudfront.net/static/2023/06/trump-indictment.pdf

[338] Ibid.

[339] Ibid.

[340] Ibid.

Trump claimed the staff at the National Archives did not help him pack in his final days before leaving office in January of 2021.[341] Because they were not present, he unknowingly took classified documents to Florida.[342] Trump's attorneys told Congress that the National Archives "unfortunately has become overtly political and declined to provide archival assistance to President Trump's transition team."[343]

Trump's lawyer later turned over another thirty-eight documents.[344]

In a historic move, the Federal Bureau of Investigation raided Mar-a-Lago in August of 2022 and obtained 103 other classified documents still in the president's possession.[345] With Trump's team cooperating, it is fair to question why the raid was needed if the feds were able to retain classified documents upon each request and further review. Nonetheless, on August 8, 2022, the FBI raided Trump's home—the first time in our nation's history that a former president has had law enforcement execute a search warrant on his home as part of a criminal investigation.[346]

---

[341] Susan Ferrechio, "Trump accuses 'overly political' National Archives of letting him leave W.H. with classified docs," *The Washington Times*, April 29, 2023, https://www.washingtontimes.com/news/2023/apr/29/trump-accuses-national-archives-allowing-him-leave/

[342] Ibid.

[343] Ibid.

[344] *United States of America v. Donald J. Trump and Waltine Nauta*, Indictment, https://d3i6fh83elv35t.cloudfront.net/static/2023/06/trump-indictment.pdf

[345] Ibid.

[346] Lisa Rosborough, "FBI raid on Donald Trump's Mar-a-Lago residence is the first in presidential history," Houston Public Media, August 9, 2022, https://www.houstonpublicmedia.org/articles/shows/town-square/2022/08/09/430394/fbi-raid-on-donald-trumps-mar-a-lago-residence-is-the-first-in-presidential-history/

First Lady Melania Trump has been vocal in her opposition to the raid, posting on social media two years later about the "invasion of privacy."[347] In a roughly one-minute clip highlighting the Fourth Amendment's protection "against unreasonable searches and seizures," the First Lady spoke out, saying she never thought something like this would happen to her.[348]

"I never imagined my privacy would be invaded by the government here in America. The FBI raided my home in Florida and searched through my personal belongings. This is not just my story, it serves as a warning to all Americans—a reminder that our freedom and rights must be respected," she said in the clip, posted days before the release of her memoir, *Melania*.[349]

Special Counsel Jack Smith indicted Trump over the classified documents issue in June of 2023, roughly two months before he would also issue a separate indictment against him in Washington, DC, over his contesting of the 2020 election results.

In the forty-nine-page indictment, Smith said Trump had secret information that came from the Central Intelligence Agency, Department of Defense, National Security Agency, Department of Energy, and Department of State, among other departments.[350] He claimed Trump shared some of that intel with a writer and a representative from a political action committee.[351]

---

[347] Melania Trump, Facebook, September 14, 2024, https://www.facebook.com/watch/?v=551457454240828video

[348] Ibid.

[349] Ibid.

[350] *United States of America v. Donald J. Trump and Waltine Nauta*, Indictment, https://d3i6fh83elv35t.cloudfront.net/static/2023/06/trump-indictment.pdf

[351] Ibid.

It was the first time the president faced a thirty-eight-count federal indictment, with allegations ranging from an alleged scheme to conceal, making false statements, withholding and concealing documents, and obstruction of justice.[352] Remember, his previous New York indictment was on state charges, not federal. Of course, Smith later lobbed four federal counts against Trump over his challenge to the 2020 election results, claiming he committed election fraud.

Between the federal indictments and state indictments out of both New York and Georgia, Trump faced roughly 121 criminal counts against him. They were all announced between April and August of 2023 and continued to plague him as he campaigned throughout 2024.

But the treatment of Trump in the documents case appeared one-sided to the public, because classified documents kept by Biden in his unsecured Delaware garage, office, and basement were not the subject of a criminal prosecution and amounted to zero charges against him. That's even despite Special Counsel Robert Hur, tasked with reviewing Biden's document handling, having found that Biden "willfully retained and disclosed classified materials after his vice presidency when he was a private citizen."[353]

The material included national security, foreign policy, and military information, including intel on Afghanistan.[354] The doc-

[352] Ibid.

[353] Robert K. Hur, *Report on the Investigation Into Unauthorized Removal, Retention, and Disclosure of Classified Documents Discovered at Locations Including the Penn Biden Center and the Delaware Private Residence of President Joseph R. Biden Jr.*, February 5, 2024, p. 1, https://www.justice.gov/storage/report-from-special-counsel-robert-k-hur-february-2024.pdf

[354] Ibid.

uments spanned the course of Biden's political life—not just from his time as president, and also included secret information from his time as a senator.[355]

Trump's Mar-a-Lago, by contrast, was secured by both Secret Service and outside security. Americans are left wondering why a former president cannot retain classified documents, but a former vice president and senator could do so without facing any repercussions. Trump's team had argued in one of their legal filings that the president had declassified the documents because it is within his authority to do so, and that the Presidential Records Act clashed with the federal criminal charges.

The conflicting treatment between Biden and Trump from two separate special counsel probes reeked of double standards. The answer given for the differential treatment—whether acceptable or not—was in Hur's report, where he said a jury would be too friendly to Biden because they would view him "as a sympathetic, well-meaning, elderly man with a poor memory."[356]

"Based on our direct interactions with and observations of him, he is someone for whom many jurors will want to identify reasonable doubt. It would be difficult to convince a jury that they should convict him—by then a former president well into his eighties—of a serious felony that requires a mental state of willfulness," Hur wrote.[357]

Hur also noted in his report that "many former presidents and vice presidents have knowingly taken home sensitive materials related to national security from their administrations without being charged with crimes.[358]

---

[355] Ibid.
[356] Ibid., p. 6.
[357] Ibid.
[358] Ibid., p. 10.

"This historical record is important context for judging whether and why to charge a former vice president—and former president, as Mr. Biden would be when susceptible to prosecution—for similar actions taken by several of his predecessors. With one exception, there is no record of the Department of Justice prosecuting a former president or vice president for mishandling classified documents," he said, referencing Trump.[359]

Smith came out differently in his calculation to go after Trump, a former president about the same age as Biden.

It took federal District Judge Aileen Cannon, a Trump appointee, to put an end to the double standards, two days after a gunman attempted to assassinate Trump at a campaign rally in Butler, Pennsylvania, on July 13, where one of Trump's supporters was killed. Judge Cannon issued her decision that Smith was illegally appointed special counsel. She said that under the Constitution's Appointments Clause, the attorney general did not have the authority to appoint a special counsel that was not confirmed by the Senate. Smith was a private citizen when he was named special counsel.[360]

"The Appointments Clause is a critical constitutional restriction stemming from the separation of powers, and it gives to Congress a considered role in determining the propriety of vesting appointment power for inferior officers. The Special Counsel's position effectively usurps that important legislative authority, transferring it to a Head of Department, and in the

---

[359] Ibid.

[360] CNN staff, "Read: Judge Aileen Cannon dismisses classified documents case against Trump," CNN, July 15, 2024, https://www.cnn.com/2024/07/15/politics/aileen-cannon-order-classified-documents-case-trump

process threatening the structural liberty inherent in the separation of powers," she wrote.[361]

Judge Cannon was only thirty-nine years old when she was appointed to the Southern District of Florida by Trump during his first administration. She took to the bench in 2020. Then, four years later—in one of the federal criminal prosecutions against the very president who tapped her for her lifetime appointment as a judge—she decided his fate.

The decision was bold. It was the first time her jurisdiction took up the question on whether a special counsel appointment was lawful, and she delivered a victory for the president. She was not bound by any other precedent or interpretations made by other courts—like those in DC.

Josh Blackman, a professor at South Texas College of Law, had argued before Judge Cannon's court that the appointment of Smith ran afoul of the Constitution. In an interview with me, he said the mainstream media was unfairly critical of Judge Cannon's decision against Smith:

> I found her to be one of the most well-prepared district court judges I have ever met. She knew the case inside-out, was familiar with all of the precedents, as well as the complex statutory regime. When I raised some historical points that were not in the briefing, she immediately took interest and started writing down notes. A few of the points I raised made it into her opinion. Judge Cannon was tough on all sides. At one point, I tried to go a bit too far with an argument, and she pushed me back very quickly.

---

[361] Ibid.

> Judge Cannon no doubt has a very conservative approach to the law, but her final decision was well-reasoned, and I think would survive appellate review.

Trump was used to facing backlash from Democrat-appointed judges in New York and the nation's capital. They repeatedly issued head-scratching, one-sided decisions for the government. It was refreshing to see Trump notch a victory in his uphill climb against Democrats' lawfare.

Of course, Smith was not going to give up. He tried to appeal the documents case to the Eleventh US Circuit Court of Appeals, which hears appeals from Florida, Georgia, and Alabama. But after Trump won the election in November, the case was dismissed due to Justice Department policy not to prosecute a sitting president.

Shortly after Trump's election victory, Smith moved on his own to dismiss both his appeal pending in the Eleventh Circuit and his federal case in Washington, DC, over Trump's contesting of the 2020 election results based on that Justice Department policy.[362]

In his dismissal requests, Smith said he consulted with the Office of Legal Counsel and was told that the department's policy not to prosecute a sitting president extends to the situation where

[362] Alex Swoyer, "Federal appeals court dismisses Jack Smith's documents case against Trump," *The Washington Times*, November 26, 2024, https://www.washingtontimes.com/news/2024/nov/26/11th-circuit-dismisses-jack-smiths-classified-docu/

the president-elect had been a private citizen at the time of indictment and is now readying to enter the White House.[363]

The prosecution over the handling of classified documents still included some of Trump's alleged co-conspirators like Walt Nauta, a personal aide at Mar-a-Lago. But with the change of administration at the Justice Department, once Trump took office, those cases were dismissed with prejudice, meaning they would not be revived.

House Judiciary Committee Chairman Jim Jordan told me that there is some concern among GOP lawmakers that Smith's team acted improperly when communicating with Nauta's lawyer, Stanley Woodward, who was being considered for a judgeship on the DC Superior Court.[364]

"There is a concern that…in a meeting, Jay Bratt (a Justice Department lawyer) and others on the Smith team said to that lawyer, Stanley Woodward, 'We didn't know you were a Trump guy. We thought you were interested in the judge position?' So that is a veiled threat," Jordan said. "That is certainly something we need to explore relative to Jack Smith."

Jordan told me that he's going to work with the incoming Trump administration to get more answers—and that could also include calling Smith to testify in the future before his committee, if necessary. "We haven't taken anything off the table," he said. And Jordan said his inquiry just does not stop with Smith's

---

[363] Tom Howell Jr., "Jack Smith moves to dismiss election interference case against Trump," *The Washington Times*, November 25, 2024, https://www.washingtontimes.com/news/2024/nov/25/special-counsel-jack-smith-moves-dismiss-election-/

[364] Letter to Jack Smith, Special Counsel, from Jim Jordan, US House of Representatives, September 7, 2023, https://judiciary.house.gov/sites/evo-subsites/republicans-judiciary.house.gov/files/evo-media-document/2023-09-07-jdj-to-smith-re-woodward-allegations_0.pdf

handling of the Trump lawfare, but spans the allegedly improper conduct of both DOJ and FBI leadership.

> There are lots of questions Americans still have about subjects like the school boards spying on parents going to school board meetings; the memorandum written by the Richmond field office at the FBI that said if you're a pro-life Catholic, you're an extremist; Mark Houck—the way they used the FACE Act (Freedom of Access to Clinic Entrances Act) when they arrest Mark Houck (a pro-life protester) in front of his wife and children; and we still would like to know, there is information we think the country needs to know, about the twenty-six confidential human sources from the inspector general a month ago that were present on January sixth. Those are things we still have questions about.

Returning to Smith's lawfare crusade: He was forced to have both his federal cases against the president dismissed without prejudice by the courts. That means, technically, they could be renewed in the future, so long as the statute of limitations does not run.[365] Trump's legal team did not move to dismiss the cases against him with prejudice. They may have figured the request would not be granted by a judge, or that it would be a waste of time, but some legal experts say it was at least worth a shot. Although

---

365 Alex Swoyer, "No prejudice here: Jack Smith's legal move keeps federal cases against Trump waiting in the wings," *The Washington Times*, November 29, 2024, https://www.washingtontimes.com/news/2024/nov/29/prejudice-jack-smith-legal-move-keeps-federal-case/

most federal crimes carry a five-year statute of limitations, some of the charges Trump was facing, especially those related to national security information, could arguably carry a much longer statute of limitations. A court could also hear other considerations—like the defendant being unavailable for prosecution—to extend the time that has lapsed.

With all that said, there is a possibility—even if slim—that if a Republican does not win the White House in 2029, when Trump is leaving, a Democratic Justice Department bent on vengeance could try to resurrect some of these charges against the president once he is out of office...unless Trump and his new administration are able now to put the lawfare cork back in the bottle.

Curt Levey, president of the Committee for Justice, said to me that while it is possible the same charges or similar ones could return in the future, it is unlikely.

> By the beginning of the next administration, more than eight years will have passed since the events of January 6, and almost eight years will have passed since the events at issue in the classified documents case. While it's possible that a federal prosecutor in the next administration who is as unabashedly aggressive as Jack Smith could rush to bring classified document charges with an eight-year statute of limitations, or come up with a legal theory that extends the statute of limitations, that would seem to be not just legally difficult but politically difficult as well.

"After all," he added, "the nation will have moved on after eight years."

I hope, as we all should, that he is right.

SMITH'S ELECTION INTERFERENCE

Special Counsel Jack Smith had a fail-safe should his documents prosecution against President Donald Trump fizzle. Less than two months after issuing his first, historic federal criminal indictment of a former president in June, Smith announced a second one in August—this one targeting Trump for his challenge to the 2020 election results.

When Smith was named special counsel in November of 2022 to probe Trump's January 6, 2021 actions, onlookers suspected the Biden administration—through Smith—would attempt to criminalize Trump's Ellipse speech, where he rallied his supporters outside the White House ahead of Congress's certifying his opponent, Joe Biden, the winner of the 2020 election. Shortly after his speech, a small percentage of the rally-goers journeyed to the Capitol, breaking in and entering.

But knowing the high bar it takes a prosecutor to criminalize speech—especially political speech, which is given the upmost protection under the First Amendment—Smith went another route: using federal fraud and conspiracy laws to ding the president.

Attorney General Merrick Garland gave Smith authority to investigate "whether any person or entity violated the law in connection with efforts to interfere with the lawful transfer of power following the 2020 presidential election or the certification of the Electoral College vote held on or about January 6, 2021, as well as any matters that arose or might arise directly from this investigation."[366]

Smith charged the former president with four federal criminal counts surrounding his allegations of fraud in the 2020 election, and Trump's contesting of the January 6 election certification. Smith said Trump committed a conspiracy to defraud the country "by using dishonesty, fraud, and deceit to impair, obstruct, and defeat the lawful federal government function by which the results of the presidential election are collected, counted, and certified by the federal government."[367] He also said the conspiracy involved obstructing Congress's meeting to certify the vote, and that by doing so, Trump conspired to violate the right to vote.[368]

"Each of these conspiracies—which built on the widespread mistrust the Defendant was creating through pervasive and destabilizing lies about election fraud—targeted a bedrock function of the United States federal government: the nation's process of collecting, counting, and certifying the results of the presidential election," Smith alleged.[369]

---

[366] Attorney General Merrick B. Garland, Order No. 5559-2022, "Appointment of John L. Smith as Special Counsel," November 18, 2022, https://www.justice.gov/archives/opa/media/1260551/dl?inline

[367] *United States of America v. Donald J. Trump*, Indictment, US Justice Department, August 27, 2024, https://www.justice.gov/archives/media/1366521/dl

[368] Ibid.

[369] Ibid.

Smith alleged that the president, through using his First Amendment right to speak out about his belief that there were fraudulent and questionable election activities in key swing states, created mistrust of the electoral process. But it was Smith—and Democrats' use of lawfare against Trump—that actually created a mistrust of the judicial system.

The American public made that evident in their votes on November 5, 2024, giving Trump an electoral landslide—voting in mass for the man Smith alleged had violated their right to vote just four years prior. The irony was not lost on me.

Unlike the Manhattan hush-money trial, which was rushed by Manhattan District Attorney Alvin Bragg and the Democrat-aligned Judge Juan Merchan, Trump's lawyers successfully delayed for months this criminal proceeding, which was pending in federal court in Washington—an unfriendly venue for Trump, before an Obama appointed judge.

Critics of the president, though, wanted him to face yet another trial on the Smith charges ahead of the election. That would have put the president's case on record pace compared to those of other defendants. Most defendants have a two-year span between indictment and trial.[370] In Trump's cases, though, his opponents wanted to see him stand trial in under a year and a half for both federal prosecutions.

The documents indictment—discussed earlier—came down on June 8, 2023, and most cases in the Southern District of Florida take about seventeen months to go to trial.[371] That would

[370] Alex Swoyer, "Election catalyst for hurried Trump trial; average case takes 26 months to go through federal courts," *The Washington Times*, April 10, 2024, https://www.washingtontimes.com/news/2024/apr/10/defendants-not-named-trump-usually-go-to-trial-yea/

[371] Ibid.

have put the documents trial right at November 2024, if the case had not been dismissed.

And in Washington, DC, federal trials tend to take twenty-six months from indictment to trial, which—had all things been fair—would have put Trump's trial past August 2025, since he was indicted in that dispute on August 1, 2023.[372]

Luckily, his election win sidelined Smith's political prosecutions and his opponents' rush to lock him up.

So, though detractors claim Trump successfully delayed most of the lawfare against him until after the election, the truth is the two federal trials should not have taken place by then, had Trump been treated like other defendants in those jurisdictions.

During the pendency of the federal election fraud case, the Supreme Court had to step in and decide two issues that impacted the president's federal prosecution.

First, the justices took a look at Title 18, Section 1512(c)(2) of the US criminal code, which federal prosecutors and Smith used to charge January 6 defendants and Trump with obstructing an official proceeding. The charge carries with it a twenty-year prison sentence.[373]

Joseph Fischer, a former police officer who went to the January 6 "Stop the Steal" rally to support Trump's challenges to the 2020 election, was one of roughly three hundred

---

[372] Ibid.

[373] "18 U.S. Code § 1512—Tampering with a witness, victim, or an informant," Legal Information Institute, Cornell Law School, https://www.law.cornell.edu/uscode/text/18/1512

defendants—including Trump—who faced the charge.[374] He brought a challenge to the statute all the way to the Supreme Court, arguing the law was actually used for tampering with evidence, and that the federal prosecutors were trying to stretch it too far against January 6 defendants.[375]

Fischer and a friend had been in Washington for the rally and then left town, but returned to the Capitol after the Electoral College count was paused due to the disruption from some of the rally-goers-turned-rioters.[376] The electoral count was delayed for roughly six hours.[377]

Fischer went into the Capitol—only making it about twenty feet inside before being pepper-sprayed. He was inside the federal building for a total of four minutes, yet he was charged with seven counts, including obstructing a proceeding.[378]

The high court, in a 6–3 ruling, sided with Fischer.[379] The decision, issued on June 28, 2024, said that the Sarbanes-Oxley Act, passed in 2002 in the wake of the Enron accounting scandal, applied to obstructing an investigation and

---

374 Alex Swoyer and Stephen Dinan, "Supreme Court sides with January 6 defendant against obstruction charge," *The Washington Times*, June 28, 2024, https://www.washingtontimes.com/news/2024/jun/28/supreme-court-sides-jan-6-defendant-against-obstru/

375 Ibid.

376 Ibid.

377 Oyez, *Fischer v. United States*, June, 28, 2024, https://www.oyez.org/cases/2023/23-5572

378 Swoyer and Dinan, "Supreme Court sides…," https://www.washingtontimes.com/news/2024/jun/28/supreme-court-sides-jan-6-defendant-against-obstru/

379 *Fischer v. United States*, US Supreme Court, June 28, 2024, https://www.supremecourt.gov/opinions/23pdf/23-5572_l6hn.pdf

evidence-gathering—such as records and documents.[380] The justices reasoned that Congress did not intend for it to apply to obstructing a congressional proceeding.[381]

That meant federal prosecutors had to go back and reconsider whether the government could meet the burden of proving the charge against roughly three hundred January 6 defendants that it had previously tried to inculpate. It was a decision that—unless there was evidence a January 6 defendant had obstructed records or documents in some manner—made the charge hard to prosecute for the feds. The ruling was seen as a major victory for Fischer, Trump and other January 6 defendants.

While covering the unfolding events surrounding the high court's decision, I found myself in a federal courthouse in a press room, where a reporter from NBC News opined that the Fischer ruling was narrow and did not mean that it would be unsuccessful in Smith's attempt to nab Trump on the charge. Clearly, I thought, this reporter did not understand the law, yet the reporter was responsible for explaining the legal developments to NBC's millions of readers and viewers. How disheartening, but not at all surprising, given the trend with the mainstream media in losing public trust. It would be yet another butchering of reporting on the Trump lawfare, which I had witnessed over the past several years.

Back at the Supreme Court, the justices were not done pushing back against Smith's charges.

---

[380] Swoyer and Dinan, "Supreme Court sides…," https://www.washingtontimes.com/news/2024/jun/28/supreme-court-sides-jan-6-defendant-against-obstru/

[381] Ibid.

They also decided, on July 1, 2024, what is likely the most significant ruling the high court has made in recent history. The justices took up a challenge from Trump himself over presidential immunity.

The president had argued that he was absolutely immune from criminal prosecution. It was the first time the Supreme Court had to grapple with the immunity of a president from criminal charges.

In 1982, the high court had weighed in *Nixon v. Fitzgerald* whether a president can be held civilly liable. The justices ruled that a president has absolute immunity against civil lawsuits for all conduct within the "outer perimeter" of his presidential duties.[382]

But for the first time in the nation's 248-year history, the justices had to evaluate a president's *criminal* liability. Democrats' lawfare against Trump led to this monumental, historic precedent having to be set.

In the legal battle, the justices somewhat sided with Trump; however, despite how liberal outlets have portrayed it, it was not a slam-dunk win for the president. The 6–3 decision said that a president is absolutely immune from criminal charges regarding core presidential functions, which the justices described as the pardon power, laid out in the Constitution.[383] The president is also presumed immune for other official duties, but is not immune from criminal prosecution for unofficial actions.[384]

---

382 "ArtII.S3.5.1, Presidential Immunity to Suits and Official Conduct," *Constitution Annotated*, https://constitution.congress.gov/browse/essay/artII-S3-5-1/ALDE_00013392/

383 Stephen Dinan and Alex Swoyer, "Supreme Court rules presidents have absolute immunity for official acts, but not unofficial acts," *The Washington Times*, July 1, 2024, https://www.washingtontimes.com/news/2024/jul/1/supreme-court-rules-presidents-have-absolute-immun/

384 Ibid.

Trump had argued that his duties to protect the integrity of the election fell within official duties. But the lower-court judge never had to apply the high court's decision to Trump's specific election-fraud charges because the clock essentially ran out on Smith when Trump won the election.

Judge Tanya Chutkan, an Obama appointee, was overseeing the prosecution at the trial-court level when it was paused for roughly seven months while the justices decided the immunity issue. She held the first hearing following the lengthy pause in September of 2024, two months after the high court's immunity precedent, to set a new timeline in the proceeding. She said it was unreasonable to set a new trial date; but instead of allowing the defense team to file a new motion to dismiss—traditionally the next step in the process, after Smith updated his indictment following the Supreme Court's two decisions on the Fischer and immunity cases—she allowed the prosecutors to file a new opening brief.[385] Judge Chutkan green-lighted Smith's request to file an oversized motion, arguing why all the election-fraud charges still applied to Trump, despite what the justices had ruled.[386]

So, less than six weeks before the presidential election, Smith laid out in detail—in 180 pages—facts supporting his indictment of Trump over January 6, 2021. A normal filing is just forty-five pages, which reveals the lengths to which Democrats wanted to go to detail their case before the public.

Most of the contents remained under seal until early October, when it was revealed in public court records that Smith said

---

[385] Alex Swoyer, "Judge sets schedule in Trump election-fraud case, lets prosecution file briefs first," *The Washington Times*, September 5, 2024, https://www.washingtontimes.com/news/2024/sep/5/trump-again-pleads-not-guilty-to-federal-election-/

[386] Ibid.

Trump could be charged as an "office-seeker, not office-holder."[387] He alleged Trump knew his claims about election fraud were false, based on comments he made to a family member, and that his communications with former Vice President Mike Pence over Pence's duty to oversee Congress's certification of the election results were not official conduct of a president, but rather that of a candidate and running mates.[388] He said that meant the Supreme Court's immunity decision did not apply to Trump.

It was Smith's—and Democrats'—last-ditch effort to influence the 2024 election. And it was an unfair move by the judge to allow this filing to take place before Trump had a chance to file a motion to dismiss.

Trump's team responded by saying Smith's oversized filing was riddled with falsehoods and that Democrats were "hell-bent on weaponizing the Justice Department in an attempt to cling to power."[389]

In the end, both Smith and Chutkan had to dismiss the prosecution after Trump's massive election victory. Citing Justice Department policy, Smith said in November court filings that the Office of Legal Counsel at the Justice Department reasoned that a sitting president cannot be prosecuted, and that the longstanding

---

387 Alex Swoyer, "Special counsel contests Trump immunity, says he's charged as an 'office-seeker, not office-holder,'" *The Washington Times*, October 2, 2024, https://www.washingtontimes.com/news/2024/oct/2/jack-smith-says-donald-trump-not-immune-from-prose/

388 Ibid.

389 Ibid.

policy applies to Trump's current posture, now that he was reentering the White House.[390]

The filings came with a request to dismiss the legal battle without prejudice in both the federal election fraud trial in Washington, DC, and in Smith's appeal over the classified documents case. The latter was pending at the Eleventh US Circuit Court of Appeals over the issue of Smith's authority to bring the prosecution as special counsel.[391]

Because the cases were dismissed without prejudice, they could potentially be refiled in 2029 when Trump leaves the presidency, depending on how a court would decide the issue of statute of limitations and whether or not the charges have lapsed.[392]

David Schoen, Trump's impeachment lawyer, told me that if Smith had a solid case, he would have been able to charge Trump with criminal insurrection for his January 6 speech.

"It is not a case that should have been criminalized, ever, which they take the speech out of context," Schoen said. "Those who hate Trump, and the threat they recognize he poses to their business-as-usual advantages, often take things out of context and rely on the notion that the listener won't bother to fact-check."

Democrats, though, still were able to silence Trump, as they had through other prosecutions. Smith had requested—and Judge Chutkan had granted—a gag order on Trump related to the election-fraud federal case for more than a year—which ran from

---

390 Alex Swoyer, "No prejudice here: Jack Smith's legal move keeps federal cases against Trump waiting in the wings," *The Washington Times*, November 29, 2024, https://www.washingtontimes.com/news/2024/nov/29/prejudice-jack-smith-legal-move-keeps-federal-case/

391 Ibid.

392 Ibid.

October 2023 through the case's dismissal in November of 2024, while Trump campaigned for the White House.[393]

It was all part of the Democrats' lawfare strategy, a full-court press to silence and censor the political opponent of President Joe Biden and Vice President Kamala Harris.

The attempt backfired, though, when the American people saw through it.

---

393 Robert Legare, "Trump gag order back in effect in federal election interference case," CBS News, October 30, 2023, https://www.cbsnews.com/news/trump-gag-order-back-in-effect-federal-election-interference-case/

FAWNING FANI WILLIS

The fourth and final criminal indictment Democrats lobbed at President Trump during his 2024 campaign came out of Fulton County, Georgia. It also stemmed from his contesting the 2020 election results. And it was issued about two weeks after Special Counsel Jack Smith announced his federal election prosecution.

The legacy media applauded the Georgia case, suggesting that out of all the criminal prosecutions, this one was the best built.

In 2023, *Time Magazine* opined that of his long list of legal troubles, the criminal election-related charges against Trump out of Georgia "carries the most risk" for him.[394] The publication said that the "Georgia case may be the most durable, most threatening, and most important headache facing Trump."

And *Time Magazine*'s analysis did not stand alone. For example, the *Georgia Law Review* cast the Fulton County, Georgia, prosecution as catastrophic for Trump's litigation war. "This

---

[394] Philip Elliott, "Why Donald Trump's Indictment in Georgia Carries the Most Risk," *Time*, August 14, 2023, https://time.com/6304861/why-donald-trumps-indictment-georgia-carries-most-risk/

Indictment is the Most Consequential Yet" read the headline detailing Trump's charges.[395]

The lawfare found its way to the Peach State in August of 2023, when Fulton County indicted Trump and eighteen of his allies, alleging they conspired to overturn the 2020 election results. The county claims the defendants violated Georgia's Racketeer Influenced and Corrupt Organizations Act.[396]

The prosecution, though, has been on hold for months as an appeals court scrutinizes Fulton County District Attorney Fani Willis's behavior. At issue was her appointment of Nathan Wade, her boyfriend, as the special prosecutor overseeing the case.[397] Willis was paying Wade with county tax dollars while the two took luxury vacations together. It was alleged she was profiting from the prosecution, creating a conflict of interest.

County judge Scott McAfee analyzed the situation and said Wade could not stay on the case, but Willis could. His decision was appealed and remained in limbo for much of the 2024 campaign season.[398] Judge McAfee had been appointed by GOP Georgia Governor Brian Kemp, but was up for reelection at the time of his decision, in a county where Willis is vastly popular. In fact, he ruled Willis could stay on the case just a week before the

---

[395] Jake Shatzer, "Trump Has Been Indicted in Georgia. Here's Why This Indictment is the Most Consequential Yet," *Georgia Law Review*, August 21, 2023, https://georgialawreview.org/2023/08/21/trump-has-been-indicted-in-georgia-heres-why-this-indictment-is-the-most-consequential-yet

[396] Alex Swoyer, "Georgia prosecution could follow Trump into White House even as other legal battles wind down," *The Washington Times*, November 18, 2024, https://www.washingtontimes.com/news/2024/nov/18/georgia-prosecution-could-follow-trump-white-house/

[397] Ibid.

[398] Ibid.

nonpartisan election, which he won, defeating civil rights attorney Robert Patillo.[399]

That left court-watchers wondering if he had made his ruling in a calculated manner, knowing his own job was on the line.

Judge McAfee said that there was no evidence of an actual conflict of interest, but that there was an appearance of impropriety between Willis and Wade in handling the case.[400]

"Whether this case ends in convictions, acquittals, or something in between, the result should be one that instills confidence in the process," he wrote. "A reasonable observer unburdened by partisan blinders should believe the law was impartially applied, that those accused of crimes had a fair opportunity to present their defenses, and that any verdict was based on our criminal justice system's best efforts at ascertaining the truth. Any distractions that detract from these goals, if remedial under the law, should be proportionally addressed."[401]

Now, nearly two years later, the Georgia prosecution is still durable and a thorn in Trump's side. As other federal lawfare cases against him have been wrapping up after his 2024 election win, the Georgia case has remained unresolved.

In December of 2024, seven months after Judge McAfee's decision, a Georgia appeals court correctly booted Willis from

---

[399] Antonio Pequeno, "Trump Prosecutor Fani Willis Easily Wins Her Democratic Primary, While Judge In Georgia Case Reelected," *Forbes*, May 22, 2024, https://www.forbes.com/sites/antoniopequenoiv/2024/05/21/trump-prosecutor-fani-willis-easily-wins-her-democratic-primary-while-judge-in-georgia-case-reelected/

[400] Scott McAfee, "Order on Defendants' Motions to Dismiss and Disqualify the Fulton County District Attorney," Superior Court of Fulton County, State of Georgia, March 15, 2024, https://www.documentcloud.org/documents/24482779-order-on-defendants-motions-to-dismiss-and-disqualify-the-fulton-county-district-attorney/

[401] Ibid.

the case due to her appearance of impropriety. Had Willis not eventually been disqualified from the case, it was expected she would proceed in her lawfare against Trump and his eighteen codefendants, especially after winning reelection by roughly forty points.[402]

"Fani Willis is a formidable prosecutor and politician," B. Michael Mears, a professor at Atlanta's John Marshall Law School, told me when I wrote for *The Washington Times* about how the Georgia case could potentially follow Trump into the White House. "She feels she has a mandate based upon the public."[403]

"I would not suspect she would be dropping these charges," he added.[404]

Although Willis was removed from the prosecution, the case is still open. It is up to other state prosecutors whether or not to take over the dispute. Lawyer John Eastman, who had counseled Trump on his January 6, 2021, challenge to the 2020 election results certification, was indicted with Trump as a co-conspirator. He told me the Cobb County prosecutor now may move to take over Willis's prosecution against them. Like Willis, Cobb County District Attorney Flynn D. Broady Jr. is a Democrat.

One problem with the Georgia indictment for Trump and his allies is that even Republican Governor Brian Kemp cannot step in and pardon Trump, or anyone else.[405] The pardon authority in

---

402 Dan Gooding, "Fani Willis Wins Election After Raising $2.5 Million for Campaign," *Newsweek*, November 5, 2024, https://www.newsweek.com/fani-willis-fulton-county-disrict-attorney-result-1978623

403 Alex Swoyer, "Georgia prosecution could follow Trump into White House even as other legal battles wind down," *The Washington Times*, November 18, 2024, https://www.washingtontimes.com/news/2024/nov/18/georgia-prosecution-could-follow-trump-white-house/

404 Ibid.

405 Ibid.

Georgia belongs to the Georgia Board of Pardon and Paroles. A defendant, usually after a conviction and sentencing, must petition the board.[406]

Trump's best-case scenario, though, has already occurred. Willis, who brought the charges against Trump, has been sidelined, and the prosecution has been kicked to the nonprofit Prosecuting Attorneys' Council of Georgia.[407] If a district attorney within that organization does not wish to proceed, the case would be dropped altogether.[408] It's unclear if Broady—or anyone else—is taking it up at this time.

Democrats had such high hopes for Willis's chances to lock Trump up.

They pointed to the fact that this was a state case, in which—unlike his federal indictments—he would not be able to pardon himself or instruct his Justice Department to drop the charges, should he win reelection.

But just five months after the favorable coverage of Willis's indictment against the former president, her legal battle—and her reputation—began falling apart.

The demise started in January of 2024 when a defense attorney, Ashleigh Merchant, representing a co-defendant of Trump's in the criminal racketeering and conspiracy charges, filed a lengthy motion to dismiss the case, arguing Willis was benefiting

---

[406] Ibid.
[407] Ibid.
[408] Ibid.

financially from the prosecution.[409] If a prosecutor or judge has a financial interest in any prosecution of a criminal defendant, that presents a conflict and jeopardizes the defendant's Sixth Amendment right to a fair trial. It typically means the prosecutor cannot be involved in the case, or that the charges have to be dismissed altogether.

Merchant, in her monumental filing, said that the case could not move forward because Willis did not have authority to appoint Wade as special prosecutor, and that he assisted in obtaining the indictments from the grand jury.[410] She alleged that Willis had to have county approval before she appointed Wade as special prosecutor, and that there was no evidence of such an approval by the county, which is required by the Georgia Supreme Court.[411]

Willis hired Wade while the two were having an affair, as Wade was seeking a divorce at the time. According to the filing, Willis paid Wade with public money, and then they would take lavish trips together to Napa Valley, Florida, and the Caribbean.[412] Willis defended the behavior, saying she would reimburse Wade for trips and they would split costs.

---

409 Donald Watkins, "Ashleigh Merchant: The Lawyer Who Turned Fani Willis's RICO Case Against Donald Trump on Its Head," DonaldWatkins.com, February 14, 2024, https://www.donaldwatkins.com/post/ashleigh-merchant-the-lawyer-who-turned-fani-willis-rico-case-against-donald-trump-on-its-head

410 Ashleigh Merchant, "Defendant Michael Roman's Motion to Dismiss Grand Jury Indictment as Fatally Defective and Motion to Disqualify the District Attorney, Her Office and The Special Prosecutor From Further Prosecuting this Matter," Superior Court of Fulton County, State of Georgia, January 8, 2024, https://s3.documentcloud.org/documents/24352579/motion-to-disqualify.pdf

411 Ibid.

412 Ibid.

"Even assuming this type of nepotism might be forgiven in the abstract, a review of the amount of money that the special prosecutor has been paid by the district attorney and the personal activities of the district attorney and the special prosecutor during the pendency of this prosecution shed light on just how self-serving this arrangement has been," Merchant's filing read.[413]

Willis also paid Wade more than one hundred dollars per hour over what Merchant estimated his value on the case would be worth.[414] Willis had obtained funds from the county to clear a backlog of COVID cases, but according to Merchant, much of that money was used towards Wade's special-counsel prosecution, instead.[415]

The personal relationship created a conflict of interest that eventually required the two lawyers to be disqualified from the case, under the Georgia Rules of Professional Responsibility.[416] And, Merchant said, Willis's use of taxpayer dollars without disclosing her conflict of interest to the public violated 18 U.S.C. § 1346, making it a crime to defraud.[417]

"The issues raised herein strike at the heart of fairness in our justice system and, if left unaddressed and unchecked, threaten to taint the entire prosecution, invite error, and completely undermine public confidence in the eventual outcome of this proceeding," Merchant wrote.[418]

The motion was so charging and detailed that the judge scheduled a hearing over the matter and allegations. It was

---

413 Ibid.

414 Ibid.

415 Ibid.

416 Ibid.

417 Ibid.

418 Ibid.

televised across national news networks, where the country watched the Fulton County, Georgia, prosecution—once hailed as a nail in the coffin for Trump—unravel.

Willis also did not do herself any favors by taking the stand in her defense against the motion, and attacked Merchant over the allegations of her affair with Wade. Her behavior was aggressive, defensive, and unprofessional. Wade, meanwhile, also testified, but remained calmer. The two did admit to having dated at one point, and Wade acknowledged his pending divorce.

Judge Scott McAfee, to his credit, interjected to redirect Willis when she was coming undone on the witness stand.

"Ms. Willis, I am going to have to caution you," said Judge McAfee. "If this happens again and again, I am going to have no choice but to strike your testimony."[419]

Out of the allegations, it was uncovered that Wade had been paid by Willis's office more than $1 million for working on the case.[420]

Beyond their relationship, the decision to hire Wade was a curious one, as pursuing a conviction under the state's Racketeer Influenced and Corrupt Organizations Act (RICO) is not Wade's expertise.

In fact, as court filings detailed, Wade had never tried a felony RICO case before and would not be qualified under the county's standards to be appointed to the case.[421] While Willis made a little more than $198,000 as district attorney, Wade had made more than $1,000,000 on the prosecution. That's more than the

---

[419] 11Alive, "Judge warns Fani Willis," YouTube, February 15, 2024, https://www.youtube.com/watch?v=J9f-NG_9pgA

[420] Merchant, "Defendant Michael Roman's Motion to Dismiss…," https://s3.documentcloud.org/documents/24352579/motion-to-disqualify.pdf

[421] Ibid.

justices that sit on the Supreme Court of Georgia make each year. Based on Wade's lack of experience, the pay did not add up.

RICO is a hard federal charge to prove. It targets organized crime and is quite complex. However, Georgia has its own version, and legal experts say that law is broader and allows the prosecution to use activities outside the state to try to prove a criminal conspiracy.[422] Typically, with a RICO charge there has to be a personal or financial benefit.[423] If convicted, one could go to jail, or pay a fine, or both.[424]

Willis has used the statute against others. Against Trump and his allies, she charged they were working in an organized conspiracy to unlawfully overturn the 2020 election results in the Peach State, where President Biden had won.[425]

What also came out during the heated testimony over Willis's financial and love interests with her special prosecutor, was his billing for sixteen hours' worth of meetings with the Biden White House counsel. To put it mildly, that revelation is head-scratching, because there is zero reason why a local county district attorney's office would need to meet with the president's lawyer over a local criminal case involving his political opponent.

David Schoen—Trump's impeachment lawyer, who has remained a Trump defender—said the involvement between a local prosecutor and White House counsel was definitely unusual.

---

422 Devan Cole, "What is RICO, the law at the heart of Trump's Georgia criminal case?," CNN, September 6, 2023, https://www.cnn.com/2023/08/15/politics/rico-explainer-georgia-trump-indictment/index.html

423 Lawson & Berry, "Have you Been Charged with Georgia Racketeer Influenced and Corrupt Organizations (RICO) Act?," GeorgiaCriminalLawyer.com, https://www.georgiacriminallawyer.com/rico

424 Ibid.

425 Ibid.

"Never seen it before in any kind of case, other than maybe a national security kind of case, arguably—not this kind of case, for sure," Schoen told me. "It just lends to the idea that it is all part of a political agenda."

House Judiciary Committee Chairman Jim Jordan, Ohio Republican, also said the connections reveal the political nature behind the Georgia charges.

"One of the reasons all these cases fell apart is because they were all based on politics—not based on the facts or the rule of law or equal treatment under the law—not based on the Constitution," he said.

Jordan is hoping his committee will get more details during the new Trump administration on the federal government's interactions under President Biden with state and local prosecutors, suggesting that incoming Attorney General Pam Bondi and new director of the Federal Bureau of Investigation Kash Patel could aid in getting lawmakers more transparency.

"One thing we want to get to the bottom of is: We want to know how extensive were the interactions between Fani Willis, Nathan Wade, and the DOJ, and the White House—and frankly, it looks like Nathan Wade may have had communications with the January sixth Committee," Rep. Jordan told me. He added: "We think there is something there, and we think that is something the American people need to understand, and by getting that information, we hope we can stop that sort of stuff from ever happening in the future."

House GOP lawmakers have been probing the Georgia prosecution (among others) against Trump, and quizzed Wade on why he had billed for a trip to the White House. During an exchange, it was suggested the meeting could have been made to discuss executive privilege issues with some witnesses, but Wade said he could not recall what was discussed.[426] He pushed back on any wrongdoing.

"No one at the White House, the White House counsel's office, the Department of Justice, or the January 6th committee directed, ordered, asked, coerced, or pressured me or any member of my investigative team to seek or not to seek an indictment against anyone," he said.[427]

Willis's controversy—and performance in court—is an example of Democrats' lawfare making a mockery of the judicial system, but backfiring.

The legacy media, though, helped run cover for her, failing to disclose her political identification.

The three major outlets—ABC, CBS, and NBC—did not routinely note that Willis is a Democrat.[428] She even ran again in 2024 to be reelected as a Democrat, which was a timely event that should have been properly addressed during the news coverage, to give the viewer or readers context and potentially suggest a motive for her lawfare crusade.

---

[426] *Deposition of: Nathan Wade*, Committee on the Judiciary, U.S. House of Representatives, October 15, 2024, https://judiciary.house.gov/sites/evo-subsites/republicans-judiciary.house.gov/files/evo-media-document/2024-10-15 Nathan Wade Deposition_Redacted_Errata.pdf

[427] Ibid.

[428] Rich Noyes, "Study: At Least 90% of TV News Fails to Call Trump Prosecutors 'Democrats,'" MRC *NewsBusters*, April 15, 2024, https://www.newsbusters.org/blogs/nb/rich-noyes/2024/04/15/study-least-90-tv-news-fails-call-trump-prosecutors-democrats

But Media Research Center's *NewsBusters* discovered that the mainstream media largely failed to disclose that fact, as they did in other legal battles against Trump.[429]

ABC's *World News Tonight* and *CBS Evening News* aired around ninety-nine stories about the Georgia case, according to a *NewsBusters* report in April of 2024, which discovered that none identified Willis as a Democrat.[430] *NBC Nightly News*, meanwhile, rightly identified her as a Democrat in just eight out of fifty stories.[431]

"Add it all up, and out of 149 evening news stories about the Georgia election case against Trump, a scant five percent revealed that Willis was a Democrat, vs. 95% that kept viewers in the dark," the April research from MRC revealed, which came just seven months ahead of the November election.[432]

Georgia lawmakers, like members of Congress, are also reviewing Willis's conduct.[433] She and Wade have also faced complaints brought to the state bar, where sanctions could potentially be issued.[434] The Georgia State Bar, though, would not give me any indication, or even acknowledge, these complaints when I inquired about an update as to their status.

---

[429] Ibid.

[430] Ibid.

[431] Ibid.

[432] Ibid.

[433] Deidra Dukes, "Georgia Senate committee investigating Fani Willis probes use of special purpose juries," Fox 5 Atlanta, August 9, 2024, https://www.fox5atlanta.com/news/georgia-senate-committee-fani-willis-investigation-misconduct-trump

[434] Tim Darnell, "Fulton board of ethics taking up 2 complaints against DA Fani Willis," Atlanta News First, February 22, 2024, https://www.atlantanewsfirst.com/2024/02/22/fulton-board-ethics-taking-up-2-complaints-against-da-fani-willis/

Ultimately, though, Fulton County voters did reelect Willis despite knowing of her handling of the Trump prosecution and their tax dollars. When voters do not hold elected officials accountable for wrongdoing, the lawfare will continue, unless an entity like the Georgia lawmakers, members of Congress, or the state bar take action. But it is unlikely that any of those authorities will second guess the people's choice.

LETITIA JAMES'S UNCIVIL DISORDER

Like her fellow elected Democrat colleague, Manhattan District Attorney Alvin Bragg, New York Attorney General Letitia James campaigned on targeting Donald Trump and his businesses.

"I will never be afraid to challenge this illegitimate president."[435]

"He should be charged with obstructing justice."[436]

"I believe that the President of these United States can be indicted for criminal offenses."[437]

"I will be shining a bright light into every dark corner of his real estate dealings."[438]

---

[435] CNN, "See what New York AG said while running for office about charging Trump," https://www.cnn.com/videos/politics/2023/10/03/letitia-james-prosecute-trump-2018-comments-running-office-cnntm-vpx.cnn

[436] Ibid.

[437] Ibid.

[438] Ibid.

Those were just a few snippets of some of her 2018 campaign promises, which drew applause and support from her deep-blue liberal base.[439]

After those statements, how could anyone with the last name Trump feel like they would get a fair shake at justice from James's office?

An attorney general is expected to follow ethical standards that apply to all lawyers—and even more importantly, to those working on behalf of the government. James is expected, as attorney general, not to make any sort of public remarks that could prejudice legal proceedings[440] and not to make disparaging comments about election candidates. Those requirements come under rules for professional conduct set forth by the American Bar Association.[441]

James, however, spent time bad-mouthing Trump in the press, which gives an impression that she was out to get him from the very beginning and lacked impartiality towards the presidential candidate—and defendant—all for her own political gain.

Although James made good on her campaign vows to get Trump by charging the president with civil fraud violations—scoring a more than $350 million fine against him—she ran into trouble on appeal. That fine, meanwhile, grew to about half a billion dollars, due to interest.

---

439 Ibid.

440 "Rule 3.6: Trial Publicity," American Bar Association, https://www.americanbar.org/groups/professional_responsibility/publications/model_rules_of_professional_conduct/rule_3_6_trial_publicity/

441 "Rule 8.2: Judicial & Legal Officials, *Maintaining the Integrity of the Profession*," American Bar Association, https://www.americanbar.org/groups/professional_responsibility/publications/model_rules_of_professional_conduct/rule_8_2_judicial_legal_officials/

In September of 2024, seven months after James's civil-fraud conviction of Trump, a New York appellate court—composed of five Democratic-leaning jurists—finally raised questions during oral arguments about the fairness of the verdict against the president.[442]

A couple of the judges asked the state's attorney arguing on behalf of James's office for other examples of the attorney general using state law, Executive Law Section 63(12), to probe transactions between private parties, as the office had done with Trump.[443]

The law, which is basically a regulation aimed at stopping fraud in the marketplace that would harm large swaths of consumers, has been criticized as being too broad and vague, giving the attorney general authority to probe allegedly fraudulent activity sans any intent or malicious *mens rea*, meaning state of mind.[444]

"Every case that you cite involves damage to consumers, damage to the marketplace," Justice David Friedman, a Democrat, said to the state attorney.[445] "We don't have anything like that here."

In fact, no one lost any money.

There were no actual victims.

---

[442] Jack Queen and Luc Cohen, "Appellate judges skeptical of New York civil fraud case against Trump," Reuters, September 26, 2024, https://www.reuters.com/world/us/trump-ask-new-york-appeals-court-toss-nearly-500-mln-civil-fraud-judgment-2024-09-26/

[443] Ibid.

[444] Mark Kelley and Lois Ahn, "Trump's NY Civil Fraud Trial Spotlights Long-Criticized Law," Law360, April 5, 2024, https://www.mololamken.com/assets/htmldocuments/Law360_Trumps NY Civil Fraud Trial Spotlights Long-Criticized Law_April 2024.pdf

[445] Queen and Cohen, "Appellate judges skeptical…," https://www.reuters.com/world/us/trump-ask-new-york-appeals-court-toss-nearly-500-mln-civil-fraud-judgment-2024-09-26/

Nevertheless, after a five-week trial conducted before only Judge Arthur F. Engoron, a Democrat, the president, his family members, and business associates were found to have inflated personal worth to obtain loans at lower rates.

The judge, at least in part, recognized the law that the attorney general brought the charges under was broad. "The statute casts a wide net," Judge Engoron wrote in his lengthy opinion.[446]

But he went on to find that the attorney general had started an exhaustive probe into Trump in 2020 and first filed a complaint in 2021 over alleged fraud and conspiracy to commit financial misrepresentations.[447] In his ninety-two-page ruling, Judge Engoron said Trump and his team inflated the value of Trump Tower, Mar-a-Lago, The Seven Springs Estate, his Scotland golf course, and other properties.[448] In one example, the judge suggested that Eric Trump, Trump's second son, inflated the value of one property by nearly $100 million.[449]

The Trump family denied any wrongdoing. Donald Trump said he thought the properties were actually undervalued.[450] During the initial trial, the judge was the only fact-finder, as there was no jury involved. Judge Engoron said there's no right to a jury trial due to the case being equitable in nature, so the Seventh Amendment right to be judged by one's peers did not attach for Trump.[451]

---

[446] Arthur Engoron, "*People of the State of New York v. Donald Trump, et al.*" February 16, 2024, https://www.scribd.com/document/706231478/452564-2022-People-of-the-State-of-v-People-of-the-State-of-Decision-After-Trial-1688#1fullscreen=1

[447] Ibid.

[448] Ibid.

[449] Ibid.

[450] Ibid.

[451] Ibid.

But the judge has been criticized—even in legacy media—over his valuation of Trump's assets. Like Mar-a-Lago, whose value he estimated somewhere between $18 million and $27 million.[452]

CNN quoted financial experts who questioned the judge having relied on tax assessments for property values, saying the tax assessments are often lower and do not equate to market value.[453] And property experts said the Palm Beach estate could list for more than $300 million[454] and potentially up to $600 million.[455] Trump has argued it should be valued even higher, sayings it's worth at least a billion to $1.5 billion.[456]

Meanwhile, the penalty Trump was handed down itself is rather high, bringing forward questions of due process and constitutional concerns on appeal. In fact, the bond Trump was required to post was $175 million while he appeals Judge Engoron's decision. But that bond was supposed to be the full

---

[452] Ben Kochman, and Priscilla DeGregory, "Judge at Trump civil fraud trial implores media to stop saying he valued Mar-a-Lago at $18M," *New York Post*, October 2, 2023, https://nypost.com/2023/10/02/judge-implores-media-to-stop-saying-he-valued-mar-a-lago-at-18m/

[453] Matt Egan, "Real estate insiders question how Trump fraud judge valued Mar-a-Lago," CNN, October 3, 2023, https://www.cnn.com/2023/10/03/business/trump-fraud-judge-mar-a-lago/index.html

[454] Kochman and DeGregory, "Judge at Trump civil fraud trial…," https://nypost.com/2023/10/02/judge-implores-media-to-stop-saying-he-valued-mar-a-lago-at-18m/

[455] Terry Spencer, "Is Mar-a-Lago worth $1 billion? Trump's winter home valuations are at the core of his fraud trial," Associated Press, October 9, 2023, https://apnews.com/article/trump-maralago-lawsuit-palm-beach-51fea4e520b1901c1c045590b2a7bdc0

[456] Engoron, "*People of the State of New York v. Donald Trump…*," https://www.scribd.com/document/706231478/452564-2022-People-of-the-State-of-v-People-of-the-State-of-Decision-After-Trial-1688#1fullscreen=1

amount of the judgment.[457] The court, and Trump's attorneys, came to an understanding that would be an unrealistic and unreasonable figure for him to post on appeal.[458] In New York, usually 120 percent of an award is posted as bond during the appeals process, due to interest.[459] But given the large sum, Trump's attorneys challenged that figure, and an appeals court sided with them, lowering the amount.[460] That could be a sign that the overall judgment is in trouble on appeal, too. If even the bond had to be negotiated down, so too could the final judgment. Part of the president's punishment is also not running a business in the state of New York for three years. The Trump Organization is, under the ruling, also required to have an independent monitor.

The law James used against the president had been manipulated in an unusual way to nab him.

The Associated Press reported that the civil fraud law at issue had only been used to dissolve businesses in roughly a dozen cases in the course of seventy years, but that Trump's legal battle stood apart from the others.[461] "It's the only big business found

---

457 Michael Sisak, "6 things to know about Trump's appeal of his $489 million civil fraud verdict," PBS, September 25, 2024, https://www.pbs.org/newshour/politics/6-things-to-know-about-trumps-appeal-of-his-489-million-civil-fraud-verdict

458 Ibid.

459 Dareh Gregorian, "From 'practical impossibility' to done deal: How Trump posted the $175 million bond in his civil fraud case," NBC News, April 2, 2024, https://www.nbcnews.com/politics/donald-trump/trump-posted-175-million-bond-civil-fraud-case-rcna146043

460 Ibid.

461 Bernard Condon, "Dissolving Trump's business empire would stand apart in history of NY fraud law," Associated Press, January 29, 2024, https://apnews.com/article/trump-fraud-business-law-courts-banks-lending-punishment-2ee9e509a28c24d0cda92da2f9a9b689

that was threatened with a shutdown without a showing of obvious victims and major losses," the Associated Press stated.[462]

Kudos to the legacy media for calling out the uneven treatment in Trump's case, even if not wanting to outright label it lawfare.

The banks that James had argued were allegedly defrauded by Trump inflating his net worth ended up testifying favorably for Trump, in another ding against the attorney general's office. Deutsche Bank, which loaned millions for projects across the country to the Trump Organization, had a representative testify on behalf of Trump, stating that the bank would understand clients gave estimates, and the bank would do its own due diligence and "make some adjustments." Trump's team pounced on this, arguing that the banks took responsibility and understood the loan risks, too.[463]

Having a victimless crime under a consumer-fraud statute is likely problematic on appeal, given there is no consumer injured. Everyone left the negotiations paid and happy. The loans were also completely paid back, which the trial judge recognized in his opinion. Nevertheless, he slapped Trump with the massive penalty.

James, additionally, could also run into trouble on appeal with whether she overstepped her authority in using the fraud statute in this manner. One of the appeals court judges questioned during oral arguments if an attorney general had ever gotten

---

[462] Ibid.

[463] Jennifer Peltz, "Banker involved in big loans to Trump's company testifies for his defense in civil fraud trial," Associated Press, November 28, 2023, https://apnews.com/article/trump-fraud-lawsuit-trial-new-york-53313f64d57b0aa99f756c2c791d29ab

involved with this law between two private parties' financial dealings before now.[464]

The attorney general's office is holding out, though, refusing to dismiss the case, despite Trump's November 2024 victory.

"The ordinary burdens of civil litigation do not impede the President's official duties in a way that violates the US Constitution," the state's solicitor general told Trump's lawyer in December 2024, less than a month before Inauguration Day.[465]

Even as Trump returned to the White House in January of 2025, the appeals court had not issued a decision as to the civil fraud verdict. The president should be able to focus on the country's well-being and not be distracted by defending his personal financial interests.

As the appeals court continues weighing what to do with the dispute, the interest continues to accumulate, reaching just about $490 million as of December of 2024—one month before Trump returned to Washington, DC.

James's lawfare—although not in a criminal court, but through civil penalties—was part of Democrats' attempts to financially drain Trump and silence him as a political opponent.

Judge Engoron, the trial judge, took note and was in lockstep.

He gagged Trump from speaking freely about the civil-fraud trial as the president campaigned for a second term. The president

---

[464] Jordan Rubin, "Letitia James's massive Trump civil fraud victory in question after appellate argument," MSNBC, September 27, 2024, https://www.msnbc.com/deadline-white-house/deadline-legal-blog/trump-fraud-trial-appeal-rcna172946

[465] Aaron Katersky and Peter Charalambous, "New York AG will continue to pursue $454 million civil fraud judgment against Trump," ABC News, December 10, 2024, https://abcnews.go.com/US/new-york-ag-continue-pursue-454-million-civil/story?id=116639628

was not permitted to—nor were his attorneys, at one point—criticize the judge's law clerk, whom Trump categorized as "Trump Hating" on social media and shared a picture of her.[466] The clerk would apparently pass notes to the judge and roll her eyes during witness testimony.[467]

While passing notes during court proceedings is not unusual, facial expressions are considered inappropriate conduct on behalf of courtroom staff.

Again, this is another appearance of the lack of impartiality from the New York justice system. It was also another use of a weaponized gag order to silence a political opponent.

James's obsession with targeting Trump and his business is yet another episode of Democrats' lawfare that is continuing to unravel. And as usual, unfortunately, the media failed to serve as a check on the one-sided proceedings.

Media Research Center's *NewsBusters* found in December of 2023 that the press was intensely focusing on the civil-fraud lawsuit. The catch, though, was that mainstream media were not calling out the political nature of the proceedings.

The group found that from September 2023 to December 2023, the civil-fraud lawsuit was the networks' top campaign

---

[466] Adam Reiss and Dareh Gregorian, "Appeals court temporarily lifts Trump gag order in civil fraud case," NBC News, November 16, 2023, https://www.nbcnews.com/politics/donald-trump/appeals-court-temporarily-lifts-trump-gag-order-civil-fraud-case-rcna125588

[467] Ibid.

story.[468] NBC, ABC, and CBS dedicated seventy-seven minutes to covering it.[469]

By comparison, the presidential primary debates did not get as much coverage, as *NewsBusters*' research uncovered just over fourteen minutes went to debate analysis.[470]

The most offensive aspect of the news coverage might be that just 10 percent of the airtime identified James as a Democrat.[471] We saw this before, with major outlets not noting Willis, the Fulton County, Georgia, District Attorney prosecuting Trump was a Democrat, either. Even fewer told the audience that the judge—also a Democrat—was making anti-Trump rulings.[472]

But unfortunately, the media's indifference to the Trump- and MAGA-targeted lawfare became the norm, striking a blow to the journalism trade and to the judiciary.

---

468 Rich Noyes, "TV News Won't Call Anti-Trump Attorney General and Judge 'Democrats,'" MRC *NewsBusters*, December 13, 2023, https://www.newsbusters.org/blogs/nb/rich-noyes/2023/12/13/tv-news-wont-call-anti-trump-attorney-general-and-judge-democrats

469 Ibid.

470 Ibid.

471 Ibid.

472 Ibid.

MEDIA MISINFORMATION

Less than two weeks before the November 5, 2024 election, I was tracking and reporting on President Donald Trump's legal cases when I shared on the social media platform X a post from an attorney that worked in the first Trump administration and is well-known as an ally to Supreme Court Justice Clarence Thomas. The attorney, Mark Paoletta, posted about negative experiences with General John Kelly, who became quite the Trump critic after serving as his chief of staff during the first Trump administration.

Kelly was in the news at the time for yet another swipe at the president—calling him a fascist[473]—as Trump was competing against Vice President Kamala Harris. She had by that time replaced President Joe Biden at the top of the Democratic ticket due to him dropping out of the race following a poor debate performance.

---

[473] Eric Bradner and Kate Sullivan, "Trump's former chief of staff says he fits 'fascist' definition and prefers 'dictator approach,'" CNN, October 23, 2024, https://www.cnn.com/2024/10/22/politics/trump-fascist-john-kelly/index.html

"I worked in the White House with John Kelly, and I don't believe a word he says. He was a terrible chief of staff who dishonestly kept information from the President to pursue his own agenda, an unelected former military official substituting his judgment for the duly elected President," Paoletta posted on the social media platform, going on to give examples of Kelly being insubordinate, in his opinion.[474]

Since Paoletta's post was timely in response to Kelly making new criticisms of Trump, which the mainstream media happily pounced on ahead of Election Day, I shared the post, thinking it was newsworthy. Little did I know that my sharing of Paoletta's response to Kelly would trigger a former journalism professor of mine, whose comment landed in my direct message inbox shortly thereafter.

"Never been more disappointed of a former student. You have become a biased journalist and you didn't learn that at Mizzou," the professor wrote.

This professor had been a good mentor to me, so I was surprised to see his note. When I went to the professor's page, I saw nothing but negative posts about Trump. I realized my former professor had a case of Trump Derangement Syndrome.

I chose not to respond.

Overall, I've had a great experience with former professors who taught me journalism at the University of Missouri nearly two decades ago. I have received kind messages from at least two others, checking on me and noting how difficult it is to report in the legal world, recognizing my success since leaving the journalism school, which I appreciated.

---

474 Mark Paoletta, X.com, October 24, 2024, https://x.com/MarkPaoletta/status/1849609777225011262

I do not hold it against this former professor for his message. But with that brief comment, it became obvious to me that even those who are supposed to teach how to report the news from all sides are unable to avoid their own bias when it came to Trump. Good thing this professor no longer teaches at the school.

Journalists are supposed to question politicians and push back on government leaders. That is at the heart of being a watchdog, which is the duty of the press.

When you have one candidate—like Harris, echoing Kelly—calling Trump "a fascist," it is right for reporters to challenge that narrative.[475] Curiosity and challenging authority are essential characteristics for making a good newsman or woman.

Our Founding Fathers understood that point when they gave the press recognition and protection in our First Amendment to the US Constitution.

> Congress shall make no law respecting an establishment of religion, or prohibiting the free exercise thereof; or abridging the freedom of speech, or of the press; or the right of the people peaceably to assemble, and to petition the Government for a redress of grievances.[476]

---

[475] Alex Seitz-Wald, and Megan Lebowitz, "Kamala Harris calls Trump a 'fascist' as she argues he's 'dangerous' and unfit for office," NBC News, October 23, 2024, https://www.nbcnews.com/politics/2024-election/kamala-harris-calls-trump-fascist-argues-dangerous-unfit-office-rcna176713

[476] "Amdt1.9.1 Overview of Freedom of the Press., Constitution Annotated, https://constitution.congress.gov/browse/essay/amdt1-9-1/ALDE_00000395/

The media is said to be the fourth branch of government. That is how important the news industry used to be back at the time of the nation's founding and the adoption of the First Amendment of the US Constitution, which specifically recognizes "the press" by name.[477] The Founders understood how powerful a free press is—one that is liberated from government influence. This principle became evident as the press covered America's increasing independence from Britain, and once independent, Virginia became the first state to pass a law protecting the press.[478]

Scholars of law and history have interpreted the First Amendment to mean that the media is given heightened protection because of its important role in disseminating news and fomenting public debate.[479] This is still true today. But the public perception of the media has tanked since our nation's founding.

Gallup has polled media trust for decades. It found that in 1973, 74 percent of Democrats and 68 percent of Republicans had confidence in the press. But by 2023, that had dropped to just 58 percent of Democrats and 11 percent of Republicans having confidence in the media.[480]

---

[477] ShareAmerica, "The importance of an independent press," US Embassy & Consulates in Russia, https://ru.usembassy.gov/the-importance-of-an-independent-press/

[478] History.com editors, "Freedom of the Press," History.com, December 7, 2017, https://www.history.com/articles/freedom-of-the-press

[479] "Amdt1.9.1 Overview of Freedom of the Press," Constitution Annotated, https://constitution.congress.gov/browse/essay/amdt1-9-1/ALDE_00000395/

[480] Jesse Holcomb, "Media Mistrust Has Been Growing for Decades—Does It Matter?," Pew, October 17, 2024, https://www.pewtrusts.org/en/trend/archive/fall-2024/media-mistrust-has-been-growing-for-decades-does-it-matter

A May 2024 poll from The American Press Institute and The Associated Press-NORC Center for Public Affairs Research revealed that more than 80 percent of those surveyed believed that during the 2024 election, corporate media would "report inaccurate information or disinformation."[481] A Pew Research Center study also found during the 2024 election cycle that Republicans were as likely to trust information they saw on social media posts as they were to believe reports from the national news.[482]

Trump was able to tap into this growing distrust of the media with how he ran his 2024 campaign. He used social media platforms and podcasts to get his message out rather than relying on the legacy media, which he had determined was biased against him ever since he launched his 2016 presidential campaign nearly a decade before.

When Trump first took to Twitter—now known as X—in March of 2017 to react to revelations that the previous administration had been "spying" on his campaign, many in the media dismissed his concerns. Somehow, some still do, despite all the evidence, and continue to question the validity of this story.[483] It

---

[481] Tristan Justice, "Poll: More Than 8 In 10 Americans Don't Trust Corporate Media To Report Facts," *The Federalist*, May 2, 2024, https://thefederalist.com/2024/05/02/poll-more-than-8-in-10-americans-dont-trust-corporate-media-to-report-facts/

[482] Kirsten Eddy, "Republicans, young adults now nearly as likely to trust info from social media as from national news outlets," Pew Research Center, October 16, 2024, https://www.pewresearch.org/short-reads/2024/10/16/republicans-young-adults-now-nearly-as-likely-to-trust-info-from-social-media-as-from-national-news-outlets/

[483] Marshall Cohen, "'They spied on my campaign': How Trump transformed a conspiracy theory into a political rallying cry," CNN, August 29, 2020, https://www.cnn.com/2020/08/29/politics/trump-spying-campaign-obama-fact-check/index.html

was one of the first examples of the media ignoring and failing to call out the lawfare against the president.

The surveillance of the Trump campaign was, in part, based on a now-debunked dossier from former British spy Christopher Steele, as I discussed in earlier chapters. The press ran with the dossier story, which was salacious in claiming Russians had blackmail on Trump, reportedly having a tape of prostitutes urinating on a hotel bed in Moscow.

Even when it became obvious that the claims were not substantiated—and that they were being pushed by his political opponent at the time, Hillary Clinton, and the Democratic National Committee (which were fined $113,000 by the Federal Elections Commission for funding the Steele dossier[484]), there were no media retractions.

The Russia, dossier saga is where the lawfare against Trump began and remained unchecked by the so-called press watchdogs.

Reporters were used by Democratic lawmakers like former Representative Adam Schiff—now a California senator—to peddle allegations that there was evidence of conspiracy and collusion between the 2016 Trump campaign and the Kremlin. When Special Counsel Robert Mueller's report found no criminal correlation or coordination, Democrats and Americans were still skeptical, since they had been consuming 24/7 news reports of just the opposite.

Two campaign cycles later, the Russian collusion story still remains the focus of the press, with *The Economic Times* pondering "Is Trump secretly helping Putin" in his quest for America

[484] Jill Colvin, "DNC, Clinton campaign agree to Steele dossier funding fine," Associated Press, March 31, 2022, https://apnews.com/article/russia-ukraine-2022-midterm-elections-business-elections-presidential-elections-5468774d18e8c46f81b55e9260b13e93

to take back control of the Panama Canal,[485] and Yahoo reporting "Kremlin Insiders Reveal How Trump Is Already Secretly Helping Putin."[486]

Experts that study news coverage and consumption agree that the one-sided "Russiagate" coverage contributed to the Trump lawfare. "It certainly undermined his credibility with many Americans who are not a fan of his," said Brent Baker, a senior fellow and research expert at Media Research Center.

> Independents, liberals assumed he was a total fraud and got into office inappropriately by using a foreign power, and I think that really hurt him politically. He had much less political power to get things done because he was fighting this whole storyline of being a Russian operative.

I personally was not confident as to whether the media butchered covering the lawfare against Trump because reporters simply did not understand the complexities of the law—or if their coverage was intentionally supporting the Democrats' political litigation.

I thought about the NBC News reporter that I referenced while detailing Trump's federal election fraud case, who claimed

---

[485] *ET Online*, "Is Trump secretly helping Putin? Russia's take on US President-elect's bold Panama Canal annexation proposal," *The Economic Times*, December 30, 2024, https://economictimes.indiatimes.com/news/international/global-trends/donald-trump-putin-russia-us-ties-is-trump-secretly-helping-putin-russias-take-on-us-president-elects-bold-panama-canal-annexation-proposal/articleshow/116831476.cms?from=mdr

[486] Julia Davis, "Kremlin Insiders Reveal How Trump Is Already Secretly Helping Putin," *Daily Beast,* December 30, 2024, https://www.yahoo.com/news/kremlin-insiders-reveal-trump-already-110025930.html

to me the Supreme Court's *Fischer* ruling (where the justices sided with a January 6 defendant, striking down one of the feds' obstruction charges) was "narrow," and that was why it was still part of Trump's updated indictment. Maybe that reporter did not understand the justices' decision—or maybe the reporter was just doing Jack Smith's public-relations work, trying to bolster the special prosecutor's case against Trump after Smith had suffered a significant high court loss.

In the *Fischer* ruling, the justices actually narrowed the application of the federal criminal law, which elevated the burden for the government to prove charges against January 6 defendants, including Trump. There was no evidence that Trump altered or destroyed documents or records, which was what the high court suggested the government must show to make that criminal charge stick. So, clearly, the NBC news reporter misunderstood—willfully or by ignorance—the actual holding that the Supreme Court made in its decision. His error, though, creates misinformation that is then disseminated to his readers.

The lawfare was given full focus in the legacy media especially leading up to the 2024 election.

Media Research Center's *NewsBusters* research uncovered that Trump's legal cases got more coverage than issues like the economy, immigration, and abortion.[487] A January 2024 report showed that evening newscasts devoted 992 minutes in 2023

---

[487] Rich Noyes, "Exclusive: TV Ignores Issues & Rivals, Fixates on Bashing Trump," MRC *NewsBusters*, January 11, 2024, https://www.newsbusters.org/blogs/nb/rich-noyes/2024/01/11/exclusive-tv-ignores-issues-rivals-fixates-bashing-trump

to Trump's legal trouble, which was eight times more than was allocated to the GOP candidates' discussion of policy matters.[488]

The advocacy outlet highlighted the media's legal breakdown, showing that Special Counsel Jack Smith's January 6 election-fraud case got 290 minutes while his classified documents charges got 224 minutes.[489] Manhattan District Attorney Alvin Bragg's hush-money trial received 172 minutes of coverage, while the Georgia case brought by Fani Willis, the Fulton County district attorney, received 132 minutes.[490]

"Each of these cases drew more network evening news airtime than all of the policy discussions involving these candidates in all of 2023," MRC's report revealed.[491]

House Judiciary Committee Chairman Jim Jordan said the media assisted in pushing the "ridiculous cases." He said calling out the lawfare was not the only issue the press failed to properly address.

"They did the same thing with censorship. There was all kind of, 'There wasn't censorship.' I was like, don't take my word for it, take Mark Zuckerberg. He sent me a letter where he said, 'The Biden administration pressured us to censor. We did it, we are sorry, we won't do it again,'" Jordan recalled. "So it was like the whole left just pushed this narrative, and it was just wrong."

Part of the problem with the media misinformation and spreading the Washington establishment's political propaganda is that reporters thrive on leaks, and those leaks are more reliable when they come from those in power in Washington. So, reporters cozy up to power and thus become mouthpieces for government

---

488 Ibid.

489 Ibid.

490 Ibid.

491 Ibid.

leaders and politicians, rather than questioning them at every turn and being the watchdogs our Founders had envisioned.

The Washington press enjoys riding its First Amendment privileges when it is self-serving to do so, but when it came to Trump's rights, the media was mum. After facing more than a year of gag orders, unable to speak in detail about the criminal charges and proceedings he faced, Trump found no major legacy media outlet moved to question or challenge the courts' gag orders during much of the 2024 campaign cycle.

It is the press' responsibility to ensure voters hear from both sides on any issue, and especially during an election reporters should strive to cover all candidates impartially. But in their lack of curiosity, the media failed to achieve that balance.

There was, though, one podcaster and member of the New York press, *Good Lawgic*'s Joseph Norman, who took his application all the way to the Supreme Court. He sought a stay of the Trump gag order from Associate Justice Sonia Sotomayor, who reviews requests out of New York. Norman's argument was that the gag order issued by Judge Juan Merchan in the Manhattan hush-money case ran afoul of the freedom of the press.

Justice Sotomayor, an Obama appointee, rejected the application.

Trump arguably won the election by using social media and podcasts as well as influencers to help advance his 2024 campaign, largely sidestepping a legacy media that instead focused on his criminal charges. He was forced to go around the usual media streams—which were simply echoing Democratic prosecutors in their news coverage of the Trump trials—to present his defenses to the American people as best he could, given he was subject to a handful of gag orders.

The mainstream media did discuss Trump's gag orders. But that coverage largely lacked any substantial questions as to the constitutionality of the courts' orders.

Brent Baker, the previously cited research expert at the Media Research Center, told me the press's lack of interest in challenging a gag order that silenced a former president and leading presidential candidate "added to the viewpoint that somehow [Trump's] viewpoint was illegitimate and improper, that anything he would say would be a lie anyway, so why report it? That is what came across to the public."

Baker told me the mainstream media failed to cover how novel the Democrats' legal arguments were. "These are theories that have never been put forth in court by a prosecutor," he said, noting Democrats had waited two years since Trump had left office in 2021, and until Trump announced he was going to run for reelection, before announcing the string of indictments. "That entire context was given short shrift."

The media went into covering the lawfare assuming Trump was guilty, Baker explained. "They all gave it massive coverage. That, pretty much all last year and all this year, was the only thing in the campaign they covered.... It was all Trump trials. They were enthusiastic backers of the whole idea of lawfare."

In the end, the public tuned out the all-day negative coverage, and the legacy media lost influence.

"People have to move on and try to support and promote the alternative media out there," Baker said. "Media hitched the wrong horse because the prosecutors moved so slowly that Trump beat them and all these terrible things that were going to be proven in court never happened."

A staunch critic of government corruption is Senator Ron Johnson, Wisconsin Republican. He has worked during his time on Capitol Hill—especially in the Trump era—to shield whistleblowers looking to improve transparency and accountability.

Johnson told me that truth is the way to combat the left's lawfare.

"We would not have this outrageous level of corruption inside government agencies if we had an unbiased media that held both sides equally accountable. Unfortunately, we have a highly biased media that actively promotes the radical left and its agenda. Our most effective weapon against lawfare is to relentlessly pursue and expose the truth," Johnson said.

Attorney David Schoen, who had to deal with the lawfare coverage as he represented Trump at his second impeachment trial, said the media promoted an agenda.

"The media's role in promoting and justifying the lawfare did perhaps more harm than the lawfare itself," the Montgomery, Alabama based lawyer said. "The media abandoned its critically important role of accurately informing the public, keeping public officials honest, and reporting facts—and broke its trust with the American people, and forfeited its role as the important check on government misconduct that we always had been able to depend on before this period."

As a result, Middle America does not trust the media now.

"The American people really rose above the media, and I believe the election result was, in significant part, a reaction to the bias in the media, which just did not sit well with fair-minded Americans. It was a powerful rejection of *The New York Times* and fellow travelers," Schoen said.

Despite the media's hyper focus on Trump's litigation, Robert C. Cahaly, chief pollster and strategist at The Trafalgar Group, told me the public just was not buying into Democrats' strategy.

He said that aside from the hush-money trial out of Manhattan, when it came to Special Counsel Jack Smith's prosecutions on election fraud and mishandling documents—and even the Georgia case—the public was not following the purported criminality, according to his polling.

"That's the stuff people thought was way over the top—especially the records case, where it looked like Biden did the same thing, and yet it was fine when Biden did it, but not when Trump did it," Cahaly told me. "And the Georgia thing is like, [people] didn't even know what was going on, but they keep hearing words like racketeering, and that doesn't sound like politics.

"They weren't even sure what Jack Smith was going after in DC, they didn't really understand. They just knew it was trying to indict a bunch of stuff, just to see if something will stick," he added. "It lost legitimacy."

POLITICAL TIT FOR TATS

The destructive use of lawfare knows no bounds. It spans across party lines. Lawfare should not be used against any one political party or against any single politician.

Once tolerated by one side—say, the Democratic Party—it could soon become the norm. And Republicans, now in charge of the Justice Department, could do the same.

The result, of course, would be political tit for tats.

As I previously discussed, Colorado's highest court ruled Trump could not appear on the GOP primary ballot because of the January 6, 2021 US Capitol riot, reasoning that he had led an insurrection and was therefore constitutionally unable to hold office.

On February 8, 2024, during oral arguments over an appeal of that ruling, US Supreme Court Chief Justice John G. Roberts Jr. warned that such a legal ruling could have a "daunting consequence."[492] He seemed to worry about what type of precedent

[492] *Trump v. Anderson*, US Supreme Court, February 8, 2024, https://www.supremecourt.gov/oral_arguments/argument_transcripts/2023/23-719_2jf3.pdf

it would set to allow one state court to wield such power over a federal election.

"I would expect that, you know, a goodly number of states will say, whoever the Democratic candidate is, you're off the ballot, and others for the Republican candidate, you're off the ballot. It'll come down to just a handful of states that are going to decide the presidential election. That's a pretty daunting consequence."[493]

Justice Samuel A. Alito Jr. likewise raised concerns. "The consequences of what the Colorado Supreme Court did, some people claim, would be quite severe," he said.[494]

Their remarks foreshadow eye-for-an-eye retaliation when it comes to future lawfare, as political parties would attempt to remove each other's political opponents from ballots through the use of court challenges.

The concern about the weaponization of the judicial system being used from one administration against another administration—or from a red state against a blue state, or vice-versa—continued to echo through the Supreme Court's last term.

It again came up roughly two months after the justices grappled with the Colorado ballot case, when the justices heard oral arguments over Trump's claim of absolute immunity from criminal prosecution brought by Special Counsel Jack Smith in his federal election fraud case. It was yet another unprecedented legal battle involving Trump to make it to the justices, all stemming from Democrats' lawfare.

Justice Brett M. Kavanaugh pointed out that "the concern going forward is that the system will—when former presidents are subject to prosecution…it's going to cycle back and be used

---

[493] Ibid.

[494] Ibid.

against the current president or the next president or—and the next president and the next president after that."[495]

That fear is potentially why the Supreme Court majority batted down both legal challenges—and in the case of the immunity decision, drew some guidelines for lower courts to follow so that Trump—and all future presidents—do not have to be inundated with dozens of federal charges for conduct that is related to the presidency.

Without the Supreme Court, Democrats' lawfare against Trump would have gone unchecked.

Some aides to President Joe Biden were hoping the pardon power would go unchecked, too. According to reports that emerged after Trump won the November election, they hoped to see pardons handed out before Trump could take revenge on the wielders of lawfare. In fact, on Inauguration Day before leaving office, Biden issued unprecedented pardons for family members, and lawmakers who led the January 6 investigations into Trump and his allies, among other Trump critics.

None of the individuals had been charged with a crime—like President Biden's siblings, for example, or Senator Adam Schiff, who I previously noted was a mouthpiece for lawfare in the media.

Politico reported in December 2024 that in Democratic circles there was support for these preemptive pardons, and that there was precedent for it with President Gerald Ford's pardon

---

[495] *Trump v. United States*, US Supreme Court, April 25, 2024, https://www.supremecourt.gov/oral_arguments/argument_transcripts/2023/23-939_3fb4.pdf

of President Richard Nixon.[496] Ford pardoned Nixon before any formal criminal charges came down against him, for any crime that Nixon may have committed during his presidency. Nixon was expected to be impeached over the Watergate scandal for obstruction of justice, abuse of power, and contempt. He resigned before a formal impeachment took place in the House or any trial in the Senate.

The suggestion that a president would need to issue preemptive pardons, out of fear of legal retribution coming from an incoming administration, demonstrates what a true threat political lawfare has become. Perhaps Biden recognized the precedent that his own Justice Department had set in its pursuit of Trump?

The whole narrative indicates that legal retribution is anticipated and expected.

It also signals a recognition of judicial and legal overreach.

As soon as Trump moves to correct the lawfare that rained down on him and against his inner circle and supporters, he'll face accusations of waging lawfare against his political foes.

This allegation will demonstrate the height of double standards in Washington. In other words, when it comes to taking steps to correct the legal abuse and judicial manipulation, Trump is damned if he does and damned if he does not.

Some conservatives have said the way to right the lawfare wrong is to hold open hearings and make the accountability process transparent, by punishing those who bent the law due to political bias. Others, meanwhile, have said the only way to hold the judiciary accountable for allowing elected lawyers to

---

[496] Jonathan Martin, "Biden White House Is Discussing Preemptive Pardons for Those in Trump's Crosshairs," *Politico*, December 4, 2024, https://www.politico.com/news/magazine/2024/12/04/biden-white-house-pardons-00192610

file frivolous, novel claims against a political opponent is to start sanctioning attorneys and impeaching judges who tolerated—or even participated in—the lawless lawfare.

Susan Ferrechio, my *Washington Times* colleague who I previously mentioned, said that if Trump's new administration addresses lawfare, it will be cast as "retribution," instead of him cleaning up the politically motivated probes and litigation.

"That's the irony," she said. "There is fear spreading through the Justice Department and the FBI that 'he is going to go after us.' Why not frame it this way: He is going to go in and get rid of the people who are waging the lawfare? It is all about how his actions are reported in the media."

She said Trump and his team can expect the media will push back on him.

"People that only listen to NPR and *The New York Times* will have a hard time getting a balanced perspective of the Trump administration. It is just the way people consume media," Ferrechio said. "Lawfare is the ultimate form of resistance, and people go along with that in order to resist Trump. Lawfare is a way of resisting or stopping the political figure you don't like."

General Michael Flynn, who told me about the damage he experienced from the MAGA-targeted lawfare during the Russian collusion investigation, said Trump could shut down the Federal Bureau of Investigation and reshape the Central Intelligence Agency to help prevent the political weaponization of law enforcement. It was one way he thought the new administration can combat the misuse of the courts.

"I don't think the FBI will ever recover," Flynn told me. He added, "The CIA is vastly worse than the FBI—the true deep state is the CIA. If I was POTUS, I'd put the hardest-ass military leader in charge of it."

The weaponization of government spiraled out of control from the moment Trump became a presidential candidate in 2016 and has increasingly grown even more problematic. But one former Democratic governor said he witnessed it personally nearly two decades ago.

That man is former Illinois Governor Rod Blagojevich. He viewed his criminal prosecution as a blueprint that the Washington establishment later used against Trump.

Blagojevich told me that aside from millions of dollars in legal fees, lawfare also cost him his livelihood, and "just about everything" was taken from him over his criminal prosecution.

He was convicted and also impeached from his public office after news broke of a corruption probe into him back in 2008. As a result, he now faces a law in his state that bars him from holding office in the future, the constitutionality of which he questions.

"They didn't just take away from the voters of Illinois the governor that they elected twice," he said. "They took me away from my children. They took me away from my wife. They took my reputation and they took my freedom."

> They took away from the people from Illinois the person that was blocking a big tax increase. I predicted once they got rid of me there was going to be a 60 percent income tax increase on the people of Illinois, and within months, they did that. And they also took away from most of the senior citizens the free public transportation

> I was able to get them when I was governor. So there were a lot of things that were taken away.

Blagojevich went to federal prison for nearly a decade before President Trump commuted his sentence in 2020 and later pardoned him in 2025. He suggested Congress should pass a law to strengthen its oversight of the Justice Department, legislation aimed at holding prosecutors accountable when they abuse their "uncontrolled power."

The former governor also proposed that a nonpartisan presidential commission be assembled under Trump to study reforms to the justice system that could depoliticize federal law enforcement agencies. It was a suggestion I had not heard before, as others who had been caught up in the surge of MAGA-targeted lawfare often suggested that transparent congressional hearings, or counter-prosecutions, would be the way to put the cat back in the bag.

"This is the moment in our history where we are either going to save our democracy or we are going to lose it forever," Blagojevich declared.

He said lawfare—not Trump, as liberals have claimed—is the true threat to democracy, and that something must be done because one party will continue to use it against the other. That would ultimately embolden the Washington establishment, which could mean the end of free and fair elections.

"The Democrats have taken [lawfare] to a whole new level, disgracefully abusing their power with what they have done to Trump," he said. "But don't think that it ends with them. The Republicans are certainly capable of doing that to the Democrats. So somebody has to save our democracy and think about America, and this is the opportunity now."

Blagojevich knows the reach and impact of political prosecutions. He was a twice elected governor of Illinois until he came under the feds' scrutiny in 2008.

He was arrested and charged with allegedly trying to sell President Barack Obama's US Senate seat. Although his first trial was declared a mistrial, the prosecutors decided to retry him, and he ultimately was found guilty in 2011.

"There was just this brief, shiny moment of about forty-five minutes where you think, 'This is over'—and then they come out: 'We're trying him again,'" he recalled.

Even though the former governor had no criminal record, the judge sentenced him to fourteen years in prison. And even when some of the charges were reversed on appeal, his lengthy sentence remained unchanged.

> Why is it they gave me fourteen years? Because I fought back in a free country against what I believe is prosecutorial corruption. This is no different from the Soviet Union—or from Russia, or from China. Maybe in Iran they would kill you; but how different is this from those countries? And they're doing it to Trump now.

Blagojevich ended up serving eight of his fourteen years until his commutation.

The former governor says prosecutors manipulated evidence at his trial, only playing 2 percent of the FBI tape recordings, and taking what he said on those recordings out of context. Still, years later, the rest of the tapes remain under seal.

"Ninety-eight percent of the tapes are still under court seal, under a gag order," he told me. "They did this tactically. They took snippets of conversations out of context, and then they covered up the rest of the tape, so you could never show what was actually said.

"I am not allowed to talk about those," he added. "In my case, I'm the anti-Nixon. I am not trying to protect or keep tapes from the public. I want them all played. They're the ones who were covering up the tapes, because it shows how they lied, how corrupt they are."

He's maintained his innocence, and said he watched from federal prison the same federal law enforcement agencies that targeted him use a similar playbook against Trump.

At the time of his arrest, the FBI was led by Robert Mueller, who would become the first Special Counsel deployed on Trump in the Russia collusion probe.

Characterizing the conversations that supposedly showed conspiracy, he says "It was all political horse trade and ideas. We were discussing ideas, and they criminalized it.... I really believe they saw how they were successfully able to do it with me. As long as they have their judge, who is basically a fourth prosecutor, they can do whatever they want. I think they saw they can do that."

> They were non-crimes invented by corrupt prosecutors. Non-crimes invented by corrupt, weaponized prosecutors, who did to a Democratic governor at the Triple-A level what they later went on to try to do, and have been doing, to a Republican president at the Major League level, and to the leading presidential candidate of the opposite party.

Blagojevich said the feds used other moves against him that were similar to what they employed in the former president's cases: from the over-the-top, televised FBI raid at Mar-a-Lago in the Trump documents case, which was like Blagojevich's sensational arrest, to the prosecutors creating media-marketable political slogans, like Blagojevich's alleged "selling a US Senate seat" and Trump's alleged "Russian collusion."

He also said emboldened, unchecked prosecutors in both his case and Trump's were bolstered by biased judges from tainted venues. Speaking of Trump's ordeal, he told me "I watched it all from prison. I recognized every bit of it. I recognized the corrupt practices. When it happened to you, you recognize when it happened to somebody else."

But in the end, he says the 2024 election gives him hope, because at least half of America recognized the dangers of a politicized, biased justice system. And he thinks the election of Trump could be what ends it.

> In a strange way, perhaps in a weird way, this could turn out to be a blessing—that they overreached and did what they did to him—because he will be determined to make sure this is reformed and we save the political process so it is what it was intended to be. Not something uncontrolled prosecutors can destroy.

DESTABILIZING JUSTICE

As a legal affairs reporter covering historical, politically charged legal battles, I have learned that I can often look at the judge overseeing the case and note which president (a Democrat or a Republican) appointed him or her to the bench, and to be able to predict how the legal proceedings will play out. It is not always a 100 percent accurate prediction, but I'd say at least 90 percent of the time the political affiliation of the president who appointed the judge gives me insight into which party will win.

The fact that I, as a reporter, can accurately anticipate which party will come out victorious, based on the judges' political appointment, indicates there is something more than judicial philosophy at play in these highly political disputes. Of course, a judge's jurisprudence matters as to how he or she would approach the law. But the political nature of the legal battles and their predictable outcomes reveal that Lady Justice is not blind or at all impartial, as we have been led to believe.

The judge overseeing General Michael Flynn's case, Judge Emmet Gael Sullivan of the District of Columbia, was appointed by Democratic President Bill Clinton.

Flynn said the handling of his case was corrupt and that he did not trust judges or US attorneys, especially in Washington.

"There needs to be a scrubbing out of the assistant attorney general's office of Washington, DC. They need to eliminate the national security division, and really, I would be fine with the FBI shutting its doors," Flynn told me.

Meanwhile, Peter Navarro, who served in President Trump's first administration and plans to serve in his second term, was sent to prison for four months, and ordered to pay a nearly $10,000 fine, by federal Judge Amit P. Mehta of the District of Columbia. The reason was Navarro's refusal to comply with the House January 6 Committee's subpoena. Judge Mehta was appointed by Democratic President Barack Obama.

"For the first time in our nation's history, a senior presidential advisor has been convicted of contempt of Congress after asserting executive privilege over a congressional subpoena," read Navarro's filing with the Supreme Court, which rejected his request to get involved ahead of his reporting to federal prison.[497]

Stephen K. Bannon, who worked in Trump's 2016 campaign and in the White House during part of Trump's first administration, also served four months in prison over refusing to comply with a similar subpoena. He was actually sentenced by a Trump judge for defying a congressional subpoena in the January 6 probe, refusing to sit for a deposition, and refusing to turn over

---

[497] Alex Swoyer, "Supreme Court turns down Peter Navarro's request to stay out of jail," *The Washington Times*, March 18, 2024, https://www.washingtontimes.com/news/2024/mar/18/peter-navarro-bid-stay-out-jail-rejected-supreme-c/

documents.[498] US District Judge Carl Nichols of the District of Columbia reportedly denied Bannon's attorney's planned defense avenues—looking to call as witnesses members of Congress serving on the January 6 panel.[499] The Trump appointee ruling against a Trump ally is the exception, not necessarily the norm, when it comes to these highly politicized cases.

Before Bannon and Navarro, the last time anyone was locked up for refusing to comply with Congress was in 1961, according to a report from *The Washington Post*.[500]

Supporting my theory of looking to the judge to see how a case will play out, one needs to look no further than the behavioral dichotomy between Judge Tanya Chutkan, an Obama appointee in the District of Columbia who oversaw Trump's federal election-fraud case, and Judge Aileen Cannon, a Trump appointee who oversaw his classified-documents prosecution in the Southern District of Florida.

Judge Chutkan ruled against Trump's team at nearly every turn, and in the most egregious manner allowed procedural norms—like Trump filing a motion to dismiss after the high court's immunity ruling—to be superseded, so that Special Counsel Jack Smith's team could file their enormous, oversized

---

498 Alex Swoyer, "Trump ally Steve Bannon ordered to jail by Trump-appointed judge," *The Washington Times*, June 6, 2024, https://www.washingtontimes.com/news/2024/jun/6/steve-bannon-staunch-trump-ally-ordered-to-jail-by/

499 Ashraf Khalil, "Steve Bannon convicted on contempt charges for defying January 6 committee subpoena," PBS News, July 22, 2022, https://www.pbs.org/newshour/politics/steve-bannon-convicted-on-contempt-charges-for-defying-jan-6-committee-subpoena

500 Swoyer, "Trump ally Steve Bannon ordered to jail…," https://www.washingtontimes.com/news/2024/jun/6/steve-bannon-staunch-trump-ally-ordered-to-jail-by/

evidentiary motion just weeks ahead of the November election, as I previously highlighted.

It was obvious the intention was to get the government's evidence out to the public before Election Day, before Trump's team could rebut the accusations. During a hearing in September 2024, she said she did not care that an election was just around the corner.

"I understand there is an election," she told the lawyers. "The electoral process and the timing of the election…is not relevant here.… This court is not concerned with the electoral schedule. Yes, there is an election coming…that is nothing I am going to consider," Judge Chutkan said.

But in reality, her rulings hint she was well aware of the impact the proceeding had on the election—given the defendant was the GOP presidential nominee and a former president—and wanted to ensure the special counsel got his evidence out in front of the public before November 5, 2024.

Meanwhile, in a rather bold move, Judge Cannon dismissed the special counsel's pending documents charges against Trump in Florida. She took an unprecedented step in ruling that Smith had no legal standing to bring the charges, due to his erroneous appointment as special counsel by the Attorney General of the United States. Her move halted the case altogether and made it so Smith had to argue his legal standing as special counsel on appeal. That is where the case was pending before it was ultimately dismissed—without prejudice—after Trump's victory.

And, of course, there was New York State Supreme Court Justice Arthur Engoron, a Democrat, who oversaw the unusual civil fraud dispute against Trump brought by Democratic New York Attorney General Leticia James.

And federal Judge Lewis Kaplan, a Clinton appointee, who entertained the defamation case against Trump brought by E. Jean Carroll—even sidestepping a jury decision determining that Trump did not rape Carroll, and inserting his own judgment that a rape did in fact occur, as he saw it.

Politically charged cases and favorable judges with friendly venues can bridge two of our branches of government—the legislative and the judiciary. The two are supposed to be "separate but equal"; however, we have seen that premise warped and manipulated by elected district attorneys, attorneys general, and the Biden Justice Department selectively choosing where to bring their charges.

The use of lawfare is not necessarily new. It has, however, without a doubt exploded in relation to President Trump and his allies.

Lawfare has been used across political parties to shoot down policies or block presidential executive orders. It has been utilized by red and blue states alike looking to attack an opposing federal administration.

We saw red states look to bring a challenge against the Biden administration over alleged censorship on social media about the 2020 election and COVID-19 pandemic, through the Fifth US Circuit Court of Appeals, which is recognized as the most conservative appeals court in the country. They knew it was likely they would get a favorable outcome there. However, the Supreme Court overruled that when it dismissed the case for lack of standing, reasoning the states did not prove sufficient legal injury to bring the case.

And we have seen blue states looking for a favorable outcome bring challenges to stop Trump's border policies through the

Ninth US Circuit Court of Appeals, which has been known as the most liberal circuit.

But the lawfare seen against Trump, personally, is a whole other ballgame. David Schoen, Trump's impeachment lawyer, cast the justice system as having been hijacked.

"In the cases brought against Trump, it is literally as if the criminal justice system was hijacked by political enemies willing to go to any measure to ensure that Trump would never be president again," he told me.

> It was just pure hatred, aided by, and at times driven by, many in the media who shared the prosecutors' agenda, and provided skewed accounts of facts and the law again to support their political agenda. I don't believe we ever before have seen the media and the criminal justice system so badly abused for partisan political purposes.

Ken Paxton, Texas attorney general and a Trump ally, said the lawfare exploded against this president because of his popularity. It also was used to halt the America First agenda from being implemented from the top down to the states.

"It [lawfare] exploded under Trump because he was effective, and they feared his effectiveness, and so they feared his popularity among the people, so they tried to destroy him. They don't go a little bit in—they go in to ruin your life. They want to take away your freedom, ruin your family, ruin you financially, [your] reputation—anything they can do to harm you. They literally hate you and want to destroy you. They don't care about the rules and the law," Paxton said. "They went after me."

The weaponization of the court system by Democrats to target their top political rival is truly without precedent in America. Democrats made the nation's courts appear like those of a Third-World country. They have successfully utilized the judicial system to achieve a political campaign goal—labeling their political opponent as a felon.

Curt Levey, president of the Committee for Justice, said that label is part of what motivated the lawfare.

"Consider the glee with which Trump's opponents, during the 2024 campaign, trumpeted his 'thirty-four felony convictions' for what is, at worst, a single minor offense. The practitioners of lawfare hoped that felony convictions and a potential jail sentence would make him unelectable, in addition to disrupting his ability to campaign," Levey told me.

While Trump's opponents failed to disrupt his reelection, Levey believes the lawfare did permanent scarring:

> Not only did their lawfare harm the rule of law, but it also damaged our nation's political process by discarding the 250-year-old tradition that American politicians defeat their opponents at the ballot box, rather than by trying to imprison or bankrupt them. At the peak of this spectacle, we saw—for the first time in American history—an American president, Joe Biden, try to put his leading political opponent in prison, by letting it be known that he thought his attorney general, Merrick Garland, was not going after Trump aggressively enough. Deciding political disagreements at the ballot box is a key factor that differentiates successful democracies from

> Third World, politically corrupt countries. Now that a vital 250-year-old democratic norm has been violated, the nations of the world cannot be blamed for wondering if America is becoming more like a Third World country.

He also said it was with the help of mainstream media, which "enthusiastically embraced" the lawfare, that the nation's long-standing norms were weakened.

In June of 2023, 62 percent of voters thought criminal charges against the former president were politically motivated.[501] But after a constant drip of indictments and 24/7 news coverage, a poll conducted roughly one year later showed a majority believed Trump's conviction in New York was the right result and upheld the rule of law.[502]

It is a dramatic change of opinion, and a successful turning of the tide by the Democrats' campaign. I argue it was the media coverage, which was all but one-sided, that changed public opinion.

The use of lawfare aided Democrats in climbing their way to the top of the polls—even after switching out President Joe Biden as their nominee for Vice President Kamala Harris, as they tried to keep Trump out of the White House. Ultimately, the national polls were suspect. Trump not only was able to capture

---

[501] Olafimihan Oshin, "62 percent in new poll say federal charges against Trump politically motivated," *The Hill*, June 21, 2023, https://thehill.com/homenews/4061063-62-percent-in-new-poll-say-federal-charges-against-trump-politically-motivated/

[502] Chris Jackson and Annaleise Lohr, "Majority believe prosecution of Donald Trump upheld rule of law, not motivated by politics," Ipsos, May 31, 2024, https://www.ipsos.com/en-us/majority-believe-prosecution-donald-trump-upheld-rule-law-not-motivated-politics

every swing state to win the electoral college, but he also took the national popular vote by 2,284,338 votes.[503]

Lara Trump, the president's daughter-in-law who led the Republican National Committee during the 2024 election, said voters she talked to were concerned about the litigation against Trump—and that the mug-shot photograph actually helped bolster his campaign for reelection.

"It was very heavily on their minds, actually," Lara Trump said of the lawfare. "You could see it reflected in the numbers. The more they tried to go after this man—every indictment, after the mug shot, all these things—his poll numbers personally, his direct poll numbers, would go up."

"The mug shot itself was an interesting one, because the day that that mug shot was taken, I was about to do a TV interview," she recalled. "And my father-in-law called me as he was on his way to the courthouse in Fulton County. And I was like, I am about to do some show, and he was like—okay, okay, you know I am on the way. He was like, what do you think?"

> And I was like, I think that these people are really going to do the opposite of what they think they are doing. And I think your mug shot is going to be the coolest mug shot that this country has ever seen. And it turns out that is it—that is what happened. People were like, "that is bad-ass. What a photo! That is like Elvis Presley level."

[503] CNN Politics, "Election 2024: Presidential results," CNN, https://www.cnn.com/election/2024/results/president?election-data-id=2024-PG&election-painting-mode=projection-with-lead&filter-key-races=false&filter-flipped=false&filter-remaining=false

Trump was not the only one to see the lawfare inadvertently help bolster the president's campaign. Reporters noticed, too, at least those who were ready and willing to call out Democrats' legal gymnastics.

Kerry Picket, my *Washington Times* colleague, who has been a reporter in the news business for roughly two decades, said the massive number of lawsuits against Trump helped him, from what she heard from voters as she traveled the campaign trail.

"Usually that tactic works because it is almost like a machine gun," she said of the Democrats' lawfare. "They figure he is going to be so frazzled. But in this case, it literally backfired on them, because he was able to sort of dodge and dive and block and tackle," she added.

Picket observed that, in a way, voters somewhat related to Trump over the litigation—or were at least sympathetic to what appeared to be never-ending legal battles.

"People see how the system is screwing him over. They related to him," she told me. "I don't think his opponents ever really counted on that."

Democrats even looked to lock Trump up ahead of the November election. But to New York Supreme Court Judge Merchan's credit, he delayed the sentencing until after Election Day. Once Trump won, he was left with limited options for punishment over the hush-money conviction, with jail obviously having been taken off the table. Unless, of course, the judge had postponed jailing the president for four years, until after Trump left Pennsylvania Avenue to report to the pen. I'm surprised, given Democrats' use of lawfare, that this was not Judge Merchan's preferred course of action. Instead, he sentenced Trump to an unconditional discharge, where he would serve no time and pay no fine. It was an unusual use of restraint we had not seen from

Judge Merchan when he handled the trial in a one-sided manner months prior.

Don Jr., the president's eldest son, said he believed if his father had not been reelected, he would have been sentenced to jail time, as that was the Democrats' goal. He said to avoid lawfare from happening again to his father—or any politician—the right people have to be in charge.

> It starts with personnel. People are policy. And we're delivering on that in this second term. Like I've said, my role in the transition was to keep out the bad apples. The Justice Department, the FBI, and the intelligence agencies shouldn't be making decisions whether to investigate or prosecute someone based on politics. It should be based on facts and the rule of law. Democrats used to at least pretend to believe in that. And we protect our due process and restore credibility to the legal system by making sure there is accountability for those who abuse that power—and by putting people in these positions who are committed to real reform, and not endless phony investigations.

Don Jr. said this time, the Washington establishment and Democrats' lawfare failed—at least for now—telling me that "it completely backfired."

> It only made my father stronger, my family more resilient, and our country more and more aware of just how corrupt, chaotic, and divided

> the Democratic Party made this country. It's a complete disgrace. But now, we're in a position to unleash a new golden age of prosperity for America. We'll look back on the 2024 election as the election that decided whether we were a nation of laws and prosperity, or a nation of politicized lawfare and decline. We always hear that "elections have consequences"—this past election was the most consequential ever.

But given the fact that some cases—like the Fulton County, Georgia, prosecution against Trump—are still working their way through the court system, the question remains: Just how far will Democrats sink our nation's judicial system?

ACKNOWLEDGMENTS

Lawless Lawfare is a spillover of the ranting and raving I have done with friends I've had since my law school years, about the abuses of the judicial system I've witnessed as a reporter for *The Washington Times*. I want to thank them all for hearing—*and listening*—to my tirades, and often being a sounding board on the topic of lawfare. To Lauren McEndree, John Knowles, Julianne Nowicki, John Massaro, Todd Vlazny, and Sammy Jo Baker, I appreciate you all and your friendships. Without our friendly debates, this project never would have been born.

And to my family, I owe you my greatest gratitude. To my mother Victoria Swoyer, who spent hours substituting for me with Fiona's care as I would write, and to my father Don Swoyer for pushing me to pursue a career that I am passionate about, at all costs. To my husband Ali Sajadi, who, like my father, demonstrates an incredible work ethic that motivated me to burn the midnight oil as I authored this work. And of course, to my daughter Fiona Joon, you are my best creation. I love you all deeply.

For my *Washington Times* colleagues, especially Chris Dolan, Stephen Dinan, Susan Ferrechio, and Kerry Picket, I applaud your professionalism, thoroughness, and dedication to journalism. Without your leadership, I would not be the reporter I am today. And a very special thank you to Cheryl Chumley, who helped mother me through the book-writing process by answering my countless questions.

And to Brigid Mary McDonnell, you have helped build my reputation and rapport in Washington.

I would also be amiss not to thank my colleagues from my *Breitbart* days, where I reported from 2015 to 2017. You all taught me tenacity and how to be a honey badger, not giving a damn.

To those who lent their voices to *Lawless Lawfare*, especially Don Jr. and Lara Trump, who gave me a glimpse at how the lawfare impacted the president's family. And to House Judiciary Chairman Jim Jordan and Senator Ron Johnson, I appreciate your work for the American people. Moreover, I want to thank General Michael Flynn, Texas Attorney General Ken Paxton, Governor Rod R. Blagojevich, John Eastman, Stephen K. Bannon, Brandon Straka, and all the legal and political experts who shared their personal stories and research with me, which aided in bolstering my analysis.

Of course, a special debt of gratitude is owed to Mike Davis, who has been a warrior on the frontlines battling lawfare since Trump's first administration. If I were ever in the trenches of war, I would want Davis by my side.

To my professors at Ave Maria School of Law and the University of Missouri's School of Journalism, thank you for watering, nurturing, and grooming my curiosity. You taught me not only about the news and the legal industries, but also instilled in me the importance of ethics.

To everyone at Post Hill Press and Bombardier Books, thank you for giving me a platform to share my experience and thoughts on the dangers of lawfare, as it has increasingly plagued so many courtrooms.

Most importantly, thank you to the readers for caring about this topic. Learning how to spot and combat lawfare will safeguard our nation's separation of powers.

And in the words of President Trump, I want to thank "even the haters and losers." At times, my critics have served as gasoline, fueling my passion and pursuit of the truth.

ABOUT THE AUTHOR

Alex Swoyer has a unique look at the crumbling of our nation's justice system as a lawyer, member of the Supreme Court bar, and a legal affairs reporter for *The Washington Times.* She has had a seat inside the Supreme Court, federal courthouses, and halls of Congress during her more than a decade of experience covering national politics and Capitol Hill. She's watched Trump's high stake litigation unfold and has witnessed the impact his cases have had on various industries outside the legal world—including increasing the political divide and distrust in the media. After moving from Texas to Washington, DC, she covered then-candidate Trump's primary and 2016 general election campaign for Breitbart News Network, winning exclusive interviews with the GOP frontrunner and his allies. More recently, Ms. Swoyer has interviewed some of his legal advisors while covering his court hearings for her podcast, *Court Watch*, available through *The Washington Times*, Apple Podcasts, and other streaming services.

Ms. Swoyer, who has a Bachelor of Journalism from the University of Missouri-Columbia and a law degree from Ave Maria School of Law, joined *The Washington Times* as the paper's legal affairs reporter, covering federal courts and judicial confirmations. She's licensed to practice law in Texas. Ms. Swoyer has appeared on *Fox News*, *BBC*, *HLN*, *CSPAN*, *Newsmax*, SiriusXM, and *One America* as well as local TV and radio affiliate stations throughout the country. She also has public speaking experience as she served as Miss Southwest Florida during her time in law school.

www.ingramcontent.com/pod-product-compliance
Ingram Content Group UK Ltd.
Pitfield, Milton Keynes, MK11 3LW, UK
UKHW021651190726
13853UKWH00001B/201